# CHALLENGES OF THE MIND

"During the 1960s, sensitivity training, encounter-group therapy, and a wide variety of personal 'inner-development' programs were designed to help people penetrate the many layers of tape they had wrapped around their emotions and intuitions. . . .

"This book focuses on the single, most intriguing product of this exciting new age. We shall investigate how the exploration of consciousness is encouraging us to reevaluate our understanding of the healing process and the awesome responsibility we are inheriting from the growing belief that each of us has the potential to heal our own body and to help others to heal themselves."

—Nicholas M. Regush

## A BOLD NEW LOOK INTO THE COMING AGE OF MODERN MEDICINE

# FRONTIERS OF HEALING:

## NEW DIMENSIONS IN PARAPSYCHOLOGY

EDITED BY
### NICHOLAS M. REGUSH

Foreword
a statement by
The Academy of Parapsychology
and Medicine

 **AVON**
PUBLISHERS OF BARD, CAMELOT AND DISCUS BOOKS

FRONTIERS OF HEALING—NEW DIMENSIONS IN PARAPSYCHOLOGY is an original publication of Avon Books. This work has never before appeared in book form.

AVON BOOKS
A division of
The Hearst Corporation
959 Eighth Avenue
New York, New York 10019

First Avon Printing, May, 1977

AVON TRADEMARK REG. U.S. PAT. OFF. AND IN
OTHER COUNTRIES, MARCA REGISTRADA,
HECHO EN WINNIPEG, CANADA

Printed in Canada

# Acknowledgments

The foreword "The Academy of Parapsychology and Medicine" is reprinted by permission of The Academy of Parapsychology and Medicine, Denver, Colorado. "The Power of Will" by Eileen Garrett was published in *Awareness*. © 1943. Reprinted by permission of Garrett Publications, New York, and the estate of Eileen J. Garrett. "How to Make Use of the Field of Mind Theory" by Elmer E. Green was published in *The Dimensions of Healing: A Symposium*. © 1972. Reprinted by permission of the author and The Academy of Parapsychology and Medicine, Denver, Colorado. "The Triune Approach to Healing of the Edgar Cayce Readings" by Herbert B. Puryear was published in *The Dimensions of Healing: A Symposium*. © 1972. Reprinted by permission of the author and The Academy of Parapsychology and Medicine, Denver, Colorado. "The Nuclear Mobile Center of Consciousness" by Andrija Puharich was published in *Beyond Telepathy*. © 1962. Reprinted by permission of Doubleday & Co. and Souvenir Press, Ltd., London. "Cancer: The Cell And Its Intelligence" by Harry Edwards was published in *The Healing Intelligence*. © 1965, 1971. Reprinted by permission of Taplinger Publishing Company, New York and Barrie and Jenkins, London. "Magic and Medicine" by Una Maclean was published in *Magical Medicine: A Nigerian Case-Study*. © 1971. Reprinted by permission of Penguin Books, Ltd., London. "Hexing For Health" by Lee R. Gandee was published in *Strange Experience: The Autobiography of a Hexenmeister*. © 1971. Reprinted by permission of Prentice-Hall, Inc., Englewood Cliffs, New Jersey. "Hex Death" by Joan Halifax-Groff was published in *Parapsychology Review*: Vol. 5, No. 5, September-October, 1974. Reprinted by permission of the author and *Parapsychology Review* published by The Parapsychology Foundation, Inc. New York. "The Power of Desuggestion" by Alan Spraggett was published in *Probing the Unexplained*. © 1971. Reprinted by permission

*This book is dedicated to*
*The Academy of Parapsychology and Medicine*
*and to the women and men whose work*
*is helping to bring about a revolution*
*not only in medicine but in all the sciences.*

# Contents

# Foreword

a statement by

## The Academy of Parapsychology and Medicine

### Founding

The Academy of Parapsychology and Medicine is founded on an idea that is as old as man: that spirit and matter are somehow one, and that it is the essential purpose of man to seek meaning behind all human experience if the true nature of healing is to be found.

The Academy seeks to increase man's understanding of the physical and biological sciences, metaphysics, and religion as they relate to the healing of mental and physical ills. Formed by a group of scientists and physicians. The Academy's long-range aim is to discover the conditions under which total healing is possible and bring these vital findings to bear on the actual theory and practice of medicine.

### Philosophy

The philosophy of The Academy may be stated as several fundamental beliefs which it holds to be axiomatic:

- that man is a multidimensional being whose experience and ultimate purposes are inextricably and meaningfully related, and that that meaning is made manifest in patterns of health and disease

- that medicine must adopt a new view of man: one which recognizes the unity of body, mind, and spirit, and the importance of the interrelationship of these dimensions in health and disease

- that all physical and mental disease is directive experi-

ence in human development, and that it must be viewed
as a manifestation of conditions existing on subtler levels
—whether mental, emotional, or spiritual

- that the treatment of disease must be directed to the
  whole man, and that no lasting healing of the physical
  body can be achieved where the mental, emotional and
  spiritual elements have been untouched

- that there is no condition of disease in the human body
  that cannot be successfully treated if a means is discovered for treating on the appropriate level.

There is beginning evidence now to bear out the prophetic
words of the great scientific genius, Charles Steinmetz, who
said, "Some day . . . the scientists of the world will turn
their laboratories over to the study of God and prayer and
the spiritual forces which as yet have hardly been scratched.
When this day comes, the world will see more advancement
in one generation than it has in the past four."

## Growth

The Academy of Parapsychology and Medicine was founded
in 1970 following a first serious attempt to present publicly
a representative sampling of professional research being conducted on new dimensions of healing. Enthusiastic response
revealed an unsuspected degree of interest in the whole field
of paranormal and unorthodox healing.

As a result of the high interest which was uncovered,
a number of primary public symposia were presented in
the San Francisco Bay Area and subsequently carried to
Southern California and major cities across the United
States.

During this period acupuncture burst on the American
medical scene with great impact. Early consideration centered primarily on its use as an analgesic either for surgery
or pain relief. Additional research and clinical application
indicated not only its effectiveness in a wide variety of
uses but that its study scientifically might provide a key to
the understanding of body/energy systems.

First to do so, The Academy presented a National
Acupuncture Symposium at Stanford University in 1972
which was attended by nearly 1500 medical professionals.

Subsequent to this introduction, The Academy presented nine acupuncture seminars and an equal number of workshops. Biofeedback seminars and workshops and additional acupuncture events were part of several major symposia covering a wide range of clinical applications.

Corollary to these major events, dissemination of information to the lay and professional public took place through publication of an APM Quarterly and transcripts of those symposia considered to have the highest information content in medical applications of parapsychology. These included *The Varieties of Healing Experience, The Dimensions of Healing,* and *Transcript of the Acupuncture Symposium (1972).*

In June of 1974, The Academy presented jointly with the State of Florida Division of Retardation an exploratory survey of nontraditional diagnostic and treatment techniques, together with their implications for the developmentally disabled. This addressed itself to the health care professional under the title of "New Dimensions of Habilitation for the Handicapped."

Similarly, but at the national level, The National Congress on Integrative Health (1975) was developed to present a survey of nontraditional diagnostic and treatment techniques in a holistic format to those directly involved in therapeutics, health care delivery, and policy formation.

In parallel with the National Congress, a World Congress is under development which will focus attention on alternative or nonallopathic medical practice, highlighting the distinction between medicine and health, and recognizing the need for a global perspective if world health is to be achieved.

## Goals

The principal goal of The Academy is to catalyze the serious investigation of alternative or unorthodox healing practice and its integration into a holistic system of health care. Its long-range aim is to discover the conditions under which total healing is possible and to bring these vital findings to bear on the actual theory and practice of medicine. In pursuit of this aim, The Academy will:

- establish a resource center to disseminate information to the professional community and concerned laymen on cutting-edge research wherever it is being carried out throughout the world

- stimulate trained professionals to apply the research techniques of their various disciplines to the study of the mind/body relationship

- suggest, evaluate, and screen projects for research and work toward the application of the results of this research to the regular practice of the healing professions

- coordinate research plans and provide an avenue for communication among research workers in this field

- increase the level of professional confidence in the findings of parapsychological research as it relates to the medical disciplines by welcoming critical scrutiny of all studies by the scientific community

- establish a demonstration, diagnostic and treatment center to provide a window for the medical community to view the viability of alternative therapeutics.

The Academy offers membership to all those who share its philosophy and wish to contribute toward the realization of its objectives. A nonprofit educational organization, The Academy is entirely free of ties with established educational, political, or ecclesiastical organizations. The Directors of the Academy believe that responsible exploration of the healing phenomenon has horizons limited only by the range of our collective imagination.

We welcome all who would join us in this endeavor.

# Introduction

We are living in revolutionary times. More aware than ever before of our enormous untapped human potential, we are making great strides to steadily demolish the numerous obstacles to personal growth.

During the 1960s, sensitivity training, encouter-group therapy, and a wide variety of personal "inner-development" programs were designed to help people penetrate the many layers of tape they had wrapped around their emotions and intuitions. More people became acutely aware of the active role they played in creating their own daily joys and sorrows. Many of the graduates of these programs resolved to continue to further explore the hidden potentials latent in human consciousness. And as the seventies ushered in an explosion of public interest in paranormal or psychic phenomena, a stronger scientific foundation was built for the study of the human mind.

This book focuses on the single, most intriguing product of this exciting new age. We shall investigate how the exploration of consciousness is encouraging us to reevaluate our understanding of the healing process and the awesome responsibility we are inheriting from the growing belief that each of us has the potential to heal our own body and to help others to heal themselves.

The founding of The Academy of Parapsychology and Medicine is one of numerous steps being taken by scientists and physicians who are impressed by the need to examine the unity of mind, body, and spirit and their relationships in health and disease. Well-attended symposia sponsored by the academy are strong signals that in a roundabout fashion modern medicine may be slowly returning to a more unitarian concept of disease advocated by Hippocratic physicians some twenty-five hundred years ago.

The fundamental philosophy of Hippocratic medicine was that mind and body could not be considered independently of each other. Since the time that philosopher René Descartes stressed that man consisted of two separate entities, mind and body, scientists have increasingly described the human being in machinelike terms. There are indications that the tide is turning. In particular, psychical research, or parapsychology, once considered the exclusive domain of egotists, frauds, and eccentrics and now seen as more and more relevant to almost all scientific research, is without doubt greatly responsible.

Once frowned upon and ridiculed, behavior such as telepathy, clairvoyance, prophecy, and mediumship is being seriously investigated, and in many cases by scientists who several years ago would have denied such interest. As a result, researchers in this field, many of whom have medical degrees and practice medicine, are becoming more vocal and aggressive in emphasizing the implications of this growing body of work for modern medicine. They reason, for example, that if a person can mentally influence the fall of dice or send a telepathic message to a person who is dreaming, then perhaps it may also be possible to mentally influence cellular activity in the body. For example, recent experiments in biofeedback have indeed revealed that it is possible to mentally control a wide variety of bodily functions, such as respiration, heartbeat, blood pressure, and skin temperature.

The idea that our own thoughts play a decisive role in health and illness presents us with an enormous responsibility, one which we previously delegated entirely to our physicians. In Part One of this book we shall explore the nature of this responsibility. We shall examine how willpower can influence illness patterns, how we can unwittingly "program" illness, and how according to the late clairvoyant Edgar Cayce "mind is the builder," a phrase that resonates throughout the large body of trance "readings" he had given, and which are now carefully indexed at The Association for Research and Enlightenment in Virginia Beach. We can also learn more about the mind from other peoples. Too often we maintain a cultural arrogance that obfuscates achievements elsewhere, and we take credit for ideas based on research findings that have been practiced for centuries in other cultures. In Part One, therefore, we shall also examine magical powers and healing, the power of hexing, and the role of spirit hospitals in Brazil. What is often irritating is the offhand rejection of medical practices that appear to work for other peoples. To rely entirely on Western scientific methods of observation to account for these practices smacks of irresponsibility. We have much to learn from *other methods* of experiencing the world.

While Western physicians resist new or seemingly unorthodox medical techniques, patients also are resistant. They look to their doctors as the one and only saviors. They often become ruffled by the great amount of responsibility that is required of them in more comprehensive and novel healing programs. Physicians embracing the new spirit in medicine understand that it is extremely difficult to reverse a well-conditioned role and that much of the important work ahead must take into account the general education and dispositions of patients.

Whenever new boundaries are charted in any field, there is inevitable criticism, often quite unreasonable and self-serving. The medical profession's reaction to the impact parapsychological work appears to be having on medical philosophy for the most part has focused on the claims of miracle cures, conveniently ignoring the responsible work being done. A chief target has been the faith healer who often claims to be a vehicle of a higher source of knowledge. One argument is that if a physician does absolutely nothing to help a patient, the patient will have a 50 percent chance of recovery. This figure is used to disclaim spontaneous cures attributed to the psychic and spiritual powers of a faith healer. One way to respond to this argument is to point out that many physicians are apparently completely unaware of the potential harm they can do to a patient. Callousness and negative suggestions casually communicated may have disastrous effects on a patient who might need strong support in order for natural self-healing to begin and for a more harmonious balance between mind and body to be achieved. It is entirely possible that a psychic healer stimulates this kind of positive response. It also makes little sense to attribute such a process to an intangible word such as "suggestion." This is a term frequently used to obscure our own ignorance of what actually occurs at subtle levels during a dynamic interchange between people. The modern impersonal hospital environment, moreover, places patient and physician in surroundings which often may not be conducive to sustained healing.

In a sense, all of us are always patients as well as healers, an idea which is central to most of the selections in Part One. We are only beginning to understand how the interplay of our own thoughts and those of others governs our health. Responsible healers and scientists, therefore, stress that psychic healing be conducted with proper medical supervision. It would seem that the medical associations have much to gain in cooperating in this fashion. Lack of cooperation allows the charlatan to flourish.

In Part Two the boundaries of our exploration of the dimensions of healing are extended. What does it mean to be a part of universal forces? Do the stars and planets influence our behavior? Are we born with predispositions to certain illnesses? And can these be neutralized? Does a universal life energy exist which sustains our existence? These are several of the controversial questions in frontiers-of-science research that have gradually made their way into modern medicine. They suggest that we live amongst invisible forces with which we communicate on a biological level, and that *we are part of the flow of life itself* and not detached beings merely capable of observing the environment.

The main focus will be to examine how our integral relationship with our total environment is reflected in both health and illness and how we can learn to gain better control of this relationship. The selections in Part Two also serve to help exorcise the insidious, widespread defeatist and destructive belief that we are slabs of meat, devoid of spirit, to be prodded by instruments.

This book is dedicated to the women and men whose work is helping to bring about a revolution not only in medicine but in all the sciences. That the views presented *must* be seen as preliminary should in no way cloud the insight and potential of the roads being charted. Instead, the challenges described must be seen as maps, all of which no doubt will require revision again and again.

I have included selections which I believe reflect the present impact that work in psychical research and spiritual development is having on our growing understanding of the healing process. Perhaps a few selections will appear to some to suggest the possibility of miraclelike cures for illnesses that have brought great anguish to so many. However, instant salvation is *not* the focus of this book. Nor should it be construed that it is the main preoccupation of the scientists and physicians exploring alternative medical techniques.

As for my own beliefs, it is sufficient to stress that I greatly share the following view expressed by Paracelsus, medieval alchemist and physician: "The physician who has no faith can be nothing else but an ignoramus and quack, even if he had graduated in all the medical colleges in the world and knew the contents of all the medical books that were ever written."

NICHOLAS M. REGUSH
MONTREAL, JANUARY 1977

# PART ONE

# THE POWER TO HEAL
# AND
# PERSONAL RESPONSIBILITY

The power of mind can influence the delicate balance between health and illness. It requires that we radically alter our views of the responsibilities of both physician and patient in the healing process.

# 1

## The Power of the Will

### *Eileen Garrett*

*Eileen Garrett, a well-known medium, was the founder of The Parapsychology Foundation. Her comprehensivist approach to psi made her an articulate and invaluable spokeswoman for the fight to recognize the validity of psychical research.*

*Healing to her meant reintegrating the forces of an individual's life. Here, in the shadow of World War II, she stresses the importance of "the will to live" and describes types of healers, techniques of healing, and the nature of her own ability to heal.*

● ● ●

The earth, the waters, and the atmosphere of our planet are very ancient; and through the ages they have been the receivers of all the waste of the world. They are constantly active in the process of repurification, transforming the decay of old life-forms into the reconditioned substances of new life. The substances of decay are the substances out of which new life is created at the physical level; and the soil, the waters, and the atmosphere—three of the basic factors on which all forms of physical life depend—are always more or less saturated with essences which are deleterious to physical life itself. Every exhalation of our breath tends to darken the atmosphere of our environment, and the ordinary wastes of all bodies are a menace to human existence.

This is the basic circle of all physical existence, and one of the mysteries of life—the synthesizing of diverse substances into new vitalized forms, the expression of life through these forms according to their respective capacities, the eventual withdrawal of vital forces from these forms, the deterioration of the physical synthesis into its elements, and the repurification of these elements for use, again and again, in the construction of other synthetic forms for the further expression of the life-force. No wonder life remains a mystery to the mind of man. Death supervenes upon life, and life emerges out of death. The whole process operates under natural laws; and we are not equal to the comprehension of these laws.

Consequently, the world is full of distresses for mankind. This field of distress is one in which humanity differs from every other category in nature, because, by virtue of our innate capacities, we are creators of the means and manners by which life is expressed at the human level; and since we do create, we bring into being conditions that are both useful and adverse to our own existence.

The two common factors which give rise to the problems of healing are: the elements which are destructive of human well-being, and which exist in each of the four kingdoms of nature; and the ignorance which so often robs our creative power of its constructive values.

And here let me say that, as I see it, healing is not only—or even primarily—concerned with the physical diseases and disabilities that our human nature suffers from. The taproot of human difficulties reaches far below the physical level of our lives, and the manner in which we use our physical equipment is always conditioned by the deeper qualities and purposes of our psychological selves.

I have often been asked how much I know of medicine. I know nothing of medicine or anatomy or psychology, in the technical sense. Yet I am able to heal. When I do so, I am but the agent of a norm which comes to dissipate an abnormality; under any and all circumstances there must exist, within the psyche of the distressed individual, a fertile seed of the "will to live."

This will to live—which I am using here as a symbolic phrase—is fundamentally a psychological rather than a physical factor. Though in some cases recuperative power may seem to reside at the levels of physical activity, as in the healing of wounded flesh and the knitting of broken bones, nevertheless, in all conditions of disease and disability, including these, the will to live must exist (however unconsciously) as a basic fact in the individual psychology. And I would go so far as to say that successful healing consists very simply in the establishment of a regimen which releases this will to live from whatever conditions are inconsistent with and abnormal to it, and which may dominate it at any given time.

We make a grave mistake if and when we think that "healing" is principally concerned with the correction and cure of physical disabilities. Our physical equipment is in the nature of an instrument for the expression of our inner motivations and purposes; and our psychological qualities, rising constantly to the need for expression, motivate and determine our physical activities.

Does this psychological field seem vague or remote to our understanding? It is the field which, like a landscape emerging into visibility with the dawn, is becoming the object of attention for the consciousness of mankind. It is not by chance that psychology has broken away from philosophy and become an experimental science with a field of its own. Psychiatry is already proving its thesis of the subphysical sources of abnormality and maladjustment in human life. We are experiencing the early stages of a new expansion of the racial consciousness—an expansion which is to be at least as important and definitive as that other expansion which changed man from a nomad into an agriculturist.

It is as though, having conquered four of the ancient elements of earth, water, fire, air, and ether, we are now proceeding to fresh experience in the field of the least substantial of them all, and to the discovery of the nonphysical roots of our own existence. For in this new scientific advance, man is turning the searchlight of awareness upon his own inner activities, and is discovering the immaterial energies that motivate his physical operations.

What the future effects of these new techniques may be are now unpredictable. To me it all seems to be an advance of human centralizations from the physical-emotional field into the areas of rational mind. Humanity is suffering so desperately (and so predominantly at the physical-emotional level) it seems inescapable that we shall learn something positive and definite from the race-agony. If we do, it must be in the nature of a conscious realization of what causes these wars and world distresses. What does cause them is our failure to recognize, appreciate, and accept the fundamental laws of our human nature. Through its ignorance, its present lack of development, humanity creates its own malaise. But the healing of the nations, like the healing of individuals, is approaching—is entering into—a new area of psychological rationalism.

Fundamentally, there is but one kind of healing. Of course, I do not mean to deny the inestimable values of medicine, chemistry, and surgery. But the physical areas, in which these techniques are for the most part helpful to human life, are based in the individual psyche. It is to this subtle factor in man that all healing, of whatever kind, is foundationally and finally related. To heal means to assist in the recovery of a condition of health, according to the norm, whether this recovery involves a release from physical incapacity, emotional imbalance, mental delusion, or an arrest of psychic development.

But what constitutes the norm? That is what we do not yet know. Most human distresses may be said to be due to this lack of a conception of the norm. Our current investigation of psychological abnormalities is giving us some clues, however, while medicine and dietetics have found means, in recent years, for tremendously improving the physical condition of men and women—even having extended the span of life expectation. But our future programs of true development lie in *fresh* fields of discovery, knowledge, and understanding; and we are opening up the vast continent of our own psychology because it is in that area that the norm lies hidden.

Humanity creates its own norms, its own concepts of well-being, development, and fulfillment. And it is obvious that these concepts are not modeled on the patterns of our physical environment, for the life of man transcends its environment and holds in solution all the qualities and talents of the universe. We have to learn how to use the power we possess.

Healing is achieved through comprehension—not only the comprehension of a particular given distress, but also the comprehension of that perfection of which the distress is a broken symbol. There must also be developed a comprehension of how and when the original perfection began to deteriorate into this. These factors are all to be discovered in the terms and at the level of the individual in distress; for in the last analysis, his own body and his own psyche must do their own healing, must achieve recovery according to their own conception of "perfection." In physical disability the healer can give assurance and symbols of health; in psychological distresses he can give assurance and symbols of integration; but of these only those will be helpfully effective which the deep consciousness of the distressed person can accept. In experimental hypnosis it has been learned that in every individual there exists an egoic core which will resist suggestions that are incompatible with its own nature, no matter how amenable to hypnosis the person may be. In the recorded healings performed by Jesus, the psychological state of the patient was always the key—"Thy faith hath made thee whole."

Within each individual there resides the perfect form. To build a life adequately on that insubstantial pattern, the individual must become sensitive to the subtle pressures of necessity that arise within his own nature. Like the pitcher that comes into material being in accordance with an immaterial model of intention, purpose, and usefulness, the individual human life must be molded in the terms of an efficiency which is natural to itself. This inner pattern is an individualized fragment of universal nature; and the life which is erected on this foundation is meant to—and must, as far as it goes—conform to the qualities of the Infinite.

When such conformity with the Universal is achieved by the individual in a large measure, the life becomes a coherent pattern of relationships well defined and understood, and thus duties and responsibilities become living sources of activity filled with joy.

When anyone comes to me for help or healing, I rarely listen to the story of the case. Instead, I see the condition as it is reflected in his "surround." A person's *surround* encloses and accompanies him like a misty aura, changing in color and density as his moods and conditions change; and it is in my perception of a person's *surround* that I find the clues to his inner state and conditions. Were I to listen to his story, I should be diverted from my own clear apprehension of his difficulty and his need. But seeing and feeling the brightness or the shadowed grayness of their *surrounds,* I sense the physical and psychological conditions of people—and not only of people, but of denizens of the plant and animal worlds as well.

To me, the only strange aspect of this capacity of perception is the fact that it is not common. That we do not penetrate beyond the obvious physical marks of fever, depression, pain, worry, and fear seems to me to involve a peculiar limitation of perception. Many people, without seeing any *surround,* develop this capacity of penetration in some measure, as the physician gathers an inner understanding of a "case" from the temperature of the body, the absence of vital force, stertorous breathing, or the dullness of the eyes. The expert in any line of activity is one who has learned to summarize his perception of all the symptoms or indications of a condition at a glance, and who comes very close, by "intuition," to the same sensing of a subtle state of being as I gather from the perception of the *surround.* In many cases, both for the expert and for me, it would be better if the person did not talk at all; but I have learned to leave people's words to the attention of my subconscious, while I gather my own clear understanding of their condition and their need by my own modes of perception.

In any case, the person's story, with all its positive and negative details, rarely amounts to a clear and concise statement of facts, though it does reveal the clues to the psychological state of the person. Such of these as coincide and fuse with other pertinent data which I "sense" will be contributed by my subconscious to the sum total of my perception. But very often the *key* to the problem is the one point which is missing from the person's own realization of the nature of his difficulty.

My understanding presently becomes clarified and simplified. This does not mean, however, that the process of "cure" will be simple also. The chemistry of psychology is not like the chemistry of the physical body; the emetic which will cause a person to eject a poison from his psychological system is often more subtle than any emetic known to medicine. I have often surprised and sometimes disappointed people who have asked me for help by cutting them off in the middle of their story. This has had the effect of slight shock; it also has the effect of dissociating them from their condition and diverting their attention to me—frequently in resentment. There are many cases in which help can best be given, or can only be given, through an abrupt disruption of the psychological status quo. But where resentment is already the seed of the condition—as in anger, hatred, jealousy, and spite—more resentment is not what is needed, of course, although a shattering of the destructive concentration may be primary.

In any case of physical disability I know that I am simply the agent who responds to a need, and I give of whatever I have in the circumstances. I become an aid to the sufferer's "will to live." In fact it is the sufferer's will to live which seeks additional strength to save itself.

In all kinds of cases the key to correction is to get at the root of the difficulty. Actually, perhaps, I am not interested in the slightest measure in the details of a man's life; but it is essential that he shall himself be interested in them in a certain way—a specific way: he must see clearly into himself and find there the deep relations to his present dilemma. So I ask him, "When did you first feel this pain?" or "When were you first aware that things were changing in your circumstances?" To answer, he inhales a breath; that is a breath of memory; and soon or late, it will drift down to the area of his psychological being that is waiting for its revitalizing effects. It may take time to do its work, but in any case the corrective regimen has begun.

There are many cases of distress which are purely psychological in their nature, having nothing to do with a person's physical condition as such, yet affecting the whole of the individual life. In such cases a measure of hypnosis, a play of illusion, "magic," is often the proper technique. Cases of inferiority, financial inefficiency, destructive bad habits, social maladjustments, and so on, are commonly based in some delusional attitude. The question then is, what different attitude, once induced, will let in the corrective light?

Though there are many therapies, there is but one kind of healing. Whether one "treats" a man in his physical organism or in his psychological states, one aims at the reintegration of the forces of his life. A person in an adverse psychological condition must get at the core of his difficulty through an understanding of its beginnings and through faith in his own ability to help in his cure. He often does this by some sort of objective "transfer," by fastening his attention on some object outside himself. In many cases the first requirement is just such an anchor of faith in someone else's; and when anyone comes to me in the hope or faith that I may be such an anchor, I always justify him by accepting, for the moment, the anchor role.

But such a person's attention must eventually be retransferred to himself. So one gives him the suggestion which will be self-corrective of his present state. Having thus centered his attention upon his problem, I often leave him to himself for a time, and let his own psychological metabolism do its work. Actually, I thus induce a measure of self-hypnosis in him. I have suggested a fresh concentration of energy and attention, have penetrated the confusion of a delusive attitude, and have given an anchorage to the man's faith—often an inestimable gift, as is proved by the miracles of Lourdes.

In some cases a greater measure of hypnosis is necessary than in others. This is achieved by further discussion, by the deeper concentration of the man's attention upon me as anchor, and upon the relationship between me and his difficulty. But actually, in all of this, his attention does not always have to be conscious; his subconscious will take it all in. And the subconscious will use it, moreover, in its own mysterious way.

We need to realize that in conditions of psychological confusion one's whole consciousness becomes like the atmosphere on a foggy day. Confusion, illusion, delusion —the fog has progressively thickened so that the man can no longer see out, can scarcely breathe. He suffers a state of actual psychological breathlessness. And this condition becomes so desperate—the fog crowds in so heavily —that the man is at last incapable of clearing his own immediate atmosphere. If a psychic breeze would only blow, he would be released from his deepest distress. So I raise a breeze for him, enable him to clear his own atmosphere, and presently he is able to breathe and to discern the light again.

Nobody asks for help in self-healing except when the will to live is still fertile within him. In such cases the body knows its own need, and the psyche knows its own need also. And having resorted to the search for help, both the body and the psyche—the consciousness as a whole— will accept such help when they find it. To be a conscious healer is to be always ready to give help, to the best of one's ability, and to be always sensitive to the subtle perception of humanity's various needs.

There are many unconscious healers—just as there are
many people who unconsciously carry and diffuse both
physical and psychological dis-ease, debility, and despair.
The ancient challenge, "Physician, heal thyself," constitutes the first problem of the conscious healer; and the
double duty of the conscious healer is (1) to eliminate
the elements of his own injuriousness in the world and
(2) to increase his power and capacity to heal on all the
levels of life.

There are certain types of human distress, usually
rooted in the emotions and the mind, but affecting the
physical body also, in which one who can must do more
than clear the psychological atmosphere in the ways I
have already suggested. The whole field of the life, both
natural and cultural, having been tilled to normal and
creative consummations, is abruptly shattered by hon-
orable outer forces, and one finds oneself ground and
suffering between the irresistible millstones of the gods.
There are many people—especially women—who are en-
during this type of difficulty today. Having built their lives
honestly, in conditions of peace and freedom, they find
all the normal meanings of their lives swept away by the
conditions of the war. They are patriotic, and they accept
the necessities and sacrifices in principle, but are unable
to make swift and easy adjustment to the changed order
of things that is sweeping the world. They are not stupid
people—rather they are generally simple and pure in their
private purposes. Life has suddenly become too much for
them; and like the protagonist in Greek drama, they move
as they must along the paths of an overpowering fate. And
these are paths of bitterness.

One of these women came to me, dry-eyed, but stretched
to the breaking point. Her inner tension was apparent in
her face and in her person; her nervous system was in
riot, and in controlling it, she had become rigid, taut. She
was sure that her husband, who was with the naval forces
of the United States, had been killed. She knew that his
ship had been sent into the southwest Pacific, and all the
world knew of the hazards of those seas.

The death of her husband—an inevitably tragic event
for her—would be the last phase of her descent into the
abyss of despair, possibly of madness; and she was rushing forward into that phase as though fascinated by the

idea of her own destruction. Yet she had had no notification of her husband's death, either officially or otherwise; her condition was wholy self-created.

What "treatment" could one possibly offer a person so spent and desperate? It was no time for platitudinous comforting; one could give no reassurances from one's own knowledge; the pressing need precluded all slow processes of recovery; but something positive was needed at once.

So, as I frequently do, I let her pour out her entire story. And then, with a gesture—as if I held the whole condition in my hands like a physical object—I placed it beside me on my desk. "There," I said, "I shall deal with your problem in my dream tonight."

The woman went away. And that night, in my telepathic dream, her husband came and talked with me. He assured me that he was not dead. He told me where he and his ship were. He mentioned by name people and places I had never heard of, and circumstances which were alien to my knowledge. There were references to South America, to deep waters, and to Ruby as a proper name. . . .

When I reported the whole experience to his wife, on the following day, she understood perfectly what he had meant in these references. And at the receipt of his message she recovered herself almost miraculously, realizing at once how she had permitted her imagination to undermine her fortitude. That was the beginning of her self-rehabilitation. She has entered into her new cycle of strength; she has achieved a new faith—it is as though she places her trust in her husband's existence and destiny because of a new understanding; and up to the present moment that trust has been justified. Through him she is also beginning to realize the nature and meaning of the war and of her country's part in it. In fact, she is becoming individualized.

What type of person makes the best healer? Looking at the matter in the broadest terms, the extrovert, the man of action, is potentially the best healer. He breathes deeply; his blood flow is a strong current; vital energy moves in him freely; he generates a tremendous magnetism. Though he serves many idols, he is also a breaker of crystallized attitudes. He is powerfully active at the more obvious levels; and if you can induce in him—if he can induce in himself—a sympathy so potent that it will modify his activity and encourage him to give himself to the cause of healing, you have a strong new agency enlisted on the side of human welfare.

Yet it may be said that, as a matter of fact, the more contemplative introvert is more commonly the healer. He has a more just and sympathetic understanding of causes and effects, a keener sense of other people. He has the temperament. He canvasses the field of his work subjectively, rather than through outer experimental activity. What he lacks in force, compared to the extrovert, he makes up in the quality and readiness of his service. He has some good measure of psychological awareness which, above all, is the great essential dividing line between undiscriminated activity and creative action.

The objective for all of us—here as elsewhere—is to become what we are. Under some circumstances we have all had evidence of our healing capacity; somewhere, at some time, we have all eased somebody's distress; so we know that the power is in us. What we have to do, if we wish to heal the adverse conditions of human existence, is to cultivate our own inner quality by expanding the field of circumstances in which it can operate. This is primarily a matter of realization, achieved through conscious consideration and self-analysis. It really amounts to an enhancement of our own vital being.

Generally speaking, the extrovert needs to cultivate a more objective attitude, paradoxical as this may seem, for his activities are the effects of his strong inner impulsions, and being strong, he does pretty much as he likes. He needs to learn to pause and think twice before acting, to take habitually a second look to verify his first passing impressions. He needs to learn to understand before the fact, and to perceive independently of his senses.

The true introvert, on the contrary, has to learn to consider less rather than more, to come to his conclusions more directly and swiftly, more impressionistically, with less heavy-footed circumlocution. He also needs to amplify his vital force, generally speaking, and to be more adventurous in risking his conclusions and his good intentions in the fields of criticism and activity.

At this point I should like to insert a word about the breath. Whatever theories we may hold concerning either the spiritual or the physical genesis of life itself, we must all agree that the breath is the primary key to human life on this earth. Men can survive for some time without food, drink, or sunlight—the other main essentials to physical existence; but, as I have said before, to cut off their breath is to rob them of life at once. In the breath we have a mighty instrument for the development of the forces of living, and most of us do not sufficiently appreciate it or understand how to use it.

We are all familiar with the fact that our breathing is affected by the outer events of our lives—fear and shock and the excitements of contest—while the rhythms of laughter and tears, symbolized in the comic and tragic masks of the theater, are respectively marked by the stimulation and the depression of our breathing.

In the conscious use of the breath, we have a tremendously effective technique for the development of creative capacities. I suppose the best-known indicators of the effects attainable through conscious breath control are the various yogas of the East. Processes of breath control necessarily originate in the consciousness; and this means that, in the beginning, the breather deliberately projects awareness into the subconscious and undertakes to impose new rhythm upon that region of automatisms.

There is danger in this intrusion of the conscious upon the subconscious, for in such an undertaking one assumes direct responsibility for the management of the deep physical processes of his life—responsibilities which are commonly left to nature. No such practice should be undertaken except under competent direction and supervision. But when the control of the breath is achieved through the practice of correct regimens, a new unity is developed between the subconscious past and the conscious present. This unity can be achieved only through the practice of disciplines. Such disciplines have an objective which, of necessity, can exist only in the future. It thus becomes clear that the superconscious also enters into the unification of the consciousness, and that this new unity is qualified and dominated by superconscious determinants. The whole process lies in the supersensory field. Successful activity based in this new unity of consciousness depends upon a recentering of consciousness itself; sensory perceptions are inhibited or specifically intensified, as the case may require. To the best of one's ability, one induces or negates sensory effect, according to the specific aim and purpose of the concentration.

In my own work in telepathy, clairvoyance, and trance, the control of the breath is a primary factor. The precise manipulation of it always depends upon my present supersensory purpose. . . . What I wish to emphasize here is that when the consciousness becomes unified and creatively active in a relatively high degree, much of the automatism of our habitual and routine living is transcended and we consciously transpose the forces of life and of nature to new particular ends.

By the unification of the consciousness we also achieve a new relation to time. One finds each present moment related to the future rather than to the past, to the fields of burgeoning, fresh vitality rather than to the fields of obsolescence. Precedent rises into awareness when it is necessary to the criticism of oneself or one's projects; but on the whole, one progressively escapes from the drag of history, with its cynicism, ineptitude, and conflict, and goes free in the areas of clear aspiration. Basically, time and consciousness are respectively indivisible. To unify consciousness within itself is also to condition it to apprehend the unity of time. This is a key to the mystery of supersensory activity. Consciousness is capable of perception in fields that lie beyond the reach of the five senses. But the development of perception in these supersensory fields depends upon the development, by consciousness, of its own self-control. By the proper use of the breath we vitalize consciousness as well as the physical organism.

I trust I do not need to emphasize here the moral aspects of such activities. The whole field is fundamentally moral. One becomes responsible for one's activities—and their consequences—in an imperative sense. But one also learns, savingly, as one proceeds, that the law of compensation is inescapable.

The techniques and therapies of healing are numberless —chemistry, the readjustment of physical malformations, surgery, spiritual healing, the laying on of hands, prayer, meditation, hypnosis, psychoanalysis, electricity, diet, magnetism. . . . Yet most of our cures are of the simplest kinds. It is not without natural warrant that the mother kisses her child's scratched hand or bruised knee. He comes to her in tears, and goes away laughing. Yet the mother is just a human being—sometimes a very ignorant one. But having love, she is always ready for service, and when the need arises she gives what she has—herself. Usually she contributes some kind of direct attention and a soothing bit of admonition and advice; but love is always included in her ministrations, and there is no one who can adequately fill her place.

This, I suppose, indicates the foundation on which all healing is based. One must love enough to be pure, in the sense of being quite selfless, and ready for service. The magic which is effective in the laying on of hands, or in any other type of helpfulness, must reach down to the subtle will to live that lies at the very heart of the individual existence; and it, being undeceivable, must gather the positive reassurance that it is fully related to the vitality of life itself.

There is only one kind of healing—the reassurance of the vital center within the physical form—the will to live. All states of being through which life expresses itself are therefore liable to the need of healing. A ready ear, a light in one's eyes, the sympathetic pressure of a hand, an encouraging word—any one of these is often better "medicine" than all the drugs in the pharmacopoeia. Fortunately, we are now entering into the field of human relationships in which these subtle psychological values are beginning to be really understood.

There is a certain sense in which nearly all of us are "patients" of one type or another, and subject to present healing. None of us attains to our full norm. Some of us live at a high measure of conscious efficiency and are constructive agents in the world. Such a full phase of conscious living often constitutes an excellent condition for continuous progressive development. But there are also conditions of almost utter unconsciousness in which not only healing, but even salvation occurs. Miraculous cures, which actually do happen, are of this type. Under some pressure of circumstances or dire need in one's life, one surrenders completely to the Universal—which is to say that one unites oneself wholly with the perfectly adjusted balance of natural forces in the universe; and partaking of that perfection, one is renewed in body, mind, and spirit. All healing requires some measure of this transcendence of our established individual habits and attitudes. On account of this, life frequently inhibits our usual activities quite completely, and puts the body to bed, so that the individual's inner universalistic pattern may work its way undisturbed.

It is because of this same inner necessity that, always in time of war, miraculous appearances occur on the battlefield, and men are saved, against all odds, in the most desperate situations. One reads every day, in the newspapers, of events which transcend all known laws and all the probabilities of life, and indicate that when a man is reduced to the last outer extremes of physical and psychological endurance, he finds there an unrealized increment of being in which each individual life is further related to life as a whole.

The hero in action, completely concentrated in his heroic activity, comes through a chaos of destructive fury unscathed; those very near death are delivered through the intervention of apparitions; men who have abandoned everything but faith live for weeks in open life rafts, without food or water; millions voluntarily suffer and die for causes that are completely impersonal to them . . .

In the face of such mysteries, and in the face of the ineptitudes of conscious human thought and planning, is it too much to suggest that humanity as a whole needs healing, and that the way to that healing is not to be found in the directions of ordinary sensory perception and "common sense"?

Illness or maladjustment, of whatever type, represents a conflict existing between the psyche and its environment. Healing consists in the readjustment of conditions in conformity to the needs of the psyche—the inner will to live. It is not always the individual that requires healing, however; very often it is the environment that needs readjustment. Consider the conquest of yellow fever or the present battles against syphilis and cancer; these involve not only the cure of individual cases, but the preventive elimination of environmental factors which are inimical to human life itself. . . . Healing is concerned with the establishment and maintenance of a balance, a norm of relations between fragmentary and partial phases of the one Life. As a whole, this balance is established and inviolable. The battle which mankind is constantly waging against its enemies—including many factors in human life itself—is neither more nor less than humanity's effort (partially rational, but mainly irrational still) to discover and conform to its own norm of relations with the Universal.

# 2

## How to Make Use of the Field of Mind Theory

### Elmer E. Green

*Elmer E. Green, Director of the Psychophysiology Laboratory of the Menninger Foundation in Topeka, Kansas, is a pioneer in biofeedback research and the study of "states of consciousness." In this article, he presents a theoretical framework of how "mind" may be viewed and describes his experiments with Jack Schwarz and Swami Rama who both exhibit a mastery of their bodily functions.*

• • •

Our research in "voluntary controls" at The Menninger Foundation has to do with the extent to which human beings can learn to control normally involuntary and unconscious processes. We refer to this research as the study of "voluntary control of internal states," without trying to define what "internal states" might be, beyond saying that they are physiological and psychological states. Since "internal states" concern everything in human life, we are free to consider anything, from anabolism to Zen, that might be related to man's experience and to his powers of self-regulation.

One of our first psychophysiological studies (conducted with thirty-three housewives) was a study of the ability to control blood flow in the hands through controlling the temperature of the hands. Dr. Johannes Schultz, in Germany, who developed autogenic training [1] found that self

Dr. Green wishes to acknowledge the collaboration of his wife, Alyce M. Green, in the preparation of this paper.

control of warmth in the extremities was an important part of learning to relax in the autonomic (normally involuntary and unconscious) nervous system. Increased blood flow in the peripheral parts of the body was associated with the eradication of anxiety as a response to the stress of life. It seemed to us, therefore, that research (with instrumentation) on the self-regulation of blood flow was a good way to begin an investigation of the psychological "unconscious." We finally developed a training program using a sensitive temperature indicator, a biofeedback device, by means of which people could see what was happening when they attempted to control the temperature of their hands.

Parenthetically, a particular word ties some of what I wish to discuss with what has been said by other writers today. "Faith" has been mentioned. It is interesting that if you do not have faith when you begin to use a temperature feedback machine, after about ten seconds (or at least a minute) you begin to have it. If you do not believe that you can voluntarily raise the temperature of your hands, when you attach the temperature sensor to your finger, and say, "This won't work for me," the temperature usually goes down. Our comment is, "You demonstrated what you predicted. That tends to prove *our* point, not yours. It does work for you." There are variations from this simple example, but the skeptic is usually startled because he had not previously realized that the body is so responsive to belief. After a bit of practice, the average person can learn to raise the temperature of his hand, or lower it, at will, or make one hand warmer and the other colder, though this takes more practice. How far this ability to control "involuntary" physiological processes can be extended is not yet known. From a theoretical point of view, for reasons that I will mention later in connection with the field of mind theory, we are beginning to think that almost any physiological signal that can be obtained with a sensitive transducer (a measuring device) and fed back to the person who produced it, can be self regulated.

A nice illustration of biofeedback, and the specific applications of different kinds of feedback, is contained in the "headache results" of Dr. Thomas Budzynski [2] at the University of Colorado Medical Center, at Denver, and Dr. Joseph Sargent [3] at The Menninger Foundation. Excluding relatively rare types, chronic headaches are of two kinds, migraine (a blood flow problem) and muscle tension. Many people have both kinds, migraine plus tension. In a conversation with Dr. Sargent a short time ago about his results in relief of migraine through training in hand temperature control (with over 100 patients), he said that he had come to the conclusion that patients who had pure migraine could be helped quite a bit by the temperature training program, those who had a combination of the two kinds of headache could be helped to a lesser extent, and those who had pure tension headaches could not be helped very much. That same day in a phone conversation with Tom Budzynski, I happened to mention what Sargent had said. Tom laughed and said, "Let me tell you about the other side of the coin," and he explained that his tension patients were helped quite a bit by "muscle tension feedback" (from the forehead, using an electromyographic device, EMG, to detect and feed back information about electrical activity from tensed muscles), those who had a combination of the two kinds of headache were helped to a lesser extent, and those who had pure migraine did not seem to be helped very much.

What this tells us is that specific feedback can have specific results, and it suggests that possibly a person can learn to manipulate physiological behavior associated with specific feedback from any body process. Recently I talked with two physicians in Boston about the possibility of their using the information output of a "kidney machine" as feedback to patients, instead of only to doctors, during purification of the blood of patients with malfunctioning or damaged kidneys. If biofeedback "works," these patients should begin to develop control of kidney functions. This is not as far out as may seem at first glance. Dr. Neal Miller has already shown that rats can be conditioned to control kidney functions.[4] Autogenic Therapy [5] has organ-specific formulas that modify biochemical processes, and Swami Rama, in addition to demonstrating that unlikely body processes can be brought under self regulation, says that *all* physiological functions can be controlled by gaining control of that section of the unconscious in which the functions are represented.

One physician whom I talked with about the biofeedback of kidney functions objected, however. No amount of feedback would repair a damaged kidney, he said. But possibly he was overlooking an important causal relationship between kidney damage and various biochemical processes of the body. How does a kidney get damaged, from biochemical mistreatment, from psychosomatic distortion of neurohumoral processes, from genetic predisposition? Whatever the "cause" there is no reason to assume in advance that the mind at some deep level cannot make various biochemical changes, or whatever, to bring about repairs in organs and organ systems. Too many "spontaneous cures" and so-called miracle cures (which phraseology describes our ignorance of what really happened) have occurred for us to be dogmatic about the limitations of the mind to influence body processes. It is useful to stress the fact that *biofeedback feeds back information to the mind, however it may be defined,* and through the development of awareness, a psychological state, one can learn to influence physiological states.

When patients learn to control the vascular behavior associated with migraine, they are "deconditioning" themselves from the Skinnerian-type conditioning of life. They are also to some extent controlling a genetic predisposition, because migraine has been shown to run in families. The argument may still go on as to whether or not there is such a thing as "free will," whether or not a person can self determine anything, but the implications of the field of mind theory put conditioning and genetics in a new and not-totally-controlling perspective.

Before talking more about neurological mechanisms, it is interesting to point out that from the Eastern point of view, which allows for reincarnation, one's genetic structure and the life situation in which one is found are direct projections of a previous psychological structure. In the Eastern way of thinking, genetics and conditioning are the essential tools of nature in evolving consciousness and self-mastery, nothing more, nothing less. In other words, one's personal genetic configuration and his life situation comprise a kind of "cosmic feedback," without which it would not be possible to evolve into the next state of consciousness, transpersonal consciousness. The evolutionary progression is said to be mineral, plant, animal, personal (human consciousness), and transpersonal (the beginning of another kind of consciousness).

Be that as it may, what I wish to focus attention on first is psychosomatic medicine, because psychosomatic illness is one of the internal states with which most of us are concerned. According to medical specialists, perhaps as much as 80% of human health problems involve psychosomatic effects, either totally or as a contributing factor. What this really means in any specific example is that a certain section of the brain, of which one is normally unaware, learned a bad habit—a bad neurological habit—and is functioning in an undesirable manner. Research is showing that these bad habits can be voluntarily eliminated by retraining, using biofeedback to tell us what is happening in the physiological domain so that we can become aware of, and use, specific

Figure 1

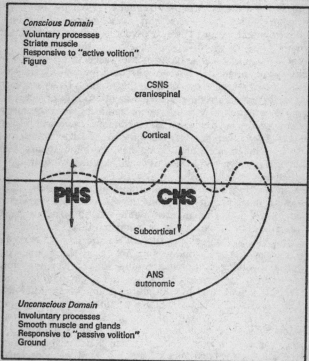

Diagram of the major psychophysiological domains and concepts, relating the conscious-unconscious psychological domain to the various sections of the central (CNS) and peripheral (PNS) nervous systems. The solid horizontal line implies the separation of the nervous system into traditional voluntary and involuntary sub-regions and the dashed line (conceptually visualized to be in continuous undulatory movement when a person is awake) separates the conscious and unconscious areas at any instant.

existential changes that are correlated with specific physiological changes. It seems reasonable to assume that if we can get physiologically sick from responding psychologically to stress in some inappropriate way, we can perhaps get well by learning to control the psychological response. Feedback devices are important for this kind of learning because they mirror what is going on beneath the skin. Visual feedback tells us when our car is going off the road, biofeedback tells us about our bodies and allows us to make existential corrections.

Figure 1 shows a diagrammatic arrangement of the nervous system. First it is useful to discuss this mind-body diagram in reference to people like ourselves, and then relate it to unusual people like Swami Rama and Jack Schwarz.

The conscious part of the diagram, above, contains both the cerebral cortex, which someone at a meeting of the American Medical Association called the "screen of consciousness," and the craniospinal nervous system that operates the muscular structure (striate muscles) in voluntary activity. The unconscious part of the diagram, below, contains both the subcortical sections of the brain, which might be referred to as the "screen of *un*consciousness," and the autonomic nervous system that controls the involuntary muscular structure (smooth muscles), glands, internal organs, and a host of involuntary processes.

The nervous system is also divided into the central nervous system, CNS, the brain and spinal cord—represented by the circle in the center of the diagram, and the peripheral nervous system, PNS, every neural network that is outside of the central nervous system. Aside from minor discrepancies taken note of in textbooks, the nervous system has four sections, then: the conscious central, the unconscious central, the conscious peripheral, and the unconscious peripheral. By "conscious" please note that I mean "that which we are conscious of." I do not mean that the muscles, etc., are themselves conscious.

Presumably when we are born the various sections have a natural harmonious interlocking way of functioning, except for genetic defects, but before long the functioning parts are modified by environmental impact; perhaps this begins even before birth. The psychological and physiological shocks of life begin to modify both conscious and unconscious behavior. Both good and bad habits are learned on both sides of the central division of the diagram.

The actual division between conscious and unconscious functions is not the fixed horizontal line, of course, but is represented by a continuously undulating line, the dashed line, "frozen" in a momentary position. When we are *un*conscious of a skill that we previously learned slowly and consciously, like walking, the dashed line moves up temporarily to include some section of the normally conscious nervous system. When we learn to control the flow of blood in our hands with the aid of a temperature trainer, we move the dashed line down over some section of the normally unconscious nervous system. In a figurative sense, one of the goals of biofeedback training is to get voluntary control over this dashed line so that we can be conscious when and where we choose inside our own being.

If we suffer from a psychosomatic disease, it is clear that somehow some section of the nervous system, whether it was originally conscious or unconscious, is now malfunctioning in an unconscious way. We may be conscious of the effects in our life, but we are not conscious of the underlying distortion in the nervous system and do not know how to correct it. If our doctor tells us we have a psychosomatic disease it does not help much and may even make us angry. After all, we know it is not "all in our heads." In actuality, it is, of course, but not in an imaginary sense but in a *real* neurological sense, with effects in our bodies.

The patient might appropriately ask two questions at this point: "How can this happen?" and "What can I do about it?" assuming, of course, that the patient does not desire to take symptom-relieving pills indefinitely, with the hope that the condition will go away, or the mind-body matrix will cure itself "for no known reason."

The origin of psychosomatic disease seems to lie in a person's response to stress. It is easy to believe that physiological stress can destroy the body or change some of its neural and biochemical functions, can strain the organic entity beyond its "elastic limits," but it is not generally understood that a stress in the psychological domain can also destroy the body by changing some of its neural and biochemical functions. The mechanism seems to be as follows:

A section of the subcortex called the limbic system, also called the "visceral" brain and sometimes the "emotional" brain, responds to emotions, and therefore to most thoughts (because few thoughts have no emotional associations) by changing neurological firing patterns. Since the limbic system is connected by multiple pathways to various other structures, including the hypothalamus (the neural control center that regulates to a large extent the autonomic nervous system), emotional response is "radiated" into autonomic control centers and modifies ongoing autonomic functions.

The evolutionary need for this mechanism is clear in the case of an at-home caveman who sees a bear coming into the cave. If his perception-to-limbic-to-hypothalamic-to-autonomic response does not quickly speed up the heart, increase the blood pressure, and bring about all the other autonomic ingredients for a fight, his genetic line might be suddenly terminated.

Having inherited a caveman's response machinery, but having to meet a chronic stress (rather than acute stress), a chronic *response* can develop—due to the psychological pressures of civilized life. Eventually a psychosomatic disease develops. The autonomic nervous system learns a bad habit.

The obvious thing to do is to change our habitual response to stress. This is where biofeedback is useful. Apparently (or at least theoretically), anything normally unconscious that we can become aware of inside the skin we can begin to change, and biofeedback makes it possible to become aware of those subtle changes of a psychological nature whose enhancement restabilizes the limbic and hypothalamic processes, with all their neurological and biochemical concomitants, and reestablishes psychosomatic health.

These considerations and various parapsychological events lead us to postulate along with Dr. Rolf Alexander [6] a "field of mind," in which control of events both inside the skin and outside the skin is hypothesized as a volitional function of mind. Parapsychology enters the picture in a crucial way because the question might be asked, "If the mind and body are so tightly hooked together that one cannot be moved without moving the other, what reason is there to believe that the mind is anything more than our cognitive perception of unconscious and uncontrollable biochemical and neurological processes in the body and brain?" The answer is that laboratory data from talented individuals imply that the mind is some kind of energy structure in its own right. The mind and body correlations we speak of appear to be functional interactions of different kinds of energy. These "fields" are not truly separable, it seems, and yet they are not exactly the same. The crucial fact of *psychokinesis*, mind-over-matter, apart from the body, is the nemesis of a physical-body-only interpretation of man's nature. The resistance of some scientists to examining the data of psychokinesis may be traceable in part to their feeling that if psychokinesis is true, then mind and body would be different from what has been accepted and mind would become one of the forces of nature, and that does not make sense, they feel, because mind is not something substantial.

Concerning mind-body correlations, however, Aurobindo suggested that we may, if we wish, think of the entire cosmos as constructed of matter (energy) with physical substance its most dense form and spirit its most rarefied form. On the other hand, he said, you may prefer to think of matter as the densest form of spirit. This idea, which is an essential concept in the field of mind theory, is consistent with the existential reports of both Swami Rama and Jack Schwarz, as research subjects in our Voluntary Controls Program, demonstrated physiological and parapsychological phenomena that imply that mind is not just body, however attractive that simplistic idea may be to some people.

Before talking further about the field of mind theory, let me review some of our laboratory findings, keep in mind the mind-brain dichotomics, conscious-unconscious, voluntary-involuntary.

### Swami Rama

The most potent of the various ideas that the Swami discussed is contained in the concept from Raja Yoga and the Yoga Sutras of Patanjali that "All the body is in the mind, but not all the mind is in the body." This simple phrase has vast theoretical implications. The control of every cell of the body is possible, according to the Swami, because every cell has a representation in the unconscious. Not only that, each cell is *part* of the unconscious. In other words each cell exists not only symbolically in mind, but also as a section of a real energy structure called mind. When we manipulate the representation of the cell in the unconscious, we literally manipulate the cell itself because the cell is part of the mind.

The second half of the phrase, "but not all the mind is in the body," is related to the extension of mind into nature in general and accounts for parapsychological events, psychokinesis, psychic healing, and all such "scientifically impossible" phenomena. The reason science has felt these phenomena are impossible is because scientists, at least the majority, have not been able to conceive of the mind as an energy structure which interlocks with energy structures both in the body and in "external" nature. These ideas seem rather far out, but consider the following facts which hopefully will lead to theories, to hypotheses, and to experimentation.

I was talking to Swami Rama about the possible control and absorption of tumors by shutting off their blood supply through the development of "internal" blood flow control. If a tiny thermistor were implanted in a tumor (or cancer) the temperature record could be used for biofeedback, and the smooth muscles that control blood flow by constriction of vascular walls could possibly be brought under voluntary control to starve the tissue. While I was outlining this, the Swami interrupted and said, "Oh yes, that wouldn't be too hard to do," but he did not mean implanting a biofeedback device, it turned out, he meant direct control of the tumor. He said that all of the soft tissues of the body were relatively easy to control. For instance, you can convert muscular tissue into something else.

I asked him what he meant. I knew that "All of the body is in the mind," suggested that psychosomatic phenomena could be controlled, but I hadn't really considered all the possibilities.

He said, "Wait a minute. I'll show you." He asked me to palpate a muscle in his hip (the top of the gluteus maximus). "Do you feel any lumps in it?" he asked. I said, "No." "Just a minute," he said. He looked to the side for perhaps five seconds and then asked me to feel it again. This time there was a big lump in the muscle, about as large as a bird's egg. I said, "What is that, a tense muscle, like a charley horse?"

"No, no," he said.

"What is it, then?" I asked.

"It's a cyst," he said.

"What's in it? Water?" I asked.

He said he didn't know. I asked if he would be willing to have an X-ray, and he replied that he was not sure because his teacher had said that cellular changes might happen as a result of X-rays that he might not be able to handle. I asked if he would be willing to have a biopsy.

"Well, maybe," he said. He asked me to feel the lump again, but to my surprise, it was gone. "Just a minute," he said, "I'll make another one." He looked away again for a few seconds, and then said, "There's another one." This one was in a different spot, where I could get my thumb on it and press it against the bone. It popped around like a cyst. I do not know if he will be willing to do that again or not. If he does I hope it takes place in our laboratory and medical colleagues are present. The Swami has been traveling and lecturing for the last year and a half, and may be "out of practice." There is a kind of "autonomic Olympics" in India for which yogis prepare, but they may not remain "in condition" all of the time.

To this point, we have discussed only inside-the-skin phenomena, but now I wish to discuss outside-the-skin phenomena, parapsychological data. To experiment is better than to argue, it is said, and even that is better than to deny without looking at the data. It may seem obvious from a scientific point of view that it is not logical to ridicule facts without examining them, but it is sometimes done. Some scientists who wish to discredit parapsychology, however, are so confident that parapsychological events can be "explained away" that they are willing to examine the data, but then are unwilling to accept the implications even though statistical probabilities in support of parapsychological hypotheses are astronomically in favor of parapsychological theories. One way of meeting this "awful fact," is to claim that the work that has been done or supported by Rhine, Soal and Bateman, Murphy, and a host of others, is fraud. From a psychiatric point of view, however, those who resort to calling "fraud" are probably defending against an unconscious fear of the unknown. What would they say to the following?

Swami Rama, in a psychokinetic demonstration in our laboratory twice caused a fourteen-inch aluminum knitting needle five feet away to rotate through ten degrees of arc. The needle was mounted horizontally on a vertical spindle that passed through it and had enough bearing friction to prevent air currents in the room from moving it. I had also taken the precaution of closing the air vents with tape. One observer felt that it might still have been done by air currents through the Swami's control of his breath, that is, by physical air currents, but six of us felt that the Swami's explanation was more acceptable than that (even if the energy involved was not detectable), because we had him wear a painter's mask with a foam rubber insert, covered with a plexiglass plate to deflect any breath downward and away from the direction of the needle.

It was interesting that while on the way to the lab for the demonstration the Swami said that one of the observers would feel that it was done with his breath and suggested that we get a bed sheet to tie over the mask and his body so that only his eyes would be exposed. Time was not available, however, and his suggestion was put aside. Later the Swami said, on being informed that he was right (that there *was* concern by one of the observers about his control of air currents), that he would (within the next half hour) be able to do it again from behind a sheet of plexiglass, or wood, or metal. It was necessary only that he be able to see over the top of it. It was not possible, however, to reschedule in less than ten days, because of other schedules in the group of observers. Since we did not wish him to perform such a demonstration with only ourselves as observers, we turned our attention to brainwave studies. We expect to continue this work when occasion permits, but in the meantime the main question in our minds is not, "Are these things facts," but rather, "How can such events be accounted for from a scientific point of view?"

### Jack Schwarz

When we heard about Jack Schwarz a few years ago, I called him on the phone and said that if he ever took a trip to the East Coast and could stop at Topeka we would be pleased to show him our laboratory. We did not know much about Jack except that apparently he and Swami Rama talked about similar things, and it was said by those who knew him that he had unusual control of physiological and psychological processes. One day, several months later, Jack phoned me in Topeka and said that he had an eight-day break in his seminar series on the West Coast and would be willing to demonstrate some mind-body coordinations as a research subject if we wished. By coincidence, the only eight days on our calendar that were free for several months concided with his suggested dates. Shortly thereafter he arrived in Topeka.

The first thing that Jack said he would like to demonstrate was voluntary control of bleeding and pain. The sailmaker's needle he used to puncture his bicep remained buried about one-half inch deep in it for about thirty seconds. Generally in this type of "experiment" I do not suggest what ought to be done, at least not the first time, for fear that I might upset a delicate psychological state of some kind and prevent the demonstration from taking place, but when the needle was buried in Jack's bicep with no particular signs of pain (with no unsual changes in heart rate, breathing rate, skin potential and skin resistance) the thought became quite strong in me that perhaps Jack did not really have control of bleeding but had a medically anomalous skin. Perhaps he was a non-bleeder (and a non-painer). If he did this a hundred times it would not prove to me that he had control of bleeding, unless we knew that bleeding was natural to him.

So I said, just before he pulled the needle out, "Jack, tell me, is it going to bleed or isn't it?" I projected that idea quite forcefully with the thought that if the control of bleeding were actually a result of Jack's control of normally uncon-scious physiological processes, then I could upset the apple-cart, so to speak, by interfering with his coordination between conscious and unconscious processes. He glanced at me with a surprised look on his face and said, somewhat uncertainly. "I don't think it's going to bleed." But when he pulled the needle out there was considerable blood flow from the two punctures. The photographer and I began mopping it up with paper tissues. While we were doing that Jack looked at his arm in a detached way and after a while said in a soft voice, "Now it stops." To my surprise the two holes in his skin drew shut, like a drawstring purse, or a tobacco sack, and not another drop of blood came out. The videotape got a good record of this but seeing it from a few inches was more impressive.

I told Jack that I was glad to find out that he was normal, could bleed when holes were poked in his skin, and that I was impressed by his ability to stop bleeding, but would he be willing to do it again and this time demonstrate that he could prevent bleeding entirely. There was a long pause. After about ten seconds I was beginning to feel rather un-comfortable, and the thought came to me that maybe I had upset the "coordination" between his conscious and uncon-scious too much. Then he said, "Okay." This time the needle passed through a small vein, when it broke through the skin. When Jack withdrew the needle, after fifteen or twenty seconds, there was no bleeding. The wounds closed up around the needle, as he pulled it out, leaving two small red spots. Of interest was the fact that no detectable subdermal bleeding took place at either trial. No discoloration was present the next day and in 24 hours one of the four holes had disappeared. In 72 hours none of the spots were visible. His skin was as smooth and unblemished as at the beginning. Jack said that he had performed this demonstration hundreds of times, but his skin was nevertheless smooth and unmarked.

I asked him if he had ever had an infection as a result of driving these needles through his arm. The first needle had accidentally fallen on the floor of the lab and when I asked if he wanted me to clean it off he said no, that he always "sterilized" his equipment that way. While talking with him about the danger of infection he suggested that infection was not possible if the mind did not allow it. This is a strange idea but agreed closely with various things that Swami Rama had said. If all of the body is part of the mind, and the mind does not permit interaction (or reaction) with foreign materials, such as microbes, there is no way that an infection can develop. I asked Jack why he had paused so long before agreeing to do it the second time. He said that he did not exactly force these things to happen. He asked the "subconscious" if it was willing to do it again and he had to wait until it said yes before he could answer me. He also said that another level of the mind, the "paraconscious," was involved and that it (part of the *un*conscious and superior to both the *sub*conscious and the conscious) had to give permission before the subconscious agreed.

In another kind of demonstration, parapsychological rather than psychophysiological (though we wired him for brainwaves, heart rate, respiration, temperature, blood flow, and skin potential resistance), Jack talked with a young lady whom he had never seen before and, after asking her not to speak or ask questions until he had finished, told her about the major events in her physical, emotional, and mental life for the preceding nine years. He did this, he said, by examining her "aura," a radiatory energy that, according to seers, surrounds the human body. The structure and color of the aura, Jack said, revealed the information. This young lady, and her husband who was with us in the polygraph recording room, were quite astonished. Jack mentioned events and problems that they had discussed with no one, and included one item of a medical nature that she had not yet told her husband. I asked Jack how he could see the names of medical problems in an aura, and he said that when he focussed attention on the various marks and colors, the names and details of the associated problems came into his consciousness as intuitive knowledge. This sounds remarkably similar to the way that Edgar Cayce worked, while in trance, and it is not unreasonable to assume that whatever the exact method, they have much in common. Of interest along this line is the fact that Swami Rama has this same ability and so does a Shoshone medicineman, Rolling Thunder, whom we have been in contact with for the last few years. These people seem to see the so-called unconscious as their link with events both inside the skin and outside the skin.

Dr. Kurt Fantl of Long Beach told me of some research he carried out with Jack in the fifties in which Jack demonstrated, among a large number of other phenomena, the ability to put his hands into a brazier of burning coals, hold the coals in his hands, and show no signs of burning or heating. This was done, he said, before a group of physicians from Los Angeles County medical and hypnosis associations. Jack's skin, he said, had been carefully examined and pronounced normal before the demonstration as well as after. I mention this here because this type of phenomenon may have psychokinetic content. The outer layer of skin is supposedly dead and should show signs of burning unless the coals or the "dead layer" itself were controlled in some way. It might be more difficult to control dead cells than live cells. Movies made by the National Geographic Society many years ago and observations by many observers in the last thirty years seem to indicate that the non-burning effect in fire walking extends not only to the body but to the garments of practitioners. This kind of demonstration, whatever the exact mechanism, seem to demonstrate that ". . . not all the mind is in the body." With the above demonstrations in mind, and also the explanations that were made by Swami and by Jack, it is interesting to consider mind as an energy structure and relate it to other ideas from both East and West.

### Field of Mind

Figure 2 is a diagram that was originally constructed for college students in explaining the relationship between Freud's and Jung's ideas of the mind, but it has been expanded so as to include additional concepts.

The most important idea about the diagram is that every line represents both a demarcation between different kinds of substance and between different kinds of consciousness. This idea is the essence of Tibetan Buddhism when its cultural peculiarities are stripped off and also represents the basic concepts of Integral Yoga (of Aurobindo), Esoteric Christianity, Sufism, Zoroastrianism, Esoteric Judaism, Egyptian and Greek Mystery Schools, Theosophy, Anthroposophy, Polynesian metaphysics, and various pre-Columbian religions in the Western Hemisphere. (For references to these different cultural views, see Item 7 in the Bibliography.)

The second important idea represented in the diagram is that the different kinds of energies and structures, physical, emotional, mental, and transpersonal, are functional parts of a planetary field of mind. Even as magnetic, electrostatic, and gravitational fields surround the planet, so does a field of mind; and furthermore, all the fields, however differentiated, are part of the basic mind field. This means that all gradations of physical substance are gradations of the field of mind. In other words, according to this theory the entire cosmos at every level is both matter and mind, and in some way evolution of living beings from mineral matter (which is not dead matter in this concept) through plant, animal, and man, is accompanied by an evolution and expansion of consciousness.

Of particular interest is the balloon-shaped section called the "conscious" at the bottom of the diagram. It is shown to have physical substance (brain and body), emotional substance, and mental substance. Surrounding the conscious is the "subconscious" substance and above the conscious is the transpersonal substance. In reality, says the theory, all these substances totally interpenetrate. There is no up or down. That is merely a convenience for purpose of illustration.

The connection between the conscious and the transpersonal structure called the Lotus, has many names in the East. This "tunnel," as it is often perceived in mental imagery, is sometimes called the "path," the "way," the antakarana, or Tao. In Christian and Judaic terminology it has been referred to as Jacob's Ladder. It is interesting to consider that this ladder, about which Jacob said, "this is the gate of Heaven," may represent a real structure, which when consciously or unconsciously constructed, brings transpersonal awareness. It is not possible in a short time to more than touch on the many references that have bearing on this

Figure 2

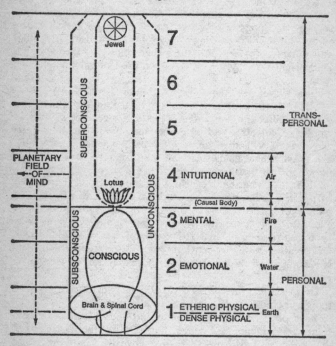

Symbolic Interpretation of Man's Substance and Perceptual Structure. (Presented at the Annual Meeting of the Association for Humanistic Psychology, Miami Beach, September, 1970, E. E. Geen.)

transpersonal level of mind, but it is interesting to note that the best known Tibetan mantra, Om Mani Padme Hum, is roughly translated by some as "Hail, Oh Thou Jewel in the Lotus," and supposedly represents the same concepts and relationships as the Father and Christ.

Whatever the parallels may be, in the field of mind theory the laws of Nature (taking Nature as the entire planetary structure, rather than merely physical nature) are the rules that govern cause and effect. Morals, in this view, rather than being arbitrary, have to do with the way Nature functions. The extent to which religious ideas are moral, then, is determined by the extent to which religious ideas correspond to the Natural Law.

Returning to the conscious envelope, however, it is possible to break the barrier horizontally between the conscious and surrounding subconscious, so that one becomes aware of what is normally unconscious in him at emotional and mental levels. These levels represent the Freudian domain of the diagram since reference is not made to transpersonal levels in Freudian psychology, as it is in the Jungian system. According to Eastern thought, especially as delineated by Aurobindo, personal safety in altered states of consciousness (which includes breaking the barrier to the subconscious) cannot exist unless one is anchored at the Lotus level, which Aurobindo calls the Overmind. He says that if the transpersonal connection is not previously established, it is possible to break through the barriers in a horizontal direction, first into the subconscious and then through the next barrier into the *extrapersonal* levels of the planetary field, and not be able to establish Self control (at least not in this incarnation). The danger seems to be that hallucinatory and delusional tendencies can grow unchecked if Self awareness is absent during exploration of "horizontal" psychic space. Mental hospitals and psychiatrists unfortunately have to handle many cases who do not appear to have a functional integrating center, or self. It is interesting in this regard that in Zen the "Lotus being" is called the True Self, and one's detours into horizontal realms of consciousness are actively discouraged. Eastern thought in general is not as adamant, but says it is necessary to find one's Self first.

It is quite easy to see that the major existential concepts held by Swami Rama and by Jack Schwarz fit neatly into the field of mind diagram. For instance, the unconscious area in the diagram contains both the subconscious and the superconscious (the personal unconscious and the transpersonal unconscious). The transpersonal unconscious is Jack's "paraconscious." In order to control physiological processes it is simply a matter of expanding consciousness at the physical level of the diagram so that all the physical being (represented here by the drawing of the brain) is held in conscious mind. When this is done, the visualization of physiological change becomes an actual physiological change because (says the theory) the body is not different from the mind. In other words, it is impossible to consciously change the "unconscious" without also changing the body. The reverse is also true in this theory. For example, changing a biochemical process in the body (as with a tranquilizer) changes the "unconscious," and this, in turn, is reflected in consciousness as a feeling of tranquility. Swallowing an aspirin has a psychological effect because the aspirin is an energy structure in the planetary field of mind. In other words, an aspirin is not different, in some respects, from body and mind. Thoughts, emotions, bodies, and aspirins are real.

LSD has intense psychological effects because, in this theory, it is a crystallized section of the general field which when taken into the body modifies (more effectively than aspirin) the physical, emotional, and mental structures and breaks some of the barriers between structural sections, horizontally and vertically. Some drugs, such as harmaline, seem to break only horizontal barriers. The dangers of drug experience without first establishing transpersonal connection, is that once the barriers have been punctured it is not always easy to close the breaks. A superior level of control is needed. In ancient initiations into altered states of consciousness, a teacher who could "see" always accompanied the student to guide him through delusional traps and protect him against "forces" he could not control.

When Castaneda was told by his Yaqui Indian teacher, Don Juan, to go away until his "gap" was healed (apparently a gap in the so-called astral plane because it was a solar plexus gap) he was probably referring to a literal break in the barrier between the conscious and the planetary field at mental-emotional levels. It is extremely interesting to note the almost exclusive use of solar plexus force by Don Juan and by his colleague, Don Genero, in training Castaneda [8]. This corresponds to the yogic idea of the third chakra in the body, the "emotion" chakra of the solar plexus. Chakras, remember, are reportedly energy centers associated with the human frame through which *perception and action* on all the different levels of being take place.

In this connection, it is illuminating to note that Don Juan said there were an infinite number of paths that *could* be followed (in the separate reality) but that only the paths with "heart" led anywhere. Since solar plexus development is associated in esoteric systems with extension of mental-emotional consciousness (what might be called "horizontal extrapersonal expansion in mental-emotional space" of the diagram) and since the "heart" is the symbol of the fourth chakra (the Lotus) it seems that Don Juan, the Yaqui Indian, and Aurobindo, the East Indian, were referring to similar existential facts. Aurobindo said it was necessary to establish a connection with the transpersonal before exploring the horizontal extensions at personal levels, in order to guard against getting lost. Don Juan said that the paths of the separate reality led nowhere, except for those that had "heart."

It is not possible to talk about existential matters without handling the problem of dangers associated with exploration in "states of consciousness." Those who are familiar with existential expansion generally agree that dangers are involved. Even to those who are no experts, it is obvious that hallucination and delusion can result from unwise use of drugs, forced meditation, or violent breathing exercises. These problems have been much discussed, but there is another kind of danger that many people are unknowingly subjected to. Recently it has become popular for people who desire existential knowledge, or wish to obtain personal psychic powers, to allow themselves to be driven by hypnotic programming through the subconscious and extrapersonal barriers into the general field of mind at physical, emotional, and mental levels.

I am referring here to commercial "mind training" programs that claim to give alpha training for developing ESP and psychic diagnostic ability. You can also learn to control other people, they say, through the psychokinetic control of their minds. Take the training course, urge the advertisements; it will make you rich, sexually potent, powerful, and also you will be able to get rid of your diseases and diagnose and treat the diseases of others.

Biofeedback training is beginning to be of value in medicine, psychotherapy, and in developing human potential. This is the research area that we have been engaged in for the last several years at The Menninger Foundation, but the "mind training" development has usurped the scientific vocabulary and is promising results that, if attained by the average person, could cause psychic disasters.

Some of these disasters have already appeared. One

psychiatrist on the East Coast told me recently that four out of thirty students in one of the popular courses (which he took for his own information) became psychotic, two having to be hospitalized. In commenting on this, he said that possibly these people were drawn to the course because they already had problems. In other words, the percentage of psychoses might be unusually high because these people were already unstable and were looking for help. In another report, a counselor in San Jose, California, told me that about a dozen of the disturbed people he was counseling had become paranoid as a result of their experiences in one of the West Coast programs.

Commercial mind-training teachers are, in general, breaking the long established rules for safety in the extrapersonal domain. They have (1) appealed to the lower emotions (with a minimal recognition of the transpersonal by suggesting that "none of these powers will be able to be used by you for evil purposes"), (2) they have known nothing about the personal hang-ups of their customers before "programming" them to break the barriers horizontally, (3) they are seldom professionally trained and cannot successfully take responsibility for psychological disasters, and (4) they generally claim that there are no psychological problems or dangers as a result of their courses.

Hypnosis is a powerful psychological and medical tool and should not be used, in our opinion, by those who are not qualified by training to handle psychic problems that may result from its use. Hypnosis is dangerous in the hands of amateurs and especially should not be used for catapulting people, as in a drug experience, into extrapersonal regions in which they are not prepared to take care of themselves. The "psychic" universe seems to be a big ocean and it is presumptuous to naively plunge in with the assumption that there are no sharks.

To return to the field of mind theory, however, it is encouraging to note that the existential experts say that a meditative effort toward the development of Self consciousness diminishes the dangers of existential expansion. According to Aurobindo, meditation releases energy that transforms the "astral plane" (the personal power-trip plane of emotional and mental substance). Don Juan's paths that have heart imply this same idea. Discriminative values are involved because results must conform to the laws of Nature and because volition seems to determine the direction of exploration. Each person chooses his path. It is worth noting that "not choosing" is also a choice, so discrimination, or lack of discrimination, becomes an essential ingredient in what "happens" in altered states.

Much more could be said along this line but perhaps a good conclusion is to paraphrase a well-known existentialist who said, "Look first for the transpersonal connection within, other powers will be added later."

This brings us back to the subject of this talk, "How to Use the Field of Mind Theory." The subject is not "how to use the field of mind," but how to use the theory. The theory can be used as a yardstick for evaluation of ideas, in studying suggestions for psychic development, in considering moral dilemmas, and for discriminating between teachers, gurus, etc. Does a teacher's behavior contradict his words? In a personal sense, what are our own goals? Do we want powers in order to dominate others? By asking such questions the field of mind theory can be used as a road map for the exploration of states of consciousness. The questions are, then, "Where are we on the map? What direction are we going?" It is a fascinating exploration— with physical, emotional, mental, and transpersonal rewards.

## REFERENCES

1. Schultz, J. H. and Luthe, W. *Autogenic training: a physiologic approach in psychotherapy*. New York, Grune and Stratton, 1969.
2. Budzynski, Thomas H., Stoyva, J. M., and Alder, C. S. "Feedback-induced Muscle Relaxation: Applications to Tension Headache." *Behav. Ther. Exp. Psychiat., 1* 1970, 205-211.
3. Sargent, Joseph. "The Use of Autogenic Feedback Training in a Pilot Study of Migraine and Tension Headaches." *Headache, 12,* 1972, 120-124.
4. Miller, N. E. "Learning of Visceral and Glandular Responses." *Science, 163,* 1969, 434-445.
5. Luthe, W. *Autogenic Therapy*. New York, Grune and Stratton, 1969.
6. Alexander, Rolf. *Creative Realism*. New York, Pageant Press, 1954.
7. Green, Elmer E. and Green, Alyce M. "On the Meaning

of Transpersonal: Some Metaphysical Perspectives." *Journal of Transpersonal Psychology*, 3, 1971, 27-46.
8. Castaneda, Carlos. *Journey to Ixtlan*. Simon and Schuster, New York, 1972.

# 3

# The Triune Approach to Healing of the Edgar Cayce Readings

*Herbert B. Puryear*

*The famous clairvoyant Edgar Cayce was capable of answering a wide range of questions put to him while he was in a trancelike sleep.*

*Herbert B. Puryear, clinical psychologist and director of the Association for Research and Enlightenment, explores Cayce's definition of illness and the stress he placed on the mind building a pattern that was not life sustaining.*

• • •

Let me begin to outline an approach to healing from the Edgar Cayce readings—a source of psychic data that accumulated over a forty-year period of work from 1901 to 1944. In considering how these readings relate to healing, we must first begin with their approach to the nature of reality and their approach to understanding the nature of man. The first principle, according to this material, is oneness. One reading says, "Oneness, oneness, oneness. This should be the first lesson for six months." The oneness of all force is especially emphasized. There is only one force, according to the readings. We sometimes refer to this force as God. The readings say that "a spark of electricity is God in motion. Life in all of its manifestations, in every animate force, is this creative force in action. For life is of, and is the creative force. It is that which you worship as God."

Going along with this principle of oneness, then, should lead us to expect some quality of this creative force in everything that is manifest. "First let it be understood that in the material plane, or physical plane, there is a pattern of every condition which exists in the cosmic or spiritual plane, for things spiritual and things material are but the same conditions of the same elements, raised to different vibrations, for all force is one force." Thus this oneness of force, this principle of oneness, carries with it the implication that may be referred to as the concept of the oneness of the microcosm and the macrocosm. There is the oneness within these and the integrating concept is vibration; this one force as unmanifested energy and the manifestations of it in the physical are different only in the vibrational level of the energy.

"So seldom is it considered by all that spirituality, mentality, and the physical being are all one, yet may indeed separate and function, one without the other, and one at the expense of the other. Make them cooperative, make them one in their purpose."

I have mentioned the concepts of physical, mental, and spiritual. Now I would like to move to a second principle from the Edgar Cayce source, and that is the use of triune concepts. There are a number of trinities that are found in these readings. . . .

The readings say that man as a spiritual being has moved into a three-dimensional awareness, a three-dimensional experience. These dimensions are time (which we understand as a measure), space (which we understand as a measure), and patience. We will have some trouble thinking of patience as a dimension, but it simply refers to that which we all know is the most important dimension of our life, and that is *value, purpose, motive, intention*. This is the dimension that he relates or correlates especially with the spirit. The readings say, "So man's concept of the Godhead is three dimensional: Father, Son, and Holy Spirit." Then the readings say, "These do not exist in fact, except in the concept of the individual as it may apply to time, space, and patience."

There is one force, but in working with this one force it will be useful for us, since we are in a three-dimensional consciousness, to work with triune concepts, whether it is of the dimensions of time, space, and patience, or of the nature of that one force which we might call God as Father, Son, and Spirit, or of ourselves as physical, mental, and spiritual.

Let me illustrate this point. If we say, "God is one," since we are inclined to think in terms of objects we are likely to say, "Then where is He?" and we look for an object or a spatial being out there. Thus we need another concept to go along with that oneness, such as the spirit, which says that He is all pervasive and everywhere. Then we need still another notion to get away from the transcendence and toward the immanence of God to enable us to say that He can express in man.

These three dimensions lead to triune concepts such as physical-mental-spiritual, subconscious-superconscious-conscious, and a physical body, a mental body, and a spiritual body. These are all one. It is simply a conceptual framework that will be especially appropriate for us in a three-dimensional consciousness to work with for better understanding.

There are other dimensions, according to this material. The readings say that in our solar system there are eight dimensions. Someone asked, "Please describe the seventh dimension," and he said, "You don't even understand the three you are in; how can we talk about seven?" However, he did describe the fourth dimension. Edgar Cayce encouraged comparative studies, so I am especially interested in a comparison between what he has said about the fourth dimension and what the great Swiss psychiatrist, Carl Jung, said about the fourth dimension. "If we wish to form a vivid picture of a nonspatial being," says Jung, "of the fourth dimension, we should do well to take thought as a being for our model."

The Edgar Cayce readings say, "The best definition that may be given of the fourth dimension is an idea. Where will it project? Anywhere. Where does it arise from? Who knows? Where will it end? Who can tell? It is all inclusive. It has length, breadth, height, and depth. It is without beginning and without ending."

Thus for both Jung and Cayce, ideas or thoughts make up the fourth dimension.

Now we come to the fundamental teaching or principle of the Edgar Cayce readings, a formula by which a great deal can be explained or conceptualized. "The Spirit is the life, mind is the builder, and the physical is the result." "The Spirit is the life." That's the one force. There is only one force; this is the Spirit . . . this is the life. "The Spirit is the life, mind is the builder, and the physical is the result." This

*physical* manifestation that constitutes all of our consciousness is the result of what has been built at a mental level.

The readings go on to say: "Truly, then, do thoughts become deeds and find a manifestation in the different manners. There then becomes the three manners, the three ways
all projections from a fourth-dimensional condition into a
third-dimensional mind."

The principle is that there is only one energy, but that any
time it manifests to our consciousness, that is, any time i
manifests in three dimensions, it will have a patterning. It i
that simple. The energy as pure force or energy will alway
have a patterning in the third dimension, and the patternin
is given it by the ideas or thought forms at the fourt
dimension. The third-dimensional projection is a manifesta
tion of the fourth-dimensional pattern.

Now, the *mind* is, of course, especially related to th
*ideas* or *thoughts* residing at the fourth-dimensional leve
There is one force; the spirit is the life; mind is the builder. I
is the mind that gives the patterning to that which is mani
fested. "Man finds himself a body, a mind, and a soul." Re
member the macrocosm-microcosm idea . . . "the body, th
mind, and the soul are as the Father, the Son, and the Hol
Spirit. Just as infinity in its expression to the finite mind i
expressed in time, space, and patience."

Another reading says, "An entity, a body-mind, was firs
a soul before it entered material consciousness. Individua
entities become aware in a material world of the earth as a
three-dimensional consciousness, having its concept or it
analysis of good or of creative forces or God in a three
dimensional concept: God, the Father—the body, the Son
or Christ—the mind, and the Spirit—the soul, or Firs
Cause. As an entity then applies itself, it becomes awar
through patience, through time, through space, of its relation
ship to the Godhead; Father, Son, and Holy Spirit."

"In self it finds body, mind, soul. As the Son is the builde
in the Godhead, so is the mind the builder in the individual."
Another reading illustrates this principle: "The mental body
the soul, and the physical body are but a shadow of the
Triune, for the body-physical is as man and the body-menta
is as the Saviour of man; and it is through the application
of the mental influences that we build that which finds expression in the physical. The soul-body is as the Creator Itself,
for it is the soul that is made in the image of the Creato
and made to be a companion to the Creator. The soul or

spirit which quickens and gives life to the physical body returns from its sojourn in the physical realm to that place that has been prepared or created by the activities of the mental body through experiences on the material plane."

This reading is saying that the mind, as the builder, not only has the physical body as the manifested result, but also is building that which the continuing consciousness will meet and experience beyond physical death. "Then the *Master* as the *mind* is the *way*, for mind is of body and of soul." It is the mediator—the mediating concept—between spirit and body. "Now, we have seen, we have heard, we know that the Son represents or signifies the mind. He, the Son, was in the earth, earthy, even as we, and yet is of the Godhead." In Philippians, Chapter Two, we are told: "Let this mind be in you which was also in Christ Jesus: who . . . thought it not robbery to be equal with God." But he was in the earth as well. Hence, "The mind is both material and spiritual. So does our mind become the builder. That which our mind feeds upon, that which our mind dwells upon, that do we supply to our body—and, yes, to our soul. Why? Because our Mind (the Son) is within us."

Another reading says, "The body and its soul are hinged upon the mental, for in a three-dimensional world, mind is the builder." Just as mind can be the Saviour here because it is that which builds, so it is the mind that gets us into trouble. "Then as the Son is the *way*, so is the mind the builder that makes for both atonement (at-one-ment) with Him and the condition of being at variance with Him."

Now we come to a definition of illness: Illness is building with the mind a pattern that is not life sustaining. If this one force is the source of all life, if this one force is creative and life-giving in its essence, then it must project through a pattern that is consistent with life and life sustaining. When the mind builds patterns that are not consistent with the flow of that energy, we find illness—or in an extreme, death. Thus death is an example of illness. What death is, is the fixing of a structure of such a nature that the life energy cannot flow through it. When we develop a pattern that is not life sustaining, we may continue in that pattern for a long time before trouble develops. Let us say, as an example, that we have established a dietary pattern of eating steak and potatoes, and every day for twenty years we have followed that pattern. This dietary pattern may be one that will not continue indefinitely to be life sustaining, because it may not keep our body in proper balance.

In the same way, death reflects the development of a behavior pattern that is not life sustaining, of which illness is an example. It would follow that healing is related to transformation, since whenever the life energy is in the earth, it takes some kind of form. If life is to be sustained, there must be a transformation process—there must be growth and the willingness to be transformed, for only in growth and the transformation process will the life energies continue to flow. This principle is illustrated in the readings' response to the question, "Will I ever get well?" to which the answer was, "Why do you want to get well? So that you can go back to the same pattern of behavior that led to the illness in the first place?"

This is very much to the point—that wanting to be healed should include the willingness to change. If we simply want to stop hurting so that we can go back to the same pattern, it follows that that pattern will get us into the same illness we experienced before. Thus healing must be basically a desire to change; not just the desire to change the symptomatic manifestations, but rather to change our behavior, our attitudes, and our thoughts.

Then the readings say, "All illness comes from sin. This everyone must take, whether he likes it or not. Illness comes from sin, whether it be of body, or mind, or soul."

I am not talking at all about a moralistic use of this word "sin," nor is the Edgar Cayce reading, but rather using the word "sin" to mean a violation of a law. There are laws; and we are beginning to discover them. Let me give you an example. These readings say that you shouldn't take orange juice and milk at the same meal; they are not compatible. There is nothing wrong with either one, but if you take them in combination, the subsequent physiological results are not satisfactory and imbalances may result. This is not a moralism at all. Yet, because the mind is so much the determiner of the physical processes, this becomes the source of many of our illnesses. For example, consider anger. The readings say, "Anger causes poisons to be secreted. Joy has the opposite effect. The adrenals are involved principally, but all the glands play a part. For example, a nursing mother would find that anger affects the mammary glands, and would also find that the digestive glands are affected."

Another reading says about resentment, "Keep the healthy

mental attitude, never resentment, for this naturally creates in the system forces that are hard on the circulation, especially where there is some disturbance of the spleen and the pancreas. An attitude of resentment will produce inflammation." Such an attitude brings about a response in the physiological processes that moves the body toward imbalance.

Another reading says, "Just as hate and animosity and hard sayings create poisons in the body, so do they weaken and wreck the mind of those who indulge in them. Then we begin to wonder why this or that has befallen us. As you may well remember, the Psalmist of old said, 'That which I feared has come upon me.' " That which we fear comes upon us. Why? Because as mind is the builder and as we invest the mind in the patterning of the way we are going to use this energy, it has an expression in the physical body as a result. Things we worry about create in ourselves mental patterns, because bodily processes naturally follow those patterns.

Now pursue with me another of these triune concepts. There is a process model in these readings: conscious, subconscious, superconscious. These are the consciousness processes of relationships or awarenesses. Along with those processes there are structures. The readings say that there is a physical body, a mental body, and a spiritual body. (There is only one body; it is simply a matter of vibrational differences, expressed in a triune concept for better understanding.)

At the physical level, in the physical processes, there is a triune that goes along with the three bodies. The conscious mind in the physical body has in the nervous system a special relationship to the sensory motor system; the subconscious and the mental body have a special relationship to the autonomic nervous system; and the superconscious and the spiritual body (or the soul) have a special relationship to the endocrine system. (See Fig. 3.)

The endocrine system, then, becomes the transducer or transformer of the life energy and information that might come from without and move through the bodies, in this order; spiritual body, mental body, physical body. Thus all psychic experience, all awareness of anything outside of oneself (and this includes information and energy—the psychic flow of energy—as in the healing energy) flows through the bodies in this way. The endocrine centers as points of contact in the spiritual body affect the autonomic

Figure 3

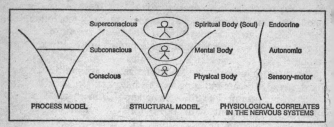

system in the mental body, and then give awareness or expression in the sensory motor system.

The point at which we may have a special effect on this system is at the mental body level, as with suggestion. For example, I can say to my adrenals, "start working," and nothing happens. But I can think of anger or resentment or fear, and I get an immediate response. The lie detector expert can get an indication of the emotional response with just a simple emotionally toned word like "Mother." You will see the whole physiological response written out there, entering the autonomic system which is amenable to suggestion, affecting the endocrine balance, and also the sensory motor system.

A reading says, "Give yourself an opportunity to function normally—mentally, physically, and spiritually. The spirit will act (and remember we are just talking about the force flowing through you) irrespective of what a body does with its physical or mental body, and it may make a very warped thing if you keep it under cover or expose it too much."

So the energy will flow through us, and the form it takes will be determined by our thoughts. It is manifested in the physical structures and processes of our body and the behavior patterns of our life.

We have considered illness as developing with the mind, or our thoughts, awakening a response, and I have given you the adrenals as an example. You see, there is within us a pattern for normal functioning. If we, with the mind, awaken a subsystem which is out of balance (if, for example, we awaken the adrenals in their activity, then that cuts off the digestive processes), a chronic condition of this kind can lead to a chronic imbalance. There is a pattern there that can be awakened, but if we keep it going out of balance to the entirety of the system, then illness is the result.

Now about healing. "No application of any medicinal property or any mechanical adjustment or any other influence is healing in itself. These applications merely help to attune, adjust, correlate the activities of the bodily functions to nature and natural forces." The readings say, "Don't look for the supernatural. Look for the natural." It's a natural law that the life-force will flow through you if your behavior patterns are consistent with these laws. All healing, then, is from life. Life is God. Healing is the flow of the energy through a pattern that is consistent with the life process. All medicines or adjustment or what have you are simply used to stimulate or awaken this kind of flow, "for all healing, mental and material, is attuning each atom of the body, each reflex of the brain forces, to an awareness of the divine that lies within each atom, each cell, of the body."

Now, speaking of each atom gets us to a point of understanding that this life energy enters into material manifestation at this subatomic level, or has its awakening effect at this subatomic level. Speaking of each cell of the body, I want to remind you again of the importance of the endocrine system, because these ductless secretions of hormones in their circulation through the body have the potential of affecting every cell of the body.

The readings say, "There is the ability within every atom, every organ, to reproduce itself, its likeness, through the assimilation of that taken within, either physically or mentally." It is through these various endocrine centers—the thyroid, the adrenals, and so on—that the physiological processes take place through which the physical body is enabled to reproduce itself. Thus the endocrine system, which the readings say is related to the spiritual processes and the spiritual body, is that which enables you to bring about a balanced and integrated system within the whole body.

Let me give you an example of the power of hormonal secretions. Here is an illustration from a biology textbook of the power of the secretion of the adrenals, known as epinephrine, which can be readily detected by biological assay. Epinephrine can be detected by biological assay in a dilution of one part in 300 million. In other words, if one ounce of this substance (that's a jigger) were so diluted with water, the diluted solution would fill nine miles of gasoline trucks apportioned 268 trucks to the mile and each truck holding 2,000 gallons. Imagine nine miles of gasoline trucks, bumper to bumper, with 2,000 gallons in each tank, and you could still detect epinephrine, with just one ounce in that dilution.

Another researcher has isolated a hormone from the pituitary so powerful that 1,560 miles of such trucks would be required to reduce one ounce to the undetectable point. That is one out of 15 billion. The point is this: with our mind, with our thoughts, with the thought of resentment or the thought of joy or compassion, there is an immediate response going through the autonomic and then through the endocrine system, and just the most unimaginably minute secretion moving throughout the whole body can affect every cell in the body. It is this that the readings say is the physiological basis of balance and healing.

Hormones are messengers. They tell the body what to do. The messengers from the adrenals tell the body, "Get ready to fight. Stop concerning yourself with digestion, get the blood going, let's get ready for a fight!" If that is continued when it is inappropriate, as in worry or resentment, then of couse it will lead to an imbalance and eventually to structural disease.

"Thus does spiritual or psychic influence of a body upon a body bring healing to any individual, where another body may raise the necessary influence in the hormones of the circulatory forces so as to take that within itself to revivify or resuscitate diseased, disordered, or distressed conditions within the body." Then one approach to understanding the laying-on-of-hands, or other kinds of healing, is that the effect is to awaken in the other person, at the spiritual-body level, at the endocrine-system level, secretions that will make for balance.

Healing, then, is an awakening, at the mental-body level, of a pattern—or in computer terminology, a program—within your body that makes for oneness so that the energy can flow through you.

Let's consider, then, the physical, mental, and spiritual. These readings say that the most important experience for any entity—the most important thing you can do—is to *set a spiritual ideal.* What does that mean? As I mentioned earlier, "spiritual" and "ideal" relate to motives, purposes. It means simply that we have built many thought patterns, we have many behavioral potentials, and these should be awakened only to serve or to help, or for constructive purposes.

The ability to be angry is a potential as a program within the body to serve, which should be awakened only for a constructive purpose. Setting a spiritual ideal means awakening all the processes, mental or physical, that you have in proper balance for constructive application, thus enabling the flow of energy to be appropriate to the occasion.

There is another reading that says, "Affinity is the ideal." This is saying that this force has an affinity to, or is drawn to, a motivational purpose that is constructive. When you set within your own consciousness a constructive motive, energy is drawn to it and is more likely to express through it.

Someone asked, "How may I best develop myself spiritually?" The answer was, "Through prayer and meditation." "What is meditation?" "Emptying self of all that hinders the creative forces from rising through the body. Properly done it must make one stronger mentally and physically. Meditation is the attuning of the mental body and the physical body to a spiritual source." Or it means thinking constructively and applying or making applicable in our physical activities that which will enhance the life flow.

The readings say, "Above all, pray. Those who are about the body should use and rely on spiritual forces, for 'prayer of the righteous shall save the sick.'" By the way, any acknowledgment of the possibility of telepathy should reintroduce to your consideration the power of prayer. If the word "prayer" is offensive to you, consider that telepathy implies that every thought we are thinking is either constructive or destructive in its potential. A student of mine came to me and said, "My mother is in the hospital. There is a very serious operation coming up. I feel that I should pray and yet I haven't been acting in any spiritual or religious way, and I don't feel right about it."

I said, "Well, do you know that telepathy occurs?"

She said, "Yes."

"You know that you can either send worry thoughts to her or constructive thoughts, and that this will affect her attitude?"

"Yes."

"Then, why worry when you can pray? Why project negative thoughts when you can project positive ones?" The readings say, "Know that all strength, all healing of every nature is but the changing of the vibrations from within— the attuning of the divine within the living tissue of a body to creative energies. This alone is healing, whether it is accomplished by the use of drugs, the knife, or what not. It is the attuning of the atomic structure of the living, cellular force to its spiritual heritage."

Here is a question about drugs. "Can those assisting in prayer do anything to prevent the body from indulging in stimulants?" Cayce says, "They can pray like the devil." Then the reading continues. "And this is not a blasphemous statement, as it may appear to some, for is there any busier body with those influences that have to do with the spirit of indulgence of any nature than that you call Satan, or the Devil?" He is equating the spirit of indulgence with the devil. "Then it behooves those who have the interests of such a body at heart not only to pray for and with him in earnestness and sincerity, but in just as continuous a manner as the spirit of indulgence works upon those who become subject to such influences, or with that attitude of being as persistent as the desire for indulgence—or 'as persistent as the devil.'" "Praying like the devil" means praying with the same persistency and sincerity as that with which you have to deal, which is the desire for indulgence, if you are going to overcome it.

There may be questions about healing through the laying-on-of-hands. Of course, this approach to healing is recommended in the Edgar Cayce readings. One reading says, "This has been aided according to the faith that has been aroused in the body. The manner of overcoming such, as has been intimated, may best be accomplished with the laying-on-of-hands that enables the individual—the entity being so aided—to have something to hold onto that is as concrete as that which it is battling." The response must be awakened in the mental body, in the autonomic system, and then the endocrine system, for the healing to begin. This is one of the ways—not the whole story—in which laying-on-of-hands is effective. For epilepsy, the laying-on-of-hands was suggested, and it was said that two, three, or four weeks may be required. We ordinarily think when we are considering faith healing that just one touch should cure. But no, it is a process. There are forces that flow; healing is accomplished by a natural law and should be made applicable consistently and in a precise way. For example, in epilepsy it was said, "This may be accomplished by placing the left hand over the abdominal region and the right hand over the ninth and tenth dorsal or the solar plexus ganglia and held there for one-half to three-quarters of an hour each day."

The healing process is seen as a growth process, step by step, here a little, there a little, and not necessarily instantaneously, although this certainly may occur, and there are instances of it reported in the readings.

Now, consider the mental level. "For thoughts are things, just as the mind is as concrete as a post or a tree or that which has been molded into things of any form. What one thinks continually, he becomes. What one cherishes in his heart, in his mind, and makes a part of the pulsation of the heart through his own blood cells, he builds into his physical being. For mind is the builder, and that which we think upon may become crimes or miracles; for as the mental dwells upon these thoughts, so does it give strength and power to things that do not appear, and they do indeed become real, as so oft given that faith is the evidence of things not seen."

One way in which mind is the builder is through the process of visualization. In seeking healing, Cayce told many people, "See the activities that are being created by the applications, and how from the vital force itself there is being supplied those energies for purposeful influence." "Any other advice?" "Keep that same healthful and hopeful attitude toward the using of the vision of the mental and spiritual self." For another, he said, "See within self that which is to be, which may be, which is being accomplished by such applications."

For another, "See, know, that that which you ask is being accomplished. As the vibrations are raised within self through this visualization, energy is directed in a healthful, hopeful, and beneficial way."

There was a caution about using the visualization with respect to particular organs. Visualization needs to be used in a more general way. There are some who would teach you that to heal you locate the affected organ and direct the energy there. This reading says, "Do not attempt to use centers, segments, or structural portions unless the body considers also that the whole physical, mental, and spiritual structure must be understood." Why? Because you have a symptomatic application without necessarily affecting the origin of the disease.

A word about hypnosis as it relates to mental healing. There was a woman who lost her voice. Her reading says, "The condition might be corrected almost instantly by the use of hypnosis. Yet that which it is necessary to be learned would not be met; hence, we would use hypnosis only as a last resort." We see this as an example again of symptomatic relief in which there is no real change, no growth process. Now, with respect to physical applications, the readings say, "That is man's end of the job. For example, prayer can be just as scientific as the knife, and the knife can be just as scientific as prayer—or as spiritual as prayer." He gives the example of the Master, in using different modes of therapy. Although the readings support the philosophy of Unity and of Christian Science, yet they say it is necessary to work at all three levels.

"Remember, the Christ in person used water, clay, spittle, or other ingredients for physical application." The readings are especially concerned that we work with the individual at his own level of consciousness.

There are many, many stories of healing from this work and from other sources that you will hear about. Let us begin to claim these promises.

Let me close with a favorite story of mine about healing from the Edgar Cayce readings. A 21-year-old Jewish woman had a dream in which she had an earache. In the dream she went into a drugstore, thinking about getting some medication, and then her mother appeared to her (her mother was deceased) and the mother said, "You don't need to do that. You can overcome that yourself."

The dreamer said, "I did; and it so surprised me that as I went driving with my friend and told her about it, she said, 'What you need is Christian Science. You ought to try it; become a Christian Scientist.'

"'No,' I replied, 'I have my *own* science, Jewish science. I cured myself, just naturally.'"

In interpreting this dream, Edgar Cayce said, "In this we see the presentation of truths as are manifested in the physical world as are loath to be gathered in a physical experience. The forces which are manifest to bring relief are not of any one faith, but a oneness of faith in the God-force will manifest in the individual. Study then those truths, for they remain a oneness, whether Jewish, Gentile, Greek, or heathen."

The lesson we have to learn, and I think the lesson of Jesus, himself, was that the God-force will manifest through the individual. We are loath to learn this, whether Jewish, Gentile, Greek, or heathen.

Brother Mandus, who has a laying-on-of-hands ministry, says that in India he saw that Indian children responded to the laying-on-of-hands just as Christians do. We are loath to learn that there is a oneness of force. It is available to the individual; and thus in talking about the ideals and purposes of his whole work, Edgar Cayce said, "This should be kept first and foremost before the individual and the public— the simplicity of the ability of the individual to apply that which may be gained from his own subconscious, his subliminal self, unconscious forces, or cosmic consciousness. Call it by whatever name the individual may choose, this is the great lesson to be learned."

There is a force that will flow through us when we begin to get our thoughts straight; and when we begin to apply what we know we can claim this. All the external applications and working with others is simply to awaken within the very cells and atoms of our bodies the willingness to allow this life-force to flow through us.

# 4

## The Nuclear Mobile Center
## of Consciousness

*Andrija Puharich*

*The growing interest in Yoga in the West has heightened the awareness that voluntary and so-called involuntary bodily functions can both be controlled. Andrija Puharich, medical scientist, inventor, and psychical researcher, describes in great detail how this is accomplished by the Yogin.*

•  •  •

Yoga is a doctrine and a practice that originated in India. Its main purpose is to gain for the individual complete independence. This is not only an independence from the external influences of nature and man, but also an independence from the internal emotions, tensions, and other impediments to what we might call an idea state of self-sufficiency. The doctrine is so widespread that it permeates every religious school in India and surrounding countries. Such widespread influence of a basic doctrine is naturally bound to give rise to many different schools of Yoga, and if we were to arrange them in a scale, at the one end would be that Yoga which is solely concerned with physical health, running through intermediate stages concerned principally with emotional and mental health, and ascending to areas where the principal concern is spiritual perfection and individual independence qualified by the desire for a union with God.

However, we are principally concerned with Yoga technique and not its ideological evaluations. The shaman and the Yogin start essentially from the same point, personal physical hardihood and athletic vigor. The Yogin also subjects himself to great extremes of cold in order to condition his body to this form of stress. Under the pressure of external cold he also seeks to liberate that "inner heat" which is thought to be the fuel and energy for spiritual liberation. This is not strictly speaking one of the techniques of Yoga, it is merely a foundation for any future development in Yoga, and it is assumed that the Yogin achieves such physical hardihood and the ability to create "inner heat." From here on there is a single-pointed technique which is followed throughout all subsequent stages of development. This can be summed under the heading of "Concentration."

The beginner in Yoga assumes one of the traditional sitting postures, and placing a candle before him, attempts to gaze at it with fixity and steadfastness. He seeks to keep his attention unwaveringly fixed upon the candle as long as possible. This develops control of the tides and fluxes of the mental stream of association. The Yogin may dispense with an external object to exercise the power of concentration, he may, in fact, simply pick a point between his eyes, an imaginary point, and concentrate upon it just as he would upon the candle. Basic to the exercise of mental concentration is the act of visual concentration. Later on such concentration may be extended to other sensory systems.

The psychological conditioning based upon concentration takes two different forms. The first one is the one called "restraint," and this is concerned with those things which one is not to do, and this is in the area of personal hygiene, abstinence in sex, food, and of course mental and emotional restraint. The other form is that called "disciplines," and these are more in the direction of achieving moral purity.

In striving to achieve mastery over the random internal mental noise of the mind, and the random external noise of the mind whose origin lies in physical sensations, the Yogin moves through a gradation of controls. He begins with the control of sensory perception. He learns to look upon the candle for what it is. From this factual perception he learns to draw the correct inferences. And from his precise perception and correct inferences he learns to give what is called reliable testimony about his perception. In other words, he tries to see things as they are, and not as his mind would color them or preconceptions interpret them.

The Yogins have a term for the random noise of the senses, and the noise of the subconscious mind, it is called *cittavrti*. This term has a rather interesting meaning—whirlwinds. The Yogins look upon the unrestrained and uncontrolled activity of the senses and the subconscious mind as whirlwinds without purpose which must be harnessed and brought under control.

The Yogin goes from the control of his senses and his understanding of the information gained therefrom to studying the internal activity of his own mind. In our day we can illustrate this by examples from studies made on what is called the restricted environment. Here an individual is placed in an environment that reduces the amount of physical stimulation to his sensory system. The flow of energy from the outside world is cut down to an absolute minimum. In this state the subject lies in an environment without sound, without light, with temperature fixed, and with all the other physical sources that make for sensation controlled. When the noise of the outside world dies down he suddenly becomes aware of the internal noise of his body. He hears in an exaggeratedly loud fashion the beat of his heart, the rumble of his intestines, the noise of respiration, etc. In addition to these noises of purely physical origin in the body he becomes aware of the background noise of his own mind. He begins to hallucinate, strange creatures float through his imagination, some of them terrifying, some of them benign, the form of these images being dependent upon the nature of his mind and his psychological history. Some people can stand such an environment for only a short time, say an hour, and others of greater courage and control can stand it for as long as twenty-four hours. In either case the ghosts of one's mind rise to haunt one and often the experience can be highly unpleasant.

It is with such delusions and hallucinations of the mind that the Yogin works. He too achieves a state similar to that of the subject in the experimental restricted environment. However, when he has reached this state of development he is in considerable control of himself. He is not aware of, or bothered by, the noises of the body. These have been brought under harmonious control. His mind, as a result of concentration exercises, is not disordered, and therefore he can allow a single hallucination to appear in his mind and manipulate it and control it as though it were a puppet. He controls it; it does not possess him. These exercises are long and arduous, but in them the Yogin learns not only to control delusion and hallucination but he also learns how to manipulate the "stuff" of the mind.

Having conquered the random flow of all forms of hallucination in his mind, he then goes on to more fruitful endeavors and develops his abstract imagination. By this is meant that he no longer deals with the primordial images and stuff which arise in hallucinations, but looks beyond and through these for their abstract meaning. This process can be illustrated from laboratory experiments which I carried out, and which have been done by others, using the stimulation effect of a flashing light.

This consisted of a million-candle-power stroboscopic light. The subject, in this case a telepathic receiver, looked through his closed eyelids (at a distance of about nine inches) into this powerful light. The light was so controlled that it could flash within a frequency range of two times per second to forty-eight times per second. The subject while looking into the light controlled the frequency of the flash with a knob and adjusted it to that point which pleased him the most. I worked at this phenomenon most intensively with Peter Hurkos [a Dutch clairvoyant famous for his detection of criminals and for his work in the Boston Strangler case—N.M.R.]. Hurkos found that at a frequency of nine cycles per second he would have the following experience.

As he looked into the light his whole mental field became illuminated with a multiplex geometrical pattern. Very often it was like looking at a brilliantly colored mosaic made up of small regular geometrical figures. As Hurkos carefully adjusted the frequency of the flash, the brilliantly illuminated and colored geometrical pattern in his mind began to slowly revolve in a clockwise direction as he viewed it. The clockwise motion increased and gave him a feeling of being whirled outward, in other words, a centrifugal mental effect. By sharply controlling himself he was able to ignore the sense of being whirled outward and concentrate on the center of the pattern, finding therein what appeared to him to be a long tube which gave him tranquillity. At the end of the tube he suddenly saw distant visions. While gazing into this tranquillity he could accurately describe by extrasensory perception physical scenes going on thousands of miles away, as was demonstrated in many different experiments with him.

The important finding in this study was that it was possible to artificially induce a hallucinatory mental experience which resolved into an outward reach of the mind such as had been found earlier in an association with a state of cholinergia [a state associated with relaxation and well-being—N.M.R.] in Mrs. Garrett and Harry Stone. Accompanying this verifiable heightened telepathy and/or clairvoyance was a feeling of great relaxation and peace. Hurkos best described it when he said, "Looking into the light makes me forget all of my personal problems; I get out of myself completely, and easily look into whatever it is that I wish to concentrate upon." Immersed in this stroboscopic light, Hurkos undoubtedly experienced the peace and relaxation that the Yogin finds after mastering restraints and disciplines.

In addition to controlling the external and internal noise of the body and the mind, the Yogin spends a great deal of effort in exercising his memory functions. He is very well aware of the close linkage between the memory function and the essence of mind itself. Therefore, control of memory is an absolute necessity before any higher development can occur. He exercises such memory concentration both in the wide-awake state and in the sleep state. A Yogin does much of his exercises in what we call the sleep state. However, for the Yogin, sleep is not a state of unconsciousness, he is under all of the influences that we each personally know during sleep, with the one exception that he maintains an alert consciousness within this state of "sleep."

However, the true Yogin does not begin with the stages and exercises which we have just described. These are common to many different aesthetic, ascetic, and religious exercises. True Yoga begins with the study of the so-called postures. Physical posture is a fundamental technique in Yoga. The simplest posture is one in which the Yogin sits on a mat or an animal hide on his haunches. His back is straight and his legs are crossed in the traditional lotus posture. His neck is bent forward so that his chin touches his chest. His tongue is bent backward so that the tip of it enters into the posterior portion of the nasal passage. His hands are relaxed across his knees and various positions are assumed by the hands themselves, the basic one being with the palms placed upward. In this position the Yogin carries out the exercises for concentration cited in the previous paragraph. The Yogin then goes through a long stage where he develops mental control over every one of the voluntary muscles of the body. For example, one of the simple controls is the ability to tense the right rectus abdominal muscle, while the left one is relaxed. Or he may tense one rectus abdominal muscle and have the other one undergo rhythmic contractions. Or both abdominal muscles may alternately contract rhythmically to produce a churning motion on the intestines. The chief purpose of these exercises on the voluntary muscular system is not so much the athletic feat itself, but to guarantee that the mind at least can be the absolute master of its own means of locomotion. The end purpose of such exercises is to induce a state of complete relaxation of every muscle in the body.

Basic to such voluntary muscular control is the doctrine that this should be done under complete mental control at every step of the way. This is unlike the shaman's doctrine, where rapid and violent movements are unconsciously carried out. Such movements are entirely against the tradition of Yoga. Having mastered the voluntary muscular system of the body, the Yogin turns his attention to mastering the involuntary muscular system of the body, the smooth muscle system. These are the muscles in the bronchi of the lungs, the muscles that control the blood vessels, the muscles that control the gastrointestinal organs and the excretory organs. The first system that gets attention is that which controls to a great extent the rhythm of respiration, the diaphragm. In general the Yogin tries to achieve both maximum tenseness and maximum relaxation of the diaphragmatic muscles in preparation for his future exercises on the control of respiration. In general, during rhythmic, Yogic breathing, the diaphragm is kept at a tense level.

The Yogin achieves remarkable control over the gastrointestinal tract. One of the oft-quoted examples is that of swallowing a long bandage and propelling it through the entire twenty-eight feet of the gastrointestinal canal and having it emerge at the rectum. While this may appear to be exhibitionism, the Yogin develops this technique in order to "clean out" his gastrointestinal tract. In my opinion the primary purpose of these exercises is to gain complete mental control over the autonomic functions, but the Yogin makes use of each of these exercises for hygienic purposes.

Not only does the Yogin gain complete control over the normal functions of the involuntary muscular system, but he in fact reverses the rhythms of nature. For example, one of the simpler feats of the Hathayogin is the ability to draw fluid up into the bladder to the extent of a liter, and to use this fluid to flush the bladder. More remarkable is the ability that the Yogin develops over controlling his heart rate. Reliable witnesses and scientists have actually measured the fact that the Yogin can so slow down his heart rate that it approaches the rhythm normally found just prior to death. The Yogin aims to accelerate or slow down his heart principally to exercise his newfound mental control against something. However, the Yogin's long exercises to gain complete mastery of the voluntary muscular system and the involuntary muscular system are all aimed at gaining perfect rhythmic control over his respiration. Control of respiration is one of the fundamental techniques of Yoga and from it are believed to stem many of the higher mental and spiritual powers which are necessary in order to attain personal independence.

It must be emphasized that in carrying out such exercises, particularly on the autonomic nervous system, the Yogin is able to release adrenergic chemicals at will and to the degree he desires, as well as to release the cholinergic chemicals to any degree necessary for his purposes. I believe that this is one of the great achievements of the technique of Yoga, this power to place the body at any required balance between adrenergia and cholinergia or a preponderance of one system over the other.

Yoga calls the control of respiration *pranayama*. This comes from the word for breath, *prana,* and the word for pause, *ayama.* The essential meaning of pranayama is mental control over respiration with the object of slowing down the normal respiratory rhythm, or even stopping it for long periods of time. It is the belief of the Yoga doctrine that rhythmic respiration serves to unify consciousness itself with breathing. This is based on the assumption that the act of breathing supplies the fuel of consciousness. We might say, in terms of the concepts developed here, that breathing is a vehicle for building up the power of the psi plasma.

Respiratory exercises are always carried out in one of the traditional Yogic postures. Respiratory exercise is divided into three phases. The first is that of inhalation, called *puraka.* The second phase is that of holding the breath at the top of inhalation, and this is called *kumbhaka.* The word *kumb* comes from an old Sanskrit root which means pot or a vessel, and in this instance pictures an inverted bowl. The holding phase is followed by the exhalation phase, called *rechaka.* Holding is not only holding the breath within the lungs but is conceived of as a definite phase outside of the lungs. In this latter case holding would follow the exhalation phase where the holding refers to holding back air from the lungs themselves. There is a definite ratio between these phases which can be expressed in time, 1 : 4 : 2. This is the traditional ratio although many other variations have been worked out.

In the beginning of pranayamic exercises the holding phase is usually set at the lowest limit for about 12 seconds, and the practitioner works up to an upper limit of 108 seconds. The other ratios then have a corresponding value. In the next higher stage of the development of pranayama these ratios are multiplied by a definite factor (usually 12). Then the new lowest limit for the holding phase becomes 144 seconds, and the upper limit for holding becomes 1296 seconds, or 21.6 minutes. The respiratory rate of the Yogin therefore moves in the direction of becoming slower and slower, while he still maintains the same high level of consciousness and mental control over all the functions previously cited. In fact, the ultimate aim of the pranayamic exercises is to achieve that state of slow respiration which is found in hibernating animals. Yogins and fakirs have been known to publicly demonstrate this ability by performing the feat of being "buried alive," and in some instances such burials have lasted as long as thirty days. When the Yogin arises from his long deep sleep, although dehydrated and having lost considerable weight, he nevertheless is in good health.

One of the many respiratory rhythms used by Yogins is called *ujjaye,* and [K.T.—N.M.R.] Behanan has done some oxygen-consumption measurements on this form of breathing at Yale University. When using the ujjaye technique of breathing, his respiration rate was 76 cycles per hour. During this exercise his oxygen consumption was measured. It was found that in spite of this slow rate of breathing, his oxygen consumption increased 24.5 per cent over that of control levels. Behanan also reports on his subjective experiences during such breathing exercises. He points out that the first fifteen to twenty minutes of the ujjayic breathing exercises results in a sense of tingling all over the body, and mental excitation and exhilaration. This we have come to recognize as being based on a state of adrenergia. Following this early excitatory phase, the Yogin then passes into a state of deep relaxation. Although he is sitting up straight and his mind is intensely alert, all his muscles, both voluntary and involuntary, feel at perfect ease and are relaxed. This state of deep relaxation leads the mind to an inward turning, or toward the center of the mental field, and results in increased concentration of the type peculiar to Yoga. . . .

I have made some personal experiments on the mental effects of various degrees of cholenergia. For this I used extracts from the mushroom *Amanita muscaria*, whose chief constituent is muscarine, a powerful cholinergic drug. Different doses of muscarine show a wide spectrum of effects. A very small dose of muscarine produces a feeling of relaxation, well-being, an increase of muscular strength, and a facility for telepathy. The consciousness is scarcely altered with such small doses. With massive doses which lead to poisoning there are of course all the symptoms of massive activation of the parasympathetic nervous system, nausea, vomiting, diarrhea, etc.; the mental state is that of extreme hallucination (the kind depending on the psychological history of the individual) and this can lead to the subjective experience of a mobile center of consciousness. I was seeking to find a state of cholinergia intermediate between these two extremes.

When I found the proper dose, the following effect occurred. The first was that of a state of inebriation unlike anything I have experienced from any other chemical, including alcohol. It was a highly poised, calm, and ecstatic state. There was no effect on the voluntary muscular system in the way of imbalance, staggering, or other such dysfunction. I sat perfectly still for about an hour in one of the simpler Yogic postures. I then passed through this state of inebriation, which is comparable to the state that Behanan describes as exhilaration and excitement. Thereafter I lost consciousness for about an hour; observers tell me that I sat motionless throughout this period with a pulse rate of 36 and very slow respiration. I did not seem to be in any serious difficulty, and even responded to their questions, but I have no remembrance of this. When I came out of this state, that is, recovered consciousness, I had a singular experience. I felt that I was absolutely and unconditionally detached from "everything." In short, I was the only existence. I was aware that something else existed, but I can only describe this as "everything" else, the primary reality was the knowledge of self.

I cite this experience merely to illustrate what I believe the Yogin attempts to achieve by the exercise of concentration and rhythmic breathing, which I believe culminates in the proper state of cholinergia. The entire mental flux reduces to a single point, i.e., Self. I noticed after I passed this

point of being aware only of self that I gradually related
other things to myself. First I related myself to my body.
Then I related myself and body to the floor on which I sat.
Then I related to the walls, then to the other people in the
room. In this way I took new elements into my consciousness,
one at a time, and was able to relate them with a clarity
which I have not known before.

There are other concomitants of Yogic pranayama. It
has been reported that every inspiration of the breath in
the human being is accompanied by a marked change in the
electrical potential of the skin. This can take the form either
of an increase in potential or a decrease. The order of change
is about 10 millivolts D.C. It is also known that such breathing increases the carbon-dioxide content of the alveolar
tissue in the lungs, as well as in the blood. Both of these
effects result in an increased pressure of carbon-dioxide gas
upon the nerve cells of the brain. Carbon dioxide when administered in such increased pressure is known to result in
hallucination, feeling of expansiveness, and eventually leads
to unconsciousness.

However, the Yogins themselves state that the chief purpose of perfected pranayama is to release a latent mental
energy in the mind which they call *kundalini.* The Yogins
conceive of kundalini as being latent in the body, and it has
its origin at the base of the spinal column in the form of a
tightly coiled vortex energy. The Yogin looks upon this
as the ultimate energy, therefore extremely powerful, and
its release can be accompanied by serious danger to the
individual; therefore, this must be done with absolute control and caution.

Yoga conceives that the physical source of prana comes
from the air and this is filtered out by the process of pranayama. Therefore, in spite of the fact that the Yogin attempts
to cut off all physical energies that come through the sensations, he nevertheless does draw upon one physical source,
the air, for his mental operations. We are not told whether
the filtered air is directed to the kundalini center, or whether
the filtered air simply serves to release the kundalini energy.

Air, as is well known, is composed of 20.9 percent oxygen, 79 percent nitrogen, some rare gases, and some pollu-
tants. Of these the body utilizes only oxygen. We have not
as yet mentioned the intimate dependence of consciousness
on the chemical oxygen. There is no question that the Yogin
makes maximum use of the consciousness-maintaining prop-

erties of oxygen. How oxygen is transformed by the Yogin for special use we do not know.

It is well known that oxygen under the impress of a given amount of energy (for example, a few thousand volts D.C. potential) converts easily to the ionized state and to higher polymers of which the first is ozone. Under the influence of such electrical fields, the oxygen in the air gains a negative charge (ionized). Many workers have shown that negatively ionized oxygen exerts a beneficial effect on the organism, such as slowing respiration, and lowering of the blood pressure, and a feeling of mental alertness and general well-being. Negative oxygen ions increase the action of the cilia in the respiratory passages, which are responsible for keeping it free of dust and other noxious particles. Positively charged carbon-dioxide ions on the other hand slow down the ciliary beat. Positively charged atmospheric gas ions, in general, do not have the salubrious effect shown by negatively charged ions. . . .

The relationship between the ionized states of oxygen, ozone, and carbon dioxide in the central nervous system during pranayamic breathing is not known. This is a ripe area for research. It might provide a further chemical basis for understanding some of the phenomena associated with higher states of consciousness.

Up to this point the Yogin has reached the stage where he can consciously release the kundalini energy. Prior to this he has been able to focus his mind on specific points throughout his anatomical system, and particularly those centers which control autonomic function. He now consciously directs the kundalini energy to each of these autonomic centers. In the technique of Yoga these are not precisely identified with the autonomic centers, but are spatially in the same area, and are called *chakras*. The addition of the kundalini energy to each of these chakric centers is the next step in the development of mental control by the Yogin. The kundalini energy added to these centers moves him into a higher dimension of personal control and toward his goal of complete independence.

This leads to the stage called abstraction, and is properly speaking the fifth stage of the Yoga technique. Here the purpose is to completely dissociate sensations in the mind from their physical origin in the sensory receptor system. The Yogin manipulates sensations in his mind just as though they had their origin in the physical world. For example, he creates the image of a tree in his mind from memory. He not only sees the image of a remembered tree, but begins with the seed of the tree and watches the dynamics of the evolution of that seed through the various stages of growth into the completed tree. In this process it is most important to note that he avoids illusion and hallucination completely. He believes that he is actually reconstructing the idea forces of nature and is studying their dynamics. He does this in isolation from the physical origin of such sensations and therefore the process is called abstraction.

In order to achieve this type of power he uses one principal technique, which is the control of consciousness through its four stages. Yoga defines the stages of consciousness as: (1) The awake state of consciousness. (2) The state of consciousness in sleep when one has dreams. (3) The state of consciousness in sleep when there are no dreams. (4) The cataleptic state of consciousness. This latter must not be confused with hypnosis or what we normally call trance. The essential feature of the passage of the Yogin through these four states of consciousness is that he never loses consciousness; he maintains in what appears to be normal sleep a thoroughly alert consciousness. This also holds true for what is known as the cataleptic state of consciousness, and this is the one exercised in the state of being buried alive. In going through the various stages of consciousness his principal aim is to be able to master these states so that he can go to a higher state of consciousness called *samadhi*.

The state of samadhi is the end goal of the Yogin efforts. There are three stages associated with attaining samadhi, which cannot very sharply be differentiated from one another, which are called: (1) (stage six) True concentration. (2) (stage seven) Meditation. (3) (stage eight) Samadhi. We must remember that up till now the Yogin has brought under complete control sensory noise from the physical world, internal noise of the body and all that this implies, and has achieved complete control over the states of adrenergia and cholinergia both in regard to specific organs and with respect to his general mental state. He furthermore has found ways of extracting energy from the world around him through pranayama and has learned to direct and localize this energy from the kundalini center. He now works his operations solely by mind control of what I have termed the psi plasma. I believe the psi plasma could be identified with the kundalini energy. With the beginning of true concentration we can no longer find physiological, chemical, or physical foundations for the operations of the Yogin. We are now in the realm of unconditioned mental dynamics largely unknown in the world of Western science and psychology.

Having learned to control the substance prana by mental operations alone, the Yogin goes on to the state called meditation. Here his goal is to actually control the realm of the physical by virtue of his control over what I believe to be psi plasma. There are a number of ways to illustrate such control. We have all heard of levitation, but very few people have ever seen it. I myself have not witnessed physical levitation, and have to rely on the testimony of others.

Experiments have been done in psychology laboratories to show that when an individual is placed in an isolated environment, he may very often have the illusion of being levitated. For example, one experiment with twenty subjects showed that eight of the subjects very definitely had the sensation that they were physically rising in the air, although the observers were quite aware that the individuals did not leave their chairs. The Yogin has learned to avoid these pitfalls of the mind.

Sir William Crookes has given us the best scientific studies of levitation in his researches on the famous medium D. D. Home. Crookes measured the levitation powers of D. D. Home and confirmed by means of a spring balance that (without physical contact) Home could create both an increase and a decrease in gravitational force on objects. Then Crookes attested to the most striking phenomenon of all. The instance in which Home was levitated and carried through a window at a point eighty feet above the street and then returned into the room. Crookes makes this affirmation.

"The phenomena I am prepared to attest are so extraordinary and so directly opposed to the most firmly rooted articles of scientific belief—amongst others, the ubiquity and invariable action of the force of gravitation—that even now, on recalling the details of what I witnessed, there is an antagonism in my mind between reason, which pronounces it to be scientifically impossible, and the consciousness that my senses, both of touch and sight—and these corroborated by the senses of all who were present—are not lying witnesses when they testify against my preconception."

Another example of such control, even though it is on a smaller scale, has been furnished by [Norbert—N.M.R.] Wiener. He cites the case of a Yogin in the state of meditation whose electrical brain waves were being recorded. The ordinary individual, when he has his eyes wide open and the electrical brain activity is being registered, does not show the presence of alpha waves, these being slow sinusoidal waves of the order of eight to fourteen cycles per second. The Yogin, however, was able to demonstrate prominent alpha-rhythm frequency with his eyes wide open. This means that he is able to control the molecular and electrical activity of his brain to such an extent that external light energy was not able to cause the disappearance of the alpha frequency. This type of control is developed to higher and higher degrees by the Yogin. The purpose actually is not to demonstrate control over physical nature, but rather to give the developing mind something greater to pit its energies against. The mind can only develop in the face of the proper degree of resistance, and at this stage it is the physical realm that provides the proper degree of resistance.

Having achieved this power, the Yogin now prepares to enter the state called samadhi. We have no equivalent term in the Western world to describe it. It is based upon all the factors already cited, but it is not a state of consciousness per se. If there is any description that is adequate, it is that the Yogin now realizes himself as a nuclear mental entity which is able to control the physical dynamics of his body, control physical objects and energies at a distance from his body, and is able to move freely as a mobile center of consciousness independently of his body. This is the true meaning of the independence and autonomy that is the goal of all Yogins. However, this is not the end in that the Yogin goes on to a state that we can scarcely comprehend but which can be faintly described as merging his liberated nuclear self with that of a greater entity, namely God.

[Mircea—N.M.R.] Eliade describes samadhi as having two different conditions. The first is samadhi "with support," and this means the nuclear mental entity is still dependent in some way upon either the physical world as form or energy, or upon the physical basis of sensations, ideas, and memories. The Yogin seeks to go past this state where there is no association with the world of physics, and this is called the state of samadhi "without support." In this state the Yogin enters into a state of being that has no foundations or connections with any other form of human consciousness. It is in this state that he merges with the Absolute. We cannot in our Western way of thinking expect to follow with any clear understanding the realm which the Yogin has now entered.

It is a curious fact that the Yogins who have achieved this stage of experience and who have returned to speak about it are not able to give us an adequate description of where they have been. The language used to describe this experience is couched in terms of color, radiance, and light. It seems as though the language that we have and use was devised to describe the physical world in which we live and is inadequate to describe this other world. Anyone who has read these accounts by Yogins themselves has a great feeling of disappointment in not being able to truly understand what it is they are talking about. The feeling is almost equivalent to the void that the Yogin claims to have entered.

# 5

# Cancer: The Cell and Its Intelligence

## Harry Edwards

*The belief that cancer has a psychosomatic origin is common among spiritual healers. Most often, cancer is attributed to repressed emotions. Harry Edwards, famous for healing work at his Spiritual Healing Sanctuary in England, presents a detailed account of his own conclusions.*

• • •

Every one of the billions of cells in the body is a complete, living unit. It lives and reproduces itself. It breathes, consumes nourishment, and excretes waste. It has an individual purpose to fulfill. It is subject to the law of disciplinary control. Every second millions of new cells are born in the ceaseless program of self-renewal. They possess the spirit of life.

The cells are units from which all living matter is made. They are able to undergo chemical transformations. Their diversities are many and we do not know them all. Although they exist in the billions, in good health they work in harmony with each other and play a part in contributing to their mutual health.

The cell has similarities with the human body. It has skin, it takes in protein food, it possesses a digestive system, it excretes waste. The nutrients the cell absorbs are used as fuel to maintain an abundant energy. It possesses a "brain," which is the nucleus. It has purpose and therefore a consciousness, an intelligence.

Within the nucleus are some forty-six chromosomes, each

of which houses a large number of genes. . . . It is the genes that are the cell's central intelligence. It may well be that each cell also contains a bodily intelligence to record harmony and disharmony in its mental and physical health.

Genes are passed directly from the parents to their children and have been so passed since the beginning of man. Thus the cell's potentials contain influences from earliest human life, and occasionally we unfortunately see "throwbacks" with mongolian tendencies through the presence of an additional chromosome. The genes are influenced by the conduct of the person's outlook and way of life, for it is by this process that the evolution of man has come about. It is said that there are thousands of genes within the human system.

Every cell has its own personality, its own motive for existing. Its period of life is variable according to its function. The skin cells of the fingertips are reproduced every few days, while the nerve cells do not reproduce at all.

Like ourselves, the health of a cell is maintained in two ways, through its bodily functions and its mental harmony. The mental harmony is dependent upon its being able to carry out its life's purpose. Thus, the cell has an intelligence. So long as a cell is able to fulfill its function, it is content.

Different kinds of cells need different forms of nourishment. When a cell suffers from a lack of proper nutrients, the health tone is affected, resulting in a disturbance in the functioning of an organ or part of the body, and sickness results.

When a disharmony is communicated to the brain and thence to the bodily intelligence, it is reported not only generally, but in detail. For example, if the kidney is not working properly, or if there is inflammation of the medullary pyramids, more exact information is needed, such as that the cells in that part of the body are sick from malnutrition or some other cause.

It is then that the bodily intelligence acts and directs through the digestive processes the production of the chemical needed to be conveyed through the blood and lymphatic systems to the cells to bring them back to good health. If this cannot be bodily achieved, then through spiritual healing the characterized energies that comprise the deficient nutrient are transmitted to the cells.

Just as we suffer from both physical and mental sicknesses, so the cells can suffer likewise. If they are prevented from fulfilling their purpose, they will become frustrated and rebellious. The best example of this is in cells that have a part to play in the sexual system of a person. The cells of the mammary glands in the female breast have as their purpose the creation of milk for the baby. These cells are unique and exist for this special purpose.

The consciousness of the cells lies in the genes. There is a subtle connection between these cells and the mind. An instance of this is when an inflammation of the mammary glands is aggravated by the patient who allows her mind to dwell on it fearfully. The cause of the inflammation may be traced to a disturbance of the normal functioning of the mammary cells from the ovaries and the pituitary gland, which gland plays a dominant role in maintaining the good behavior of the cells in ordinary times, but especially when the breast takes on its function of feeding the baby.

If a woman greatly desires to have children and for some reason cannot, a state of frustration exists within the mind and spirit and this is passed on to the genes within the cells in the mammary glands. If a woman conceives a child and does not want it, a condition of mind stress is built up within her inner self and this frustration is conveyed to the cells. Another source of frustration lies in strong maternal dominance over a daughter, preventing her from exercising her natural desires by placing obstacles in her way and preventing companionship with males.

In Canada and the U.S.A. investigations have taken place into the psychosomatic causes of breast cancer in women. In every case it was discovered that the woman suffered from frustrations due to one of the above three causes. The cells within the breast became frustrated, they were prevented from fulfilling their destiny, they were rebellious. (Fuller explanation of this is given later.)

It is recalled that the genes are subject to influencing from the state of the mind. Strong tendencies in life, such as the love of the arts and sciences, virtues of kindliness, love of motherhood, and the contraries of sadistic tendencies, etc., are reflected in the nature of the genes, and these qualities are conveyed to the offspring through the genes contained within the sperm and ovum. It is for this reason that a child will often have hereditary tendencies similar to those of the parent. It accounts for genius, because the genes are so influenced by parental behavior and outlook. And it follows that the genetic directive can be adversely influenced by parental frustrations, depriving the cells of the opportunity to fulfill the purpose for which they exist.

It has been established that the cell is governed throughout its life by pituitary control. How wonderful this control is can be gathered from the manner in which discipline is maintained over the billions of cells. This functions like the governor bearing in an engine. It ensures that the body mechanisms and cellular reproductions do not proceed too fast. It is the natural incentive of all living things to reproduce themselves freely and as frequently as they can under the laws of life. The ultimate purpose of all the cells, except for the nerve cells which do not reproduce, is to divide and create other cells to carry on their life story.

The pituitary control keeps our bodies in balance, with almost identical development of limbs, features, bones, and organs. When this control, for some reason, becomes slack, we have elephantiasis. The cells then multiply without restraint. Normally, not one cell is allowed to reproduce itself until an appointed time. This indicates a system of communication and control so marvelous that it is almost inconceivable.

Where there is communication and control, there needs to be a form of intelligence to maintain and use the communication and exert disciplinary influence over its subjects. It indicates that every cell has an intelligence able to receive instruction. It denotes that a state of intellectual liaison exists between each cell and the pituitary intelligence.

A parallel can be drawn beween the cellular intelligence and the mind and spirit. It is conscious of the desire to fulfill its purpose in life, of its well-being, and of its needs when there is a physical weakness. It is affected by the emotions and outlook of the human personality and accepts, in a reasonable way, the control over its life.

Some categories of cells appear to have a more active intelligence than others. For example, the cells comprising the muscle lead a more humdrum existence than the cells concerned with reproduction. They are able to fulfill their purposes more easily and there is less opportunity for frustration.

Sexual desires can be stimulated organically, as in the overproduction of spermatozoa. Or they can be encouraged by the senses, by the sight (as with "pinup" pictures), or by impressions given to the mind by talking. Perfumes can do this too via the sense of smell, and, of course, they are stimulated through the sense of touch. There exists a strong connection between mental assessments and the sex processes. This arises from thought reactions conveyed by the mind to the pituitary organization, which in turn sends the message to activate the cells concerned. In the male there is an escape route whereby expression can be given to the desire by the expulsion of the spermatozoa. In the woman this is not so, hence the degree of frustration may be greater than in a man.

With the aid of the electron miscroscope a cell can be enlarged many millions of times, so much so that a single cell will occupy the full space of a cinema screen. Thus we are able to observe the steady, orderly process of life's function within it. When a renegade cancer is viewed, it is seen that these processes carry on at a furious rate, quite uncontrolled. Every function within the cell is speeded up. The cell has become insane. All respect for the control of its life and its orderly behavior has given way to uncontrolled and irresponsible impulses. It has run amok.

The intelligence of a cell has been likened to that of the mind and an apt comparison can again be drawn. When a person's mind has become obsessed with fears, grief, shock, great disappointment, all of which come under the classification of "frustration," all the orderly mental processes suffer, breaking down the health tone, inducing bodily wastage, and creating the conditions for the acceptance of disease. If the frustrations persist in force, they will overcome mental perspective and, if continued, will lead toward insanity and suicidal tendencies.

Through mental sensual experiences the mammary glands in the female breast are activated. This demonstrates beyond all doubt that there exists a direct liaison between the intelligence of the mind and the intelligence of the cells. One form of intelligence affects the other.

It is in this that we discern the primary causation of cancer. Continual frustration of sexual desires upsets the mammary cells, and they become frustrated with despair. The genes become rebellious, frantic, intensely unhappy, and this leads toward the cell becoming insane; it throws off the yoke of control. The cell rejects the discipline of glandular influence. It reproduces itself without any restraint, as quickly as it can. Its span of life is speeded up in an uncontrolled manner. It becomes predatory. All this the electron microscope shows.

There is a further parallel between the mind and the cell.

Insanity can be hereditary, and whatever steps are possible are taken to prevent adults with symptoms of insanity from bearing children. So it is with the insane cell. When it reproduces itself, it brings into being another insane cell. This is a common denominator in all forms of cancer.

This leads to the conclusion that the primary cause of cancer is psychosomatic. It is not the product of virus infection. Swiss scientists claim to have discovered a virus which causes cellular deformities, connected with the nucleus in animals. They say the virus propagates itself inside the nucleus and when the cells propagate, they reproduce the deformity. From this tumors are formed which can grow and threaten life. These scientists express the opinion that herein lies a cause of cancer. It is agreed that a deformity can be produced in a cell, which can be reproduced in a hereditary manner, but these cells are not insane, they are not predatory. The rate of propagation is not disturbed. They come within quite a different category than cancer cells.

Medical scientists have come to the conclusion that the cause of some forms of cancer is due to irritants. Smoking and diesel fumes have been cited, with over fifty other items from drinking coffee to kissing and using chewing gum. It is not my intention to dispute conclusions reached through medical research, but there are some observations that can be made. The effects of irritants can, of course, produce ill-conditions of a physical nature. But it remains to be shown how an irritant can induce insanity within a cell. Irritants can harm the physical structure of cells in the same way that poisons affect the cells within the bloodstream. Irritants in the digestion can cause suffering—but they do not cause cellular insanity. When we hurt our bodies in any way, even with severe burning, bruising, or cutting by surgery, the cells are badly damaged, they can be destroyed, they can suffer chronic ill-conditions through septic infections—but they do not become insane. Is it not logical to assume that if an irritant like smoking can cause cancer, then surely a sustained form of injury, such as burning or deep-ray radiation, should create cancer too?

With surgery or by the burning-up process of deep-ray therapy doctors are able to remove or destroy the insane cancer cells, and if the whole of them is so destroyed, life goes on; leave but one insane cell behind and it will not be long before it multiplies and the symptoms of cancer again become evident.

A vast amount of research has taken place this century into the cause of cancer the wide world over. Many skilled minds have devoted years of study to this. Millions of dollars have been spent in setting up elaborate laboratories—and no one will begrudge this expenditure. Millions of animals have been sacrificed in the cancer laboratories, often with great suffering, yet the cause of cancer still eludes them.

Is it that medical science has been looking in the wrong direction? Is it that cancer does not have a physical origin at all? Is it that the cause of cancer is psychosomatic? If it is, then all the equipment and microscopes are useless. One cannot put emotion and frustration under the microscope.

The means by which cells within the sex system can be deprived of their balance can be easily observed, but it is not so easy to relate mind frustrations to cancers that come in other parts of the body, e.g., the lungs, liver, throat, abdomen, limbs, etc. Frustrations, anxieties, lack of mental stability, all may create gastric ulcers. It is but an extension of this that can bring into being an abdominal cancer. The essential common denominator is that there must be a reasoned process to induce a cell to become insane and run amok. This appears to be tied up with the upsetting of glandular control which seriously disturbs the cell's mentality.

In elephantiasis the control of the growth of the cells by the pituitary gland is weak. The life of the cell is speeded up and it propagates more rapidly than it should. Balance is lost, more cells are created than normal, but they are content—they are not insane. They do not prey on other cells. Apart from their speeded life cycle, they do not cause much harm and do not cause death. Elephantiasis is more often seen in women, sometimes at a young age. We observe it in boys when there is a lack of coordination and spinal weakness. Everything seems to point to a breakdown in the glandular control of the cell's functions, yet its mentality is not violently disturbed.

The general conclusion is that in all forms of cancer there is a psychosomatic origin; there is frustration that upsets orderly conduct of the human mind, consciously or subconsciously, and this is received by the cell's intelligence, frustrating the genes and causing them to go berserk. The eminent cancer specialist Sir Heneage Ogilvie expressed this conclusion so aptly in a very few words when he said, "A happy man never gets cancer." I would like to add to this, "A contented woman never gets cancer."

Relatives of those who have passed on through cancer and who know of the opinions I have expressed . . . have taken me to task by saying that their dear one was a good person in every way, with a placid, easygoing temperament, and would do no harm to anyone. This is very true; the cause of inner-self frustrations need not be apparent. The basic fact remains that there must have been a cause in order to upset the intelligent equilibrium of the cell's life purpose. This cause may have been inherent; for example, the genic directives of the individual did not have the opportunity for development and expression.

A very close friend had shown from his early boyhood years the desire to serve God in church work. At his preparatory school he braved the storm of ridicule by conducting a prayer group. This life directive has continued with him and has never flagged. In spite of obstacles and other intervening pursuits, he is now able to satisfy this inner-self ideal and all should be well.

But supposing that due to strong parental influence he was more or less forced into a profession quite unconnected with his desires, there would have been established within him a deep inner-self frustration. This young man is most considerate in all things; he is intelligent and would have made a success of a professional way of life. It would then be said of him that he was kindly, forbearing, placid, and showed no outward sign of dissatisfaction with life. If he married and had a family, there is no reason to question that his family life would not have been a very happy one.

If he contracted cancer, his relatives would have ground for disputing the opinions I have expressed; there would have been no outward sign of frustration. Yet, within his inner self, his genetic self, there would be thwarted ambition, creating a long-suffering soul sickness, a deep inner-self frustration—and from this could have developed the primary cause for the upset of the genes concerned, resulting in cell revolt.

If research could be conducted into the life directives, the primary emotions, sexual nonfulfillment, or other causes of resentment, exasperation, and discontent with those who have contracted cancer, it would be found that these basic upsetting causes exist. It has already been shown that in women suffering from breast cancer there has been a history of sexual nonfulfillment, dissatisfaction, or frustration.

In spiritual healing, records exist of permanent recovery

from cancers, the existence of which had been medically proved. The picture is this: A cancerous state is known to have existed; sometimes it was observed when the patient was opened up for exploratory surgery. Soon after the commencement of spiritual healing all signs of the cancer have disappeared. These cases of spontaneous recoveries are well known to the medical profession. In 1964 the British Medical Association stressed the need for research into the reasons why these cures took place.

I recall one case where a woman was examined due to severe internal pains. She was opened up and a chronic cancerous state with advanced infiltration was seen. The surgeon decided the condition was inoperable and sewed her up. She was sent home to die in a short while. Spiritual healing intervened, and all pain and symptoms of the cancer disappeared. She did not die. She was able to carry on normally.

Two years later, for a different reason, she was admitted into the same hospital for abdominal surgery, and it so happened that the same surgeon operated. He had the woman's medical history, and when it was pointed out to him that he had previously diagnosed inoperable cancer, he was so puzzled upon discovering no sign of the cancer in her that he disputed it could be the same woman, even though the evidence of his previous surgery was before him.

I have said that no healing can be permanent unless the cause of the trouble is overcome, so it follows that with a spontaneous healing this has taken place. It has been shown that, through spiritual healing, corrective thought influences are effective in bringing about good changes within minds that are sick. It follows that if the inner-self frustrations which cause cancer can be soothed and calmed away, then the sustaining cause can be mastered and the ill effects can be healed.

It is contended that this is the reason that persons suffering "incurably" with various diseases get well with healing. The same reasoning can surely apply to cancer as is demonstrated with spontaneous cures. Once the ill effect is disassociated from its cause, then it will yield to treatment.

For a fleshy, cancerous mass to disappear quickly, a chemical change in the matter must have been effected. Healing experience demonstrates that these changes can be made, as with arthritic deposits, cysts, goiters, etc., so it is logical to assume that the unnatural, unwanted cancerous matter can likewise be taken away. This follows upon the direction of intelligently administered, dispersive characterized energies which effect a change in the status of matter.

A digression is now introduced, but one which has a direct bearing on the ability of the spirit people to change the state of living matter. In physical mediumship there is a phenomenon known as "apporting." This means that a physical object is conveyed from one place to another in a condition superseding the physical laws, enabling it to pass through physical structures such as walls, etc.

What happens is this: Into the seance room objects are brought from a distant place. I have photographed this feat with infrared photography. I have before me a picture of a brass ornament, in the shape of a stork, weighing some two ounces, which passed through the walls of the seance room. The medium was roped to his chair. To achieve this act, the ornament's material energy state must have been rendered into a higher rate of vibration, yet retaining its personality, a rate of vibration so high that it could pass through other energy formations comprising "solid" obstacles in the same way that sound vibrations can pass through a wall. From this state it had to be transformed back into its material form when it came into contact with the medium.

On another occasion, in red light sufficiently clear for those present to observe all that was taking place including the motionless form of the entranced and roped medium, we saw a trumpet elevated to the ceiling and twirled round at an amazing speed. While it was doing this we heard a knocking come within the trumpet. It then came to me and tilted into my hands an Egyptian amulet. Later, learned Egyptologists agreed that it was made of Theban glass, dating the amulet as belonging to the age of 1,500 B.C. This tallied with the inscription, which states it was the property of the "Custodian of the Southern Countries," belonging to the pharaoh of those times. The full story of this act of apporting is narrated in my book, *The Mediumship of Jack Webber*.

We know that all objects are masses of characterized atomic energy, nothing is really "solid." In apporting, this energy is speeded up in order to convert it from a material state into a spirit one, and in this condition it supersedes the physical laws. It can travel at incredible speed without losing its substance through friction with the atmosphere, it can be passed through other forms of energies comprising walls, etc., until the planned act reaches its conclusion with its reconversion back into a material atomic formation.

It may be worthwhile mentioning, for those who consider apporting to be a romantic fantasy, that doctors today are accomplishing a comparable act when they focus disruptive energies on unhealthy matter with deep-ray therapies. They destroy the diseased cells by applying a dispersing energy force to matter energy, hoping to accomplish this in a discriminating way, leaving the healthy cells unharmed. True, there are adverse side effects, but these are not our concern here, although much can be written on this subject. The point is that if human intelligence can work along these lines, then we should give credit to the advanced spirit intelligences to accomplish the task more easily and quickly. Thus we have an explanation to account for spontaneous healings.

Dispersals of matter take place in other ways and less directly. Sometimes the disappearance of a growth is gradual, taking a period of time. In these instances it is assumed that the conditions prevailing for the spirit, the patient, and the cancer were not suitable for a spontaneous dispersal, but that a different form of chemical change is progressively induced, sufficient for the gradual dissolution of the growth and expulsion through the excretory systems. I have recorded a number of cases where, following spiritual healing intervention, patients suffering from abdominal cancers have evacuated stools of much substance, so large as to fill two or more bedpans.

In the early years of my healing ministry, I visited a woman in Streatham who was dying from an abdominal cancer. Her condition was so advanced that the doctor was frequently calling to give morphia injections. During the night following my visit she had a tremendous evacuation. All symptoms of trouble left her and in three days she was up and about doing her household work.

How clearly this indicates that the ministering intelligence is not of the human mind but of another, which has the ability to assess the situation, make a correct evaluation, form a plan of treatment, and then carry it out by the application of characterized and qualitative energies. If there is any logic in these premises (and judgment of these can best be made by minds that are liberal and free from prejudice—not condemning these ideas simply because they are new or arise from the mind of an unqualified practitioner), the basis on which they rest is worthy of consideration. If this is so, then a new vista of research opens wide.

What is more important than the curing of cancer is the

prevention of it. Study will be necessary into the potentials of the body, mind, and spirit to recognize the forms of frustration and evaluate them according to the personality of the individual.

Psychiatry today has been termed the Cinderella of the medical profession. It has been said to be the refuge of those who fail to qualify in other directions. It should become the dominant science. On the ground that the far greater percentage of physical disease and illness has a psychosomatic cause, it is clear that far more attention should be devoted to this study in the future.

Unfortunately, from the official medical viewpoint, this would entail a measure of cooperation with spiritual healers—a step it is very reluctant to take. The time must come when physicians will recognize the all-important influence the mind exerts over health and life's purpose.

In this study people would be shown how to recognize the symptoms of unrest and inner-mind stresses and encouraged to seek aid to tranquilize the mind by appeal to the intelligence. Then and then only shall we see progress made in checking the advance of cancer and other diseases of psychosomatic origin.

High tribute should rightly be paid to the medical profession and its research work for all that it has accomplished in surgery, in conquering past scourges like typhus, typhoid, diphtheria, tuberculosis, and so on. All these are diseases of infection. This good work has cut down the mortality figures and has lengthened life. Unhappily, with the mastery over infectious diseases we are seeing a growth in psychosomatic disorders. This is due to the more hectic way of modern life, with its speed, rush, more weighty responsibilities, and hazards. There is an increase in mortality due to cancer, heart diseases, strokes, and nervous disorders. All these have their inception in mental stress. To combat them we need to appreciate more the working of our intelligence systems and to learn how to cooperate with them for the maintenance of happy health.

Many years ago I wrote with some hesitation that the cause of cancer would be found in mental disharmony. At that time the idea seemed so revolutionary that I hesitated before committing it to print. Years later I saw the first signs that medical opinion was turning toward this view, and I wrote an article in *The Spiritual Healer* (Volume 3, page 418) in which I quoted from an article on cancer research, written by Sidney Katz in the Canadian journal, *Maclean's Magazine*. I am reprinting my article here, for it provides much supporting testimony to what I have written today. It is as follows:

The relentless search for the causes and cure of cancer has now led medical scientists to a new and dramatic frontier; that of the human emotions. Surprising clues are being found which may, some day, answer such provocative questions as:

Can continued fear, worry, and disappointment be an important cause of cancer?

Does cancer race through a patient's body or slow down to a snail's pace depending on his attitude to life?

Do the cancer cells deliberately choose a specific organ to attack, the choice based on the particular kind of emotional problem plaguing the patient?

Do we all carry around cancer cells and do they only run wild when triggered off by some mysterious process in which the emotions play a part?

A few years ago doctors felt that the emotions were influential chiefly in producing such conditions as asthma, peptic ulcer, hypertension, backaches, and headaches. Cancer they felt was an exception. It was purely an organic disease. If the condition were untreated or untreatable, the cells multiplied furiously, spread through the body, and death followed inevitably.

But doctors have lately been puzzled by cases where this did not happen. The patient either recovered completely from an allegedly "fatal" disease or went on to enjoy good health for several years. Furthermore, two patients with the same degree of illness given exactly the same treatment would respond differently. Such cases led to speculation that somehow the personality of the patient governed the course of cancer. This theory was then tested in various clinics and hospitals with some rather surprising results:

At the Veterans' Administration Hospital, Long Beach, California, doctors compared a group of twenty-five patients with "fast-growing" cancer with a similar number who had "slow-growing" cancer. There was a dramatic difference in the personalities of the two groups.

In Chicago, forty women who had been operated on for breast cancer were carefully studied. The women were found to have a similar pattern of personality and behavior. They had an aversion to sex; most of them did not want to have children; they had an unhealthy, unpleasant relationship with their mothers that they covered up with an outward show of sweetness and light.

The vast majority of sufferers with leukemia—the so-called "cancer of the blood"—are adults. After numerous and intimate contacts with leukemia patients, two Philadelphia physicians reported that most of them had had harrowing lives. A female patient of 57 was a case in point. At 20 she fell madly in love but her parents forbade the marriage. At 22 she married another man, whom she did not love. Her husband was cruel, domineering, and self-centered. At times she was forced to work outside the home. Overwork and worry led to a period of mental illness. When she recovered, her mother and father died, and shortly afterward her husband divorced her. Right up until her death from leukemia, her life had been a succession of disappointments.

This may be an extreme case, but all the other cases investigated told of frustrations too.

Doctors have frequently hinted that researchers could profitably look to the cancer patient's mind for clues to the mystery. Dr. Joost Meerloo, a Columbia University psychiatrist, says, "Stress, mental shock, or maladjustment may be a causative factor in cancer." Dr. Ivan Smith, director of the Ontario Cancer Foundation, states, "One would do well to look for some relationship between a retardation of a cancerous growth and the personality of the patient." Dr. John Lovatt Doust, a psychiatrist engaged in research at the Toronto Psychiatric Hospital, says, "The mind and the body cannot be separated. When a person breaks down physically, the site of the breakdown is not accidental. It is tied up with the person's inheritance and his accustomed way of responding to difficulties. This might well influence the way the site of a cancer is chosen."

Thus there is building up a weight of medical testimony in support of our contention that cancer is a result of inner-mind disharmony, and this leads us to the natural conclusion that the prevention and cure of cancer come naturally within the province of spiritual healing.

The theory that personality traits are an influence in

cancer is strengthened by the unpredictable nature of the disease. Cancer is a slower and less often fatal disease than it is commonly believed to be. Every doctor knows this from his own experience. Some patients mysteriously recover completely even after the malignant growth has been "metastasized"—spread from the original site to other parts of the body. Other patients unaccountably live on for ten or twenty years. Many a doctor has damaged his reputation by predicting how long a cancer patient had to live.

Why do these healings take place? There is a reason behind all states of change. In my book, *The Evidence for Spiritual Healing,* I quote 281 cases where growths of various kinds have disappeared or the condition greatly bettered to the amazement of the doctor. Each of these cases received spiritual healing, and we suggest that these recoveries could only have come to pass with the mastering of the cause and that this was effected from a spiritual level, which gives emphasis to the theory that the primary cause was situated in the patient's mind or spirit self.

The possibility that we are all hosts to cancer cells is described in an issue of the professional journal *Cancer.* Dr. C. N. Edwards did autopsies on several men who had died from various causes. The results were revealing. In men over forty, 16 percent had prostate cancer; in men over fifty the proportion rose to 46 percent. Obviously most of these cancers remained stationary and the individual died for other reasons. They may have had cancer for thirty or forty years, but because of some defense system in the body, it did not grow and nobody knew about it.

Doctors followed a large group of women who were found to have cervical cancer. However, in only 20 percent of the cases did the malignant cells get to the point where treatment was required. "We are confronted with the possibility," says Dr. Philip West, a University of California professor of biophysics, "that all of us may have had or will have some form of cancer, but because of the inherent control of this process, we will never know it."

All of this suggests the presence of a defense mechanism. If this is so, what part do the emotions play in the precancerous and cancerous stage? Research followed this inquiry. The results were revealing. They showed that those patients who had developed cancer in an active way were made up of individuals who were painfully sensitive, overnice, apologetic, and overanxious to please, also the frustrated, vicious, and those who had carried revengeful thoughts, hatreds, and selfish desires. In all these conditions there is a bottling-up of feelings with no way of releasing the mental tensions. The example is quoted of a man who died from cancer in a few weeks, whereas he should have lived for a very much longer time. The doctor described him as "blocked," like a man who is afraid to reach for a gun to kill a tiger because he is afraid of the tiger.

Three years ago Dr. Max Cutler, a leading cancer surgeon and former head of the Chicago Tumor Institute, and his associate, Dr. Richard Renneker, carefully studied forty women who had been operated on for breast cancer. A general pattern emerged. Of twenty childless women, nineteen said they would not want to become pregnant under any circumstances. Of twenty women with children, seventeen said they would have preferred to be childless. Almost all the women had a difficult and unhappy relationship with their mothers. They resented their close attachment and dependency on their mothers, yet were unable to express their hostility. Other clinics have made similar observations.

Dr. James Stephenson and Dr. William Grace of the Cornell Medical School in Ithaca, New York, compared one hundred women with cancer of the cervix with a similar number with cancer in other sites. The typical cervical cancer case was revealed as a woman with poor adjustment in the field of sex, maternity, and marriage. She was likely to be divorced or separated from her husband. She disliked intercourse and seldom derived any pleasure from it. Her husband was likely to be alcoholic or unfaithful.

Worry, fear, and emotional tension all subject the body to a great deal of stress. Experimental work in recent years suggests that stress is the single cause of all diseases. Dr. Hans Selye, of the University of Montreal, believes that when the human body is under stress, be it through worry, disappointment, heat, cold, or bacterial invasion, its chemistry is thrown off balance. Immediately the glands try to restore this balance by working overtime, excreting hormones. If the stress is too prolonged, the gland mechanism breaks down and illness develops. Because leukemia—cancer of the blood —responds to ACTH and cortisone, which are glandular products, there is reason to suspect a close tie between stress and cancer.

Thus I would like to sum up by saying that there is an accumulating mass of evidence that cancer has a psychosomatic cause. The removal of these causes is generally outside the scope of the physician. It does lie within the scope of spiritual healing.

What is of equal importance to the healing of cancer is its prevention; because spiritual healing is able to soothe out inner-mind disharmony, it is the most effective preventative of cancer today. It follows that those who are receiving spiritual healing for reasons other than cancer are being protected from the possibility of cancer developing.

The implications of this statement are tremendous. The British Medical Association acknowledges the assistance that can be given by the clergy and spiritual healers in general, for over 80 percent of diseases have their causes in mind unbalance. A much more definite and close alliance between the medical profession and spiritual healing is indicated today in order that humanity may profit from the lessons now before us. This is far too big a question to be treated in an offhand manner or to allow fullness of action to be smothered by regard for old-fashioned ideas of professional prestige or theological quibbles.

It may well be that the prevention and cure of cancer is in our hands. Here is the basis of a positive appeal to humanity to save itself from the scourge that kills one in six today by inducing a higher code of spiritual values in our daily life.

While I have no statistics to prove this, I can say that, within our experience, we cannot remember a single case of disease where our help has been asked for that developed into a case of cancer. This provides verifiable evidence for our confidence that spiritual healing is the best preventative of cancer today.

It is many years since that article was written, and since the findings of the cancer researchers mentioned were published. Those findings support right up to the hilt everything

I have written here. I have not seen any further printed reference concerning this line of research since then, with the one exception of Sir Heneage Ogilvie's statement that "A happy man never gets cancer."

One wonders why this is. One can imagine the banner headlines the national press would carry if any reputable medical authority had declared that the cause of cancer is psychosomatic. Is is because our dedicated scientists are so deeply wedded to the microscope that they, following out the pattern of research of the past sixty years, are hesitant to relinquish this in favor of a new outlook? Is it that such a declaration would imply criticism of the research work now taking place and, indeed, largely terminate much of the present-day activity? Is it because human emotion cannot be clinically analyzed and is unresponsive to therapeutic treatment that it has little interest for those so scientifically materialistic it is difficult for them to look further than the walls of their laboratories?

Doctors do not discover truth, they uncover it. When it is shown to them and they ignore it, that is a sin against the human family.

I can prophesy that the time will come when research will admit that man has not only a material body but a spiritual one as well and that both are intimately concerned with the total health of all.

# 6

# Magic and Medicine

## Una Maclean

*The bureaucratization of modern medicine and the processing of patients in modern hospitals has greatly changed the interaction between physician and patient. The most typical complaint is that growing specialization in medical practice has produced a dehumanized healing environment which focuses attention primarily on "diseased" parts of the human body.*

*Una Maclean, lecturer in social medicine at the Usher Institute, Edinburgh University, describes a cultural environment quite alien from ours and makes us realize just how much Western medicine has lost the sight of treating the whole human being.*

•  •  •

Although there are a number of respects in which the patient-doctor encounter in Britain and Nigeria is similar, African medicine can only be properly understood in its complete cultural context, since the way in which people respond to illness or misfortune in any culture is inevitably related to the whole religious and philosophical framework in which existence is perceived.

Yoruba religion is by no means the frantic hotchpotch of fetishism, juju, and misleading mumbo jumbo which uncomprehending explorers and missionaries were formerly delighted to describe in derogatory terms. The idea that "The heathen in his blindness bows down to wood and stone" is now regarded by serious anthropologists as a figment of the nineteenth-century hymn writer's imagination.

The Yorubas, who are the predominant tribe of Nigeria's western region, developed over many generations not only a highly complex civil and political organization, but an elaborate philosophical system in which the central figure of man is seen to be continually interacting with spiritual principalities and powers. The ancestors, the gods, and the spirits of place, plants, and animals, all have an influence on his present existence and are capable, conversely, of being manipulated to his advantage. Feeling himself in the center of a web of personal and spiritual relationships, man is first of all aware of the strong pull of his forebears, who continually demand due respect and insist that he maintain their contact with life through producing children of his own. The personal ancestors, venerated in each family, are treated practically as gods while, on the other hand, the named gods, or *orisha*, were themselves once men. The exploits of these most famous of Yoruba ancestors form the subject matter of an extensive mythology which finds expression in a voluminous oral literature of poetry and song. Now raised to the position of deities, these mythological figures still retain many human characteristics and are notable less for their morality than for the intensity with which they express mortal passions or embody the power of the elements and of the natural environment.

In this countryside of dense rain forests the sky is only partially glimpsed above settlements and farm plots. Unlike the people living in the savanna country to the north, or in the desert still further beyond, the inhabitants of this area have little awareness of the vastness of the heavens. The humid climate often clothes what can be seen of the sky with sullen clouds, and, for fully half the year, sudden thunderstorms are liable to descend precipitately at dusk. It is a myopic, green landscape where close-up detail predominates, as in the pictures of the Douanier Rousseau, and where the spirits of the bush are continually felt to be present among the dark treetops and in the depths of the dense undergrowth. Sun, moon, and stars scarcely feature in Yoruba religion. Instead, some of the oldest strands in their mythology have to do with the earth, which is the manifest source and sustainer of their daily life. Traces of earth worship are to be found in the activities of a former secret organization, the Ogboni society, whose brass symbols, or *edan,* represent a man and woman joined by a chain between their heads. And Shopanna, the god most closely connected with medicine in the sense that he brings epidemics, also has important attributes relating to fertility and the successful sowing of seed.

It is not surprising that it should be the elements rather than the planets which have captured the imagination of people living in this environment and that Shango, the thunder god, should be universally revered. Conversely, Olodumare, the supreme sky god of the Yorubas, is, for geographical as much as theological reasons, seldom invoked. Remote from mankind, he is much less intimately involved in their affairs than are the pantheon of familiar *orisha* who have their origins firmly rooted in the historical past.

The Yorubas have a strong sense of continuity between past and present and between the living and the dead. The ancestors and the gods are both perceived as continually intervening in the affairs of their descendants; their goodwill must be sought or the best-laid plans will come to nought, their presence permeates family compounds, and sacred shrines, and may at times descend upon living men and women who are in a suitably receptive state of trance.

But the gods, the ancestors, and sundry minor spirits are not the only influences which are felt to affect life. Other people in the extended family group, or ill-intentioned members of the wider community, are constantly viewed suspiciously as possible sources of malevolence. Personal ill will is thought to operate through curses elaborately prepared and delivered, or through the manipulation of various magical devices which enable hatred and envy to act effectively across time and space. But none of the individual operations of malice are feared as much as the power of witchcraft, whose pervasive influence is still widely acknowledged.

Fortunately a means is available whereby the intentions of gods and men as well as the wishes of the ancestors may all be discovered. This is the oracular system of *Ifa* as it is practiced by its diviner priests, the *babalawo,* or "fathers of mysteries."

The Yoruba method of divination is renowned throughout West Africa and is a very complicated development of other simpler inquiries into the operations of fate. It has been described by several writers, but its fascinating details are less important than the principles which underlie it. In its commonest form it involves recording the results of loosely throwing some of a handful of sixteen kola nuts from the right to the left hand. Depending upon whether an odd or an even number of nuts remains in the right hand after the throw, a single or double mark is made upon a sand-covered tray. The wooden *Ifa* tray, which is often elaborately carved, eventually bears sets of marks in double columns. As a rule, the sixteen nuts are cast sixteen times and the outcome of each set of four throws is noted in terms of the resultant pattern of single and double strokes upon the sanded tray. Patterns of marks relate to specific verses within the *Odu,* or corpus of sayings relating to *Ifa.* There are a total of 256 verses corresponding to all the possible combinations of odd or even results following upon the usual sixteen throws of sixteen nuts, so the choice of verses which can on any particular occasion be recited to a client is very considerable.

The *babalawo,* whose long training has not only involved committing all the literature to heart but who is also skilled in psychotherapy and in interpreting the contents of the oracle for each individual inquirer, solemnly pronounces the results of the divination procedure and offers appropriate advice as to what action should be taken. The oracle may indicate the necessity of sacrificing to a neglected ancestor or a god; it may suggest that the client should become an adherent of some cult other than the family one, whose god may be judged unsuitable to his personality; it may point to disturbed relationships within the family and the need to restore good feelings between relatives.

Through *Ifa,* therefore, it is possible for someone to establish what powers are at work and, armed with this knowledge, to take appropriate action. To read one's fate through *Ifa* is not to despair in a predestined universe. The Yoruba inquirer, who has been informed of his position and of how he stands in relation to the intentions of other people and the possible grievances of ancestors and *orishas,* can then proceed to manipulate the system to his personal advantage, procuring protective medicines, operating counter-charms, offering sacrifices, and so on. He will be perfectly confident that his luck can thereby be subsequently changed. Certainty takes, at least temporarily, the place of uncertainty, and anxiety can be diverted from fruitless metaphysical questions to the practical means of improving his fortunes.

Serious illness is regarded as only one out of the many possible misfortunes which may befall someone, and the type of cause which the *babalawo* uncovers in the case of an illness will be no different in kind from the causes he will specify for other personal disasters. That is to say, the cause will be expressed in terms of spiritual influences emanating from the dead, from the gods, or from the living, and requiring appropriate ritual and practical measures to counteract them.

In general the power of an *orisha* is related to the amount and fervor of the worship he receives, and thus one village may, because of some historical event or recounted miracle, pay special respect to a minor deity who is practically unknown elsewhere. The power and influence of any god will wax and wane with the devotion of his followers, for the gods cannot exist without their worshipers. If men cease to revere them, they will die and even their names will be lost forever. Like the ancestors, who cannot continue without living descendants, the existence of the gods depends upon their living followers.

The power of a god is immanent in the vicinity of the shrines which have been consecrated to him and where regular offerings and respects are paid. In each shrine, no matter how modest, there is a central vessel which contains cult objects and in this area the *orisha*'s power is concentrated. But this power is not considered to be restricted to or identified with the carvings or implements on the altar since the purpose of these things is essentially to focus the worshiper's attention upon the true object of his devotions, the god whose attributes the materials merely symbolize.

One of the most attractive and complex of the Yoruba *orisha* is the trickster god Eshu Elegba. The mischievous reputation of this individual caused early missionaries, always on the lookout for unfavorable comparisons, to identify him with the devil. In this they maligned the cheerful insouciance of Eshu, whose many exploits are recounted locally with tolerant amusement. Eshu is the god who guards entrances and exits, crossroads, markets, and shrines. Many people think it prudent to erect a small clay mound to represent him just outside their front door and that it is important to cast a small sacrifice in his direction whenever they are honoring a major deity, as the neglect of such a simple precaution may precipitate his wrath. He is neither completely good nor completely evil but thoroughly human in his unpredictable mixture of qualities. Eshu Elegba acts as messenger, or mediator, between man and the gods and so can transmit their mutual feelings in both directions. Like *Ifa*, Eshu is worshiped and called upon by devotees of all other gods and is also closely bound up in legend with the *Ifa* divination system which he is supposed to have revealed to mankind.

The shrines dedicated specifically to Eshu Elegba are characterized by a larger representation of his motif, sometimes merely featuring a mud mound or pillar several feet high but possibly containing carvings as well. Elegba is represented in his carvings with a whistle or pipe held to his mouth and with a long, curved plait of hair, phallic in shape, reaching far down his back. His headdress is usually ornamented with small gourds of the type used as medicine bottles. He wears strings of cowrie shells about his dress and carries a large pouch, and the wood of the carving is painted black. Although his color has sometimes been taken to indicate his essential wickedness, the phallic features of his hair and its ornaments may symbolize his instinctual energy and willfulness.

His relation to the *Ifa* system of divination is one of balance or opposition. Whilst people go to *Ifa* to find out what is currently ordained, Eshu Elegba incorporates uncertainty and chaos, the irreducible element of chance misfortune which may upset the most careful plans.

Not all the *orishas* are of equal stature, but the great god Ogun commands universal respect. He is the god of smiths and all those who use iron implements of any kind, and so he includes among his followers soldiers, hunters, farmers, and butchers, with the recent addition of lorry drivers and motor mechanics.

Ogun's elevated position in the hierarchy is expressed in his family connections, for, according to legend, he was the firstborn son of Oduduwa, the legendary ancestor of all the Yorubas and founder of their spiritual capital at Ile Ife.

Ogun is never directly represented in carvings but is conceived as one of the most powerful spiritual forces which can be enlisted in the service of men. His symbols of iron weapons or tools represent his ability to mow a path through all obstacles, and so his assistance is requested in connection with important enterprises of all kinds.

As in the case of Eshu, offerings to other deities should be accompanied by one to Ogun, because it is his knives which have made the sacrifice possible.

His dominating and ferocious character is epitomized in

the following extracts from the hymns of praise, or *oriki,*
which his followers chant:

Ogun, great king of all the world, who leads all other *orishas*;
Having water in his house, he chooses to bathe in blood
And to cover his head with a blood-stained cap.
High over all,
Ogun the warrior with heart of steel.

However, his attributes are not exclusively violent and his
potency also extends in the direction of fertility. Being
credited in legend with four hundred wives and fourteen
hundred children, it is not surprising that women should
frequently approach him with requests for children and that
they entrust subsequent offspring to his care.

Paradoxically it is often the very women who have lost all
their children in infancy who finally become his most devoted
followers and place themselves permanently under his protection. Perhaps they feel that by identifying themselves
with his power and plenitude they may escape the humilia-
tion of their own inadequacy.

Another highly placed member of the Yoruba pantheon is
Shango, the spectacular thunder god who formerly lived as
the fourth king of *Ifa.* Like Thor and Jove, he embodies the
terrifying aspect of the elements. His character is impetu-
ous and generous, but he is a jealous god, visiting vengeance
upon evildoers of all kinds. Death by lightning is consequently regarded as a merited punishment for sin and the
victims are buried unceremoniously outside the town.

Neolithic remains, in the form of primitive ax heads or
celts, are kept in the shrine of Shango, representing the veri-
table thunderbolts of the god. His symbols of a double-
headed ax or a pair of ram's horns may appear alone, but a
stylized shape of this kind commonly adorns the head of a
female figure (possibly representing Shango's wife, Oya) in
the carvings which decorate his altar.

The priests of Shango grow their hair long as a tribute to
his notable virility and wear it elaborately dressed and
plaited in a strictly regulated style. In the ceremonies connected with his worship they can apparently handle flames
and boiling liquids with impunity and they are celebrated
"fire-eaters" whose skills attract great popular acclaim.

Yemaja, mother of the gods, is the beautiful divinity of
the waters. Her principal shrine is at Abeokuta, not far

from Ibadan, by the banks of the Ogun River. In the worship of Yemaja pebbles and white seashells play a part. She is perceived as a shy and retiring virgin, while at the same time her carvings present her as a symbol of motherhood, heavily pregnant, with ample breasts. In the mingling of apparently incompatible features she resembles many other female deities, including the Virgin Mary, who personify the most admired qualities of womanhood.

The legends surrounding Yemaja speak of her as the source of streams and rivers which spring from her breasts. Without her abundant waters all the other gods would perish.

Among her praise songs are the following verses:

The queen who dwells in the depths of the sea
Trembles when the strong wind blows.
When Yemaja is vexed she destroys bridges and drowns
    houses.
Mother with dripping breasts,
Who rises like the rainbow from the river
To wait proudly before the king.
Mother of the world, who brings healing to mankind.


Shopanna, the god who visits smallpox epidemics upon mankind, is so greatly dreaded that his real name is seldom uttered. Instead he is euphemistically referred to as King of Earth or Lord of the Open Places. He stalks abroad at noonday, when people are advised to keep indoors, away from the midday sun. Red garments, the shade of the hot, dry earth, may invite his wrath and so Yorubas do not wear the color he has made his own.

Shopanna is not only responsible for smallpox but for all kinds of serious and fatal illnesses, both physical and mental. The Lord of the Earth may kill or maim with smallpox, or he may drive someone mad. He is related to several minor deities, some of whom are associated, like their chief, with outbreaks of pestilence and famine. But the Lord of the Earth has his creative side as well, and several of his attributes relate to fertility and the successful production of crops and children.

Rather like the Lord whom Job worshiped, Shopanna gives life and he takes it away, expecting to be congratulated for both actions. Smallpox victims will not be mourned since nothing must be done to attract more of the god's attention.

In the verses about Shopanna he is described as being

adorned with pearls or with small round calabashes, an obvious visual analogy to the pustules of smallpox.

Before the time of colonial rule the priests of Shopanna held a respected position in the community since it was their responsibility to treat cases of smallpox and to dispose of the corpses of victims during epidemics. The dead, who would normally otherwise be buried beneath the floors of their houses, where removed naked from their homes to the shrine of Shopanna, which was always some distance outside the village. Their clothes and belongings thereafter became the property of the priests who were supposed to see that they were burned.

It seems as if the priests may have practiced some kind of preventive inoculation, or variation, and they had certainly developed a variety of ointments and salves for application to the skin of established cases of smallpox. The cult also laid down strict regulations for public behavior during an epidemic. Large gatherings of people were forbidden and sweeping of compound floors had to be done with a special, soft, leafy branch instead of the usual bunch of stiff twigs. These measures, when taken in conjunction with the isolation of cases and the disposal of bodies and personal effects, may have been instrumental in reducing the spread of the disease. There was little appreciation of the difference between smallpox and chickenpox, but smallpox was the most feared for its tendency to strike and kill adults and a visitation by Shopanna was regarded as a sign of disgrace.

In 1917 the British forbade the "worship" of Shopanna and put an end to the activities of the priests, on the unsubstantiated suspicion that they occasionally acted maliciously and tried to spread the disease by using a powder made from the dried scabs. But local treatments of smallpox are still very widely quoted and many herbalists today, without admitting adherence to Shopanna, will claim proficiency in the management of serious skin diseases.

The gods mentioned so far are only a small selection of those which may still be surviving by virtue of the reverence afforded to them in certain places. They have been selected for consideration because of their specifically medical associations, their reputation for helping barren women, as in the case of Ogun, or of bringing death and disease, in the case of Shango and Shopanna. Although many Yorubas, especially in the larger Nigerian towns such as Ibadan and Lagos, may now describe themselves as Moslem or Christian, the echoes and implications of the authentic Yoruba religion remain in everyday speech while in the villages the presence of the gods is still ensured by regular public festivals in their honor and by the devotion of their personal followers. Just as Christian morality and attitudes persist in Western countries where active church membership is small and diminishing, the habits of thought which were implicit in Yoruba religion and philosophy survive the death of the gods.

It is possibly that segment of Yoruba thought which deals with the influences which proceed directly from one individual to another which shows the greatest persistence and which has at the same time the greatest relevance for the understanding of Nigerian medicine.

There is undoubtedly a realization of all kinds of simple, direct causes for illness. For example, a palm-wine tapper whose rope snaps as he is suspended high above the ground and who fractures his femur is perfectly aware that the frayed rope was involved in his misfortune. But this will not prevent his wondering why it should have happened to him in particular, on that very day, up that particular palm tree, and the demonstration that his rope must have been in a decrepit condition will not satisfy his search for the real, underlying cause of his accident.

People may use words which suggest that they have some conception of parasitic infection, for example, they may remark that some illnesses are "due" to worms or to some other kind of curious insect or creature moving around inside the body. But to speak in these terms does not mean that they regard the illness as having been adequately accounted for, since a proper explanation will still require to indicate who put the worm there in the first place.

It is held that cold drinks are dangerous in the wet season, at a time when the outside temperature is low and fevers are common. The definition of "cold" drinks may be somewhat arbitrary, including beer, for example, but not stout. Perhaps a passing chill may be attributed to some such simple source and in a day or two it will be forgotten. But if the fever should continue and be aggravated by signs of wasting and general debility, the patient and his relatives will look for a deeper cause than a can of cold lager would provide.

Symptoms and sickness which are short, self-limiting, and familiar can be put down to dietary indiscretions, chills, and minor traumata. Then there are disease names which have been picked up from contact with Europeans, terms like yaws, gonorrhea, TB, and malaria. The often quoted cause of tuberculosis is the use of another person's "chewing stick," the piece of fibrous wood which is used in lieu of a toothbrush, and this may be related to the concept of transferable bacterial infection inculcated by several generations of sanitary inspectors. But if a disease is mysterious and persists in spite of simple countermeasures, suspicions will be aroused about the operation of personal and spiritual forces whose nature must be properly defined or divined before the patient can hope for relief.

It is in relation to disorders of the reproductive system, whose efficient functioning is a matter of the greatest concern, that explanations involving witchcraft are most often invoked. Impotence in men is a common complaint which may be related to the demands of polygamy. Men continually fear this affliction, thereby increasing their liability to it, and it is at the same time the object of much mirth and ridicule if it becomes public knowledge.

In Yoruba belief witches are always female, deriving their power from Eshu. Incorporating all the worst features of their sex, witches emasculate and weaken men, who are dependent upon women for pleasure and for offspring.

In part the view of women as potential witches probably derives from the young child's early experience of his mother as a loved individual who may suddenly turn upon him in terrifying anger and deny him his desires. It is certainly significant that the dangerous Yoruba word for a witch is seldom used and that they are referred to instead as "our mothers."

There may be a further element of envy regarding women's creative powers which men cannot hope to emulate. The question of the origins of witchcraft beliefs has been deeply debated and there is still no general agreement, opinions varying from psychoanalytic explanations, such as those touched on above, to views which stress the witches' own personalities as depressed old women whose day is past.

The subject is bound up with ideas of the soul or spirit leaving the body during sleep and traveling to meet others. Witches are believed to gather secretly at night for cannibalistic feasts and orgies. Or a witch may fly alone into her victim's house where she will seduce him with sexual dreams, leaving him weak and flaccid, a prey to strange fears and wasting fevers. She may at times harm someone directly, in his own health and fortunes, or she may choose to damage another woman's child, causing it to sicken and die. Often her malice takes the form of interfering with menstruation and making it impossible for women to conceive.

Among the Yoruba the owl is the witch bird, and to hear its hooting at night or have one perch near the house are most unlucky omens. Certain trees (*iroko*) are regarded as the favored meeting places of witches and shunned accordingly. But the witch is also thought to transform herself into various other animals who are notoriously nocturnal in their habits, such as cats, bats, and rats.

The unfortunate phrase "witch doctor" has frequently been employed in connection with African medicine, tending to suggest some kind of unholy alliance between witches and traditional doctors. In fact, one of the primary functions of the doctor in traditional society was always to protect its members from the dangerous activities of witches, as witchcraft was essentially a disruptive, antisocial activity, the ultimate expression of ill will and personal spite. It is still considered an important part of the herbalists' and diviners' business to discover whether witches have had a part in causing an illness with a prolonged or puzzling course, which is failing to respond to what are conventional forms of treatment. If necessary, a client may be recommended to make sacrifices to appease the witches whose own medicine is considered so powerful that the herbalist or *babalawo* could not otherwise hope to counteract it.

# 7

# Hexing for Health

## Lee R. Gandee

*Lee R. Gandee was raised in rural West Virginia in an atmosphere very foreign to most people. It was a world where extraordinary powers of the mind were accepted as well as apparitions, hauntings, and communication with the dead. It wasn't long before Gandee began developing his own powers, and in this selection from his autobiography he gives us a fascinating glimpse of the reality of a Hexenmeister (Hex) and the "old faith" that often is used in healing.*

• • •

The realization that Christian Science is a form of magic came as somewhat of a shock. I was not surprised that holy persons can use magic, for Stud's Aunt Mat was as good as bread, and in her own way, Grandmother was a holy woman. That Grandmother spoke a verse of the Bible and stopped bleeding—even in animals, when someone phoned and asked her to try—seemed natural to me because it was familiar.

My great-great-grandfather Zachariah Lee could command rain so well, he could stop a shower at will, or bring up one in a few hours. Now *there* was a Hex! But one day he grew angry because lightning had struck his favorite shade tree and almost frightened his great-grandson to death, so he stepped to the edge of the porch, shook his fist at the clouds, and cried, "Bust my tree and scare a little boy, damn you! This is old Zach; let's see you flash one at *me* once!" A Hex should not say such things. The lightning obeyed him; he was killed instantly.

Only after I was in college did I realize that something was involved here that is not accounted for in ordinary psychology. In college I also took philosophy. When I saw that even atheists may have Puritan standards as to right and wrong, I began to wonder what unique value religion has. Its practical values seemed to come from psychology, and its helpful effects in controlling behavior, as well or better from ethics or philosophy. All that seemed left was worship, and I found that very difficult in churches. They are not big enough to inspire awe, or beautiful enough to inspire reverence, or quiet enough for meditation. More and more I became interested in magic, more and more in the God in nature, less and less in churchly religion.

Though I still used Christian Science effectively when I believed some particular affirmation, I became interested in Hex, or Pennsylvania Dutch White Magic. This was the kind Stud's Great-aunt Mat practiced, as well as did the others in our community who used "the Power" in any of its forms.

Here is a part of an incantation called "A Good Remedy for Bad Wounds and Burns," followed by three Hex crosses: "The word of God, the milk of Jesus' mother, and Christ's blood is for all wounds and burnings good. + + + "

By the way of instruction Hohman said, "It is the safest way in all these cases to make the crosses with the hand or thumb three times over the affected parts; that is to say, over all those things to which the crosses are attached." It is a typical powwow, or Pennsylvania Dutch conjuration for curing. I find it effective, though for wounds and for burns I use two separate ones which work more quickly for me.

Unless one is already himself a powwow, the instructions may not be clear. Hohman lived at Rosenthan, near Reading, Pennsylvania, and wrote the booklet in 1819. The language has not changed much since then, but John George was a Pennsylvania Dutchman, not unlike the Carolina Swiss after they began speaking English. A barrister complained of them, "Their natural way of expression is such that not all the artifice and cunning of the legal mind could, by design, contrive its equal for obscurity and ambiguity of meaning."

Here and there, with other incantations, Hohman let fall other hints, but not enough to clarify fully what one does when he powwows. When three crosses are printed after the "sympathetic words" (incantations), the following procedures should be performed: First, the words "in the name of God the Father, God the Son, and God the Holy Ghost, Amen" are spoken. Then, the powwow makes the sign of the cross three times—over the affected part of the body if the person being treated is present, or if the person is not present, in the air in his direction. In any benevolent work the crosses are made by closing the right hand into a fist. Using the thumb, first make a downward stroke, then raise the hand to the right and cross the first stroke horizontally toward the left.

The use of the left hand and of a crossing from left to right is for malevolent purposes—useful when one is cursing a malevolent condition, in which cases the two malevolencies counter each other, as do two negatives or two positives in polarity. Any effort to heal, as for a wound or a burn, that does not require the destruction of anything could be called benevolent. If healing first requires destruction, as of a cancer, a tumor, or the core of a boil, the Hex is a curse to destroy the *cause* of the trouble and could be called malevolent.

For ritualistic reasons, I stand with my back toward the east when giving present treatment, in order that help may come to the treated person from that direction in deference to the sun, and all that the sun symbolizes. When I give absent treatment, however, I face the direction of the person treated. In absent treatment I speak the powwow aloud. But if the person is present, unless the conjuration is in German or in words whose meaning is not known, I whisper them inaudibly. This is done for the same reason that one keeps prayer secret—and Jesus Himself commanded that prayer be made in secret. In speaking a powwow, as in the ancient religion, the head is covered, as I believe it still is in synagogues during prayer or worship. For this purpose the old users of powwow kept a special hat or bonnet in a dark place, and brought it out only for this ritual. In emergency cases I have covered my head with a towel, a handkerchief, or a newspaper, but I keep a hat in my wardrobe for use whenever possible.

In some old "Papers"—the handwritten incantations kept by users who knew too many conjurations to remember them all—occasionally one finds an incantation followed by J.J.J. or I.I.I., or Y.Y.Y. However written, this indicates that instead of "in the Name of God . . . etc.," the saying is to be followed by "In Jesus' name, Amen."

The incantations marked with crosses or the three letters should be said at specific time intervals. Unless there are special instructions, the first is said and the signs are made when the Hex undertakes treatment. The incantation is repeated and the signs are again made a half-hour later; the third repetition and the third signs are made an hour after the second, making a total of nine signs in the course of the treatment. The four-square cross originally invoked the Lord of the Four Directions—the Universal One God. It is the Hex symbol of power, of universality, and of the pairing of opposites—of negative and positive, of male and female, of active and passive, or of any pair of opposites which must be in balance for wholeness, for perfection, or for generation. In the context of physics, it could stand for opposite polarities.

After the old religion gave way to, or made room for, Christianity, it transferred its conjurations to the new gods. (White Hex called the new teaching the God-spell and recognized it as the highest magic—one in which priests transformed bread and wine into the very body and blood of Christ by the ritual of the Mass.) Nevertheless, when doing research for his dissertation, "The Practice of Using to Heal Among North and South Carolina Lutherans," a student at the Lutheran Theological Southern Seminary in Columbia, South Carolina, found a woman in North Carolina successfully using an incantation which invokes Thor as well as the Trinity! It must bridge the transition between pagan and Christian belief in Northern Europe.

When he remonstrated with her, incredulous that a Lutheran should still invoke Thor (albeit many powwows refer to the Virgin Mary and other saints), the good old soul, country-bred and uneducated, told him that the word *Thor* was part of the incantation that had always been handed down. But what it meant, she did not know, for she only repeated what the old ones taught her. I can believe her, for when my cat was snakebitten, I used an incantation, *"Slongabis, Slongagift, geh im sond,"* repeated thrice as one strokes down from the wound to touch the ground with the thumb, and I have no idea what *Slongabis* and *Slongagift* mean. I only know that David Shull wrote them in his "Paper" in Pennsylvania in 1859, and that the cat recovered overnight from both swelling and sickness. That incantation invokes neither the Trinity nor Jesus, and requires only that one repeat it and touch the ground at the end of each downward stroke, then draw the cross on the ground with the thumb. It may go back to the old religion, and to a forgotten language. It was titled "To Cure Snakebite in Cattle"—but it works fine for a cat, maybe because *cattle* once meant any kind of domestic animals.

In one of his comments, Hohman said that what is prescribed for man also applies to animals. I presume the reverse is also true. Still, I would not rely on this charm, not having seen it tried on a person, unless I were snakebitten where I could not induce bleeding and hasten to a doctor.

Until he decided that God must take her ignorance into account, the researcher was rather disturbed to find that the old lady's incantation worked successfully notwithstanding its suggestion of divided loyalty. He dutifully included it with the many others he collected. I gave him my favorite powwow for burns and referred him to retired Luheran Pastor Wessinger at Newberry, South Carolina, who has lived and preached among users all his life, has great respect for their powers, and enjoys their complete confidence.

Pastor Wessinger, though he still serves rural congregations that cannot attract a full-time minister, must be past eighty. He told me that in his youth there were still a few Hexes in South Carolina who could walk in front of the fire in a burning field or forest, and the flames would stop and go out at their path, and not rekindle on the opposite side even in a high wind. He said the woman who handed down my powwow for burns could thus extinguish fire, but the only recent attempt I have heard about did not succeed. The enchanter walked in front of the flames, was cut off from escape from the field, and was forced to run for his life and jump in Lake Murray. But with what sublime confidence old Granny Slice, the good witch of Dutch Fork, would start across a blazing woodland, and how people marveled when the fire died at her tracks! People in the Dutch Fork tell of a house which stood in the path of a raging fire in Little Daniel Koon's lifetime. He arrived on horseback, only in time to jump off, circle the building and gallop on to a point where he could safely begin the walk. The house was all that remained unburned in the wake of the fire.

But I know of none left like Granny Slice and Little Daniel Koon, and though I have sought the incantation they used,

I have not found it. The old pastor said he had never heard it, nor had he seen a firewalk. "But my parents saw them, and I saw a tract of pine where Granny Slice had walked and stopped the fire," he reflected. His people had known the Slice (or Schlaiss) family since the middle of the eighteenth century.

A seminary seems an unlikely place at which to present a dissertation on magic, but the South Carolina Synod is full of people who know that "using" is practiced widely among Lutherans in the state, and I suppose they wished to learn all they could about it. Before I owned a copy of *The Long Lost Friend,* I was quite put out to make a trip to Dutch Fork to ask one of the old Slice men to let me copy from his book an incantation I needed, only to find that his minister (a young man—also named Wessinger) had borrowed it ahead of me and taken it home.

At the seminary and in the synod hardly anyone is more respected than the Reverend J. Benjamin Bedenbaugh, D.D. Older South Carolina Lutherans have known him since he was a scrawny, devout, earnest young seminarian, regarded as a genius by his instructors, and affectionately called "Bennie" by the whole synod. A farm youth from near Stony Battery, in Newberry County, he had known of users all his life.

As a student, and later as a theologian at the seminary, he was subject to agonizing, prostrating headaches. (He is a bachelor, and his headaches reminded me of the migraines I used to suffer.) So when the researcher told him he had found a conjuration for headaches, Dr. Bedenbaugh allowed him to use it in his behalf. I would give much to have witnessed that powwow, for it involves pressing the fingers of both hands against the sufferer's temples, recitation of ir-relevant-sounding words, and the solemn assurance, "This I tell thee, Bennie, for thy repentance' sake. + + +" It must have been a bizarre sight.

I was told some months afterward that Dr. Bedenbaugh's headache had stopped, and though I am too much in awe of his reputation and erudition to ask him personal questions, I noticed that he took on a different look. He remained pale, but no longer corpselike; solemn, but no longer funereal; and the pinched, tormented look left his face and eyes.

The dissertation was accepted; the researcher was ordained, and the last time I heard of him he had a church of his own, and was also "using" actively for the members of a Negro

Baptist congregation. (This group was on the verge of turning Lutheran because of his wonder-working power, but I think he taught the Negro minister how to powwow, instead of leading the church away.)

At that time I was teaching at Lenoir Rhyne College, in Hickory, North Carolina, and knowing of this development in Columbia, I felt it defensible to give help to my students when I saw they should have it. Hohman wrote, "Any and every man who knowingly neglects using . . . in saving the eye, or the leg, or any other limb of his fellow man is guilty of the loss of such limb, and thus commits a sin. . . ." I feel much the same; so, though I realized fully that the administration would make fun of it, or condemn it as superstition or witchcraft, I began using "sympathy" when I was on the faculty there.

The first instance was for a boy from Virginia. He suffered a deep inward nasal hemorrhage which had persisted for more than twenty-four hours, and had gone to a doctor in Hickory who had not succeeded in stopping it. When I learned of it, he was about to start to a specialist in Charlotte with friends, who were going along, afraid he would collapse or grow too faint from loss of blood to drive his car.

I asked him if I might try to help him, and he agreed, though he said, "What do you think *you* can do?" in complete skepticism.

"I can try, that is all," I told him. "I know an old way."

"Well, try!" he urged. "If somebody doesn't do something soon, I'm going to bleed to death!"

So I took him aside and said the "words of sympathy" to stop bleeding, made the crosses, and he went on to Charlotte.

However, the bleeding stopped before he was out of Hickory, and the specialist merely examined his nose and throat and did nothing except tell him not to do anything to risk starting it again, and sent him back. Word spread in his dormitory that I was some kind of wonderworker and the boys teased me unmercifully, though a few wanted to know the method.

Next a youth from Charlotte fell on a trampoline and cut his eybrow, injuring his eyelid and eye very severely. That night he and his friends sat up and soaked the blood and fluid into towels, for it hardly slackened, and the doctor feared that he might lose his eye. It was just before Christmas holidays, but he could not travel to visit his sister in Rich-

mond in that condition. When he did not appear for the last
class before the holidays, I went to the dormitory to visit
him, for I was very fond of him.

When I offered to try to help him, he sighed, "Well, if you
helped Stu like they say, maybe you *can* do something."

I recited the conjuration, and before the vacation began
that afternoon, his injury stopped bleeding and discharging
fluid. He went on to Richmond. His eye still looked hopeless
when he returned, but he was beginning to see vaguely with
it, and though double vision persisted for months, by the
time he graduated the following spring, his eye was normal.
Another case of a youth who was one of the most strikingly
handsome athletes I ever saw, a star on the basketball team.
During practice he was struck squarely in the mouth by someone's elbow; the impact knocked out one of his teeth and
loosened the two adjoining it. The coach found the tooth and
rushed him to the dentist, who set it back in place. But his
mouth was so grotesquely swollen and discolored when he
entered class next day, I hardly recognized him. After class
I stopped him as he left and asked him what had happened.
When he told me, I exclaimed "What a shame! Does the
dentist think it will grow back?"

"He said I had maybe a 10 percent chance it might."

He opened his mouth painfully and I saw that the gum
was black, torn, and oozing blood. I touched his lip, and
it was burning with inflammation.

"Looks awful, doesn't it?" he sighed.

"Maybe I could do something to give it better than 10
percent."

"Like for Mike's eye?"

I nodded.

"Well . . ."

"Come where we won't be seen," I said, motioning him to
my office.

"What is it you do?"

"I use an old, old method."

"Witchcraft? They say you are a witch."

"I bind a charm, but it is the power of God that does the
work."

"I don't care if it's the power of the devil, if it works!"

"Close your eyes and hold your breath till I touch your
lip," I directed and whispered the incantation, which is one
of Hohman's:

Bruise, thou shalt not heat:
Bruise, thou shalt not sweat;
Bruise, thou shalt not run—
No more than the Virgin Mary
Shall bring forth another son. +++

He peeked, and being of Catholic background, he looked askance at the crosses crossed toward the left with the thumb.

"That's a queer way to make the sign," he commented. "Why the thumb and the fist?"

"When you have your fist closed, all that is left free is the thumb."

"Why close the fist?"

"It's a roborant gesture to strike against the trouble," I replied, positive he would not know what *roborant* means (who does, and him a star athlete!)—the less understood in such cases, the better the chance of success.

"And that is going to cure me?"

"I did what I can do."

For some weeks the secret was between us, for I told him to tell no one until his teeth were again sound. His face resumed its former perfection. Then one morning he waited and spoke to me after class, with a look not unlike those I had seen on Stuart and Michael.

"Yesterday the dentist told me my teeth are fine," he breathed. "They grew back as sound as ever."

"Thank God!"

"I did. Now I want to thank you—I doubted you could do anything."

"I couldn't bear to think of your beautiful teeth ruined."

"You think my teeth are beautiful?" he beamed.

"Gorgeous," I said roguishly. "You know all too well how beautiful everything external about you is. *I* certainly don't need to tell you! But the day after the accident you were not beautiful. You ought to ponder that: physical appearance is not enough. You need a kind of beauty that disfigurement cannot take away."

Perhaps he did ponder. Before he left the college, he seemed to lose some of his egotism and superficiality. He fell in love with a quiet girl I thought quite plain, and his personality took on depth and warmth. When the inner matched the outer, he was superb.

After his mouth healed, other athletes came to me frequently. "Bruise, thou shalt not heat . . ." became something that flashed to mind every time I saw a football or basketball player limping in my direction. I am told the high school coach at Newberry, South Carolina, "uses" regularly for his boys. For a time, I did almost the same for the college team.

I have no proof that this had anything to do with my replacement on the faculty. It was not the reason given me. I was told that my department needed academic strengthening and prestige for purposes of accreditation. That could not be denied: the only Doctor of Philosophy in it was striken with Parkinson's disease and the two senior professors were due for retirement. Still, Lenoir Rhyne is a church college, and as such not likely to hold any kind of mental, spiritual, or magic healing desirable.

No matter. "Any and every man who knowingly neglects using . . ." Hohman said, "*neglects*." I would consider it more sinful and contemptible to refrain from "using" for fear of the consequences in such circumstances as mine. If I saved the tooth, or the eye—to say nothing of the life of one of my students, I am satisfied. I did what I thought right, and if I have sustained any loss from use of sympathy, God has recompensed me double.

An unidentified part of my awareness informs me when I should attempt to heal. There are individuals who can be healed, and others who cannot. Perhaps there are some who *should* be healed, and others who should not. I try to detach my conscious mind and my emotions from them as individuals, allowing my intuition to suggest an attempt or not to suggest it. God knows that I attempted to heal relatives I loved, but who made no response; whereas I have felt compelled to attempt healing for some for whom I felt no personal liking, and they were healed. Detachment, and the feeling that I am a channel for healing rather than a healer, seems the most effective state of mind to be in to produce an effect. So, again limited by language, I say, "*I* heal nothing: God heals." But I might add that there is in nature a potential for healing which my mental action seems to channel when I follow the impulse to direct it, or in rare instances I am under compulsion by some unrecognizable or unnameable Influence. I do not even speculate upon what this Influence may be, but I know when it is at work. I become restless, see strange symbols, and sometimes experience unusual phenomena.

When I need to reinforce vital energy, I do so by contact. I do not know by what process I absorb it from living things (or, if they are deficient, transmit it to them). It may be a subjective experience, for a cedar tree is a symbol of immortality, and an oak a symbol of strength. Since I think in symbols, it may be that all I do is reinforce my thought. However, I find the earth healing, be it merely a plaster of clay on a wound, or the handling of it, which stabilizes the emotions, or walking on it, which in solitary places tranquilizes the spirit and opens the inner mind.

Following an article on "using" that I wrote for *Fate* magazine, a woman in a distant state wrote me saying she had tried the incantation for bruises given her to cure a sore in her son's mouth. She said it was an ulcer, which a doctor had treated for several days. The ulcer grew larger and more painful daily, and when she read the article, it occurred to her to substitute the word *sore* for *bruise*. She said he looked in the child's mouth and repeated the "words of sympathy," feeling that if God could heal a bruise, he could as readily cure an ulcer.

It worked. The boy's ulcer healed quickly and gave no further trouble. Not long afterward I was sent David Shull's "Paper," and among the other powwows was this very one, under the heading "To Cure a Sore," substituting *sore* for *bruise*.

After that, I experimented. It is quite possible to adapt a conjuration—even to create new ones. After all, they are not mystical mantras revealed by the holy angels. Someone created each of them to meet a need—and what has been done once can be done again. All that is required is a startling affirmation or command, confidence, and the power of God to bind the spell. "Pain, go; go; go. Pain go! . . ." (which some cash-in-advance "users" in Iowa employ for broken bones) sounds modern to me, but its simplicity startles almost as much as reference to the milk of Jesus' Mother. I should like to see the one above used with a drum or an *asson* by a sorcerer who did not know what the words mean. I fancy it would heal just as effectively.

One unfortunate widow whose children had all moved to the West Coast wrote me that she fell on her icy steps and broke the small bone of her leg, but had no money to see a doctor, and no one to look after her cows and pigs and her poultry. She bound splints to it and used the "Pain, go . . ." incantation and kept on about her work. When she did see a doctor after her youngest son came back from Korea, the bone had mended, and she wrote that ". . . it was kinder sore a while, but not what you'd think a broke bone would be."

Occasionally a powwow produces that effect. Last year I was cutting a small tree in a clump of old crape myrtle, and in trying to pull it free, the butt suddenly flew loose from the others which bound it and struck my leg. The bone probably wasn't broken, but a very hard lump formed on my shin, and I could not walk without limping. By using this charm and the one for bruises, I achieved a condition in which I was not conscious of pain unless I touched the lump. It did not discolor, and I doused it with turpentine daily for a few days, and forgot about it. I don't remember when I stopped limping, or when the lump went away; when bathing several days later I thought about it, felt for the lump, and it was gone.

I was brought up to believe that the *Power* to powwow had to be protected by the strictest taboos. Grandmother made a great secret of her incantations, never telling them even to her husband, who was older. When she taught me her conjuration to stop bleeding—or showed me where to find it, for it comes word for word from Ezekiel (one recites the sixth verse of Chapter Sixteen)—she told me that in her whole lifetime she could tell only three persons, each younger than she and of the opposite sex, and that I in turn could tell only three women, all younger. It was inexorable; the penalty for breaking it was the loss of the power to use it.

As long as I did not break the taboo, I could staunch the flow of blood as effectively as she could herself. But in college I told the psychology class of the incantation and the taboo, and when the need for it came, I found that I had no power whatsoever to stop bleeding. It increased my awe of the *Power* and my belief in the taboo.

For years I could not "speak blood." Ruefully I sought out wise women who could be wheedled into confiding other conjurations for other purposes—many of whom were happy to pass the charms down to someone who still believed in them. Any I secured, I kept as secret as guilt.

In the Dutch Fork, in the past century, lived "users" who had power second to none anywhere. One old lady renowned for her success was dead before I settled here, but her daughter is also a "user," so I visited her to beg any secrets she might teach me. I found her friendly, and proud to tell of her mother's "gift." Her mother's "Paper"—it was a good-sized notebook—had been stolen, but she sent me to her brother who showed me the little German trunk in which it had been kept dark, along with his mother's "using bonnet," her spectacles, her wand, and a strange dirk which I supposed was her *athalme,* or witch's ritual knife.

We were sitting on her porch as we talked about "using," and it seemed to me that she spoke far too freely, for my wife, the woman's daughter-in-law, and several children were present. When I mentioned her mother's fame as a "user" who could cure burns, she beamed. "Yes, she was a wonder at that. People came or sent to her for miles—even on your side of the river. I do it, too, but I think she was better."

When I asked for that charm, she nodded. "Sure," she said. "I believe I remember it—let me think. It's been a good while since anybody wanted a burn used for."

"Where can we go so I can hear it?"

"I'll tell it to you right here. Them others may need to help me recollect the words."

"Will it still work if you do that?" I marveled.

"You mean letting the women hear it? I know what they say, but it just ain't true. It was just for protection. You know how they used to be about witchcraft in the olden time, and anybody who knowed anything not everybody knows was a witch, even if it was for doing good. I reckon the fewer knowed about your power, the fewer there would be to blab, and they kept it in families because your kin wouldn't be so apt to get you in trouble. That's my thought on that. It don't make no difference at all who you tell, nor how many. It's a power from God to give you a way over nature when you are in need. The more that knows how to do good, the better, it appears to me; and I reckon the more good is done, the more God likes it, too."

The utter naïvety of her reasoning was convincing. I took down the incantation, and she showed me the gestures that accompany it.

"Ma always thought the motions done as much as the words," she commented, "but I ain't so sure. The girls is always getting them mixed up. I've told them and told them. When it's the white you are doing, it's the *right* hand you use, and it's down with the thumb and up to the right, slant-wise, then across to the left, but it appears to me they do as well with the wrong motions as with the right ones. I reckon the white work is all you'll be wanting to do?"

"Your mother knew how to do the black, too?" I said in surprise.

"A witch can do either kind," she said quietly. "It's the same power. Jesus could heal, and he could kill—he killed a fig tree. It all works the same. Sometimes it takes the black to do good, and sometimes you may do bad with the white. It's what you do that makes either one good or bad. Jesus knew all about the power of God, and we know."

"You think Jesus was a witch?"

She laughed. "No," she replied, "but if you was to do here in Dutch Fork what he done in Israel, a heap of folks would call *you* a witch."

"But you think it was the same power?"

"It's got to be. There is only one God, only one Power, and only one Nature. If a witch don't know nothing else, he knows that."

A new incantation is like any other new thing one gets— one is impatient to put it in use, to see how it works—and here I must say, they do not all work with equal effectiveness for all people. I know one which never failed the person who gave it to me, yet it never has done the slightest good when I tried it. (I don't like it—never did like it—and I suppose that is the reason why. I like conjurations that say surprising things, and it is as dull as lukewarm water.)

So, I was almost glad when my sister-in-law called on the phone to tell that her son, Frank, had burned his foot that morning. "Ask her if she wants me to try for it," I urged.

"Lee wants to try to talk the fire out of his foot," my wife told her. When she hung up, she turned to me and said, "Don't just stand there and fidget. Frankie burned his foot pretty bad. Go on and witch for it."

I hastened to my room, put on my hat, faced the direction of the boy's home and recited my new incantation. . . .

His foot healed rapidly. He wore a rag around the burn for several days, but it seemed to give him little trouble. I was rather disappointed, for I had been accustomed to immediate staunching of the flow of blood and felt that a burn should heal instantaneously. But it left no permanent scar, and in that respect probably healed better than it would have with ordinary treatment.

Frank was quite young then, about ten or eleven. Six or seven years passed, and I almost forgot I had ever treated him. However, he remembered—as I discovered when he appeared one evening with a chum of his who had been burned.

I had not met his friend, but I knew of his family, and the

boy himself evoked compassion. I had seldom seen minor burns which looked so painful. Frank explained that the boy had been welding under a car at school, stripped to the waist, working in a cramped position, when something caught the torch. A shower of sparks and molten particles rained on his chest and stomach. The blisters were from pinhead to dime size, and the pain from them was so acute that he had not been able to sleep the night before. As I looked at his torso— not a pleasant sight where the silky hair was burned off and the smooth skin was sprinkled with red marks, blisters, and raw spots—I could well accept his apology for coming in stripped to the waist, saying he could not bear a shirt to touch him.

"Frank thinks you can cure me," he said hopefully. "Will you?"

For a thousand years, the ritual answer to that question has been, "I will try." A "user" should never promise a cure; he may find himself unable to concentrate sufficiently. He may become involved emotionally—even find himself questioning whether the individual *deserves* help. Fatigue, distraction—and emotional, psychic, and physical factors often too obscure to recognize—may intervene. If the cure does come from God, it comes only through the agency of the human mind, and man does not know his mind well enough to make guarantees. If one can avoid emotion, hold off the temptation to judge the individual, and concentrate fully on the powwow, usually one succeeds if he has any power at all.

The etiquette of powwow requires that the sufferer ask the "user" to "try," but those who come seldom know that, so they always begin by requesting a cure. If I feel led to use sympathy for the case, I reply, "I do what I can do; I will try." It is not the most confidence-building reply one might make, but it is the only safe answer. If a powwow has success in 90 percent of his attempts, he is excellent. If in 70 percent of his attempts he succeeds, he should not be discouraged. But I left Frank's poor burned friend standing while I digressed; so now back to him.

"Sure, I'll try for you," I told him. "Cross my threshold and advance toward the east, and I will get my hat."

"Which way is east?" he asked, bewildered by the unusual directions.

"That is the east wall where the drawing of the star in a circle hangs. Stand to face that."

He looked at the Hex drawing of a double earthstar so made that it enclosed a circle in which a serpent climbed a staff upon a heart. There were smaller hearts between each of the points of the star, and a large heart beneath was flanked with bluebirds standing on branches of olive. "What does the German on it say?" he asked.

" 'Haymet iss wau da Hotz iss'? It's dialect. It should read *'Heimat ist wo das Herz ist.'* It means 'Home is where the heart is.' "

"Where did you get anything like that?"

"I drew it."

"What does it all stand for?"

"It's for love and happiness."

"Does it work?"

"I don't look unhappy, do I?"

"Frank says you know about all kinds of queer stuff."

"Maybe," I breathed. I moved between him and the wall after I raised my hands to the east, and turned to face him. "Now close your eyes," I said, "and don't look till I say so. When I touch you, hold your breath and slowly count three times three three times, and I will do what I can do." (I wanted to puzzle him as to the counting to distract him.)

He flinched when I touched his forehead and tensed as if in dread. It was his first experience with the occult, and I imagine he was a little uneasy in the room, strange to him with its dried herbs, symbolic objects, bones, its clutter of books and curious drawings, its prehistoric relics, and its oddities.

"That is all," I breathed, "Open your eyes and check the time. In half an hour I shall use for you again, then again after a full hour."

"The burns don't seem to hurt quite as bad," he commented.

We played rummy while we waited for the second treatment, and I observed that he began toying with the burns unconsciously as he studied his hand. He had not touched them before. When the time was up, I said, "It's time again. How do they feel by now?"

"Why—they don't hardly hurt none at all! I'd quit thinking about them."

I am not sure what degree of sensation his statement describes, but it cannot be very acute. I repeated the treatment, reminded him to watch for the hour to be up, and we returned to our series.

When Frank won it, he turned to Frank and said "We'd

best leave now. I'm dying for sleep, and I can't afford to stay out of school no more than I have to."

"It's fifteen minutes yet till the time," I reminded him.

"You don't need to do it again; the burns are okay," he said.

"I'd better finish it," I insisted. "It's better to go the full set."

So he stayed for the final try and went home. Next afternoon he passed me on Main Street, with his shirt on, honked his horn, waved, and, smiling from ear to ear, yelled "Hi!" Frank later told me the burns healed and never caused him any further discomfort.

This incident was proof to me that a taboo can be broken without impairing the effect of a powwow. However, my most astonishing experience with the charm for burns came when I used it on myself. On July 3, 1968, I was working at renovating my house and had a pile of scrap to burn. Weeds and brush had grown to the edges of the lawn, so no clear spot was available for the burning. In a lightly weeded area behind the former slave cabin lay a brush pile of cedar branches four or five years seasoned, so I decided to clear a firebreak around this old heap, burn it, and use the spot to burn the trash from the house. I felt that the light branches would make a very quick fire with not enough sustained heat to dry the weeds past the firebreak, even though the weather was dry and here and there the field had much old broom sedge from previous years. So I kindled the heap of branches and stood by with a rake to put out any sparks.

It was burning briskly when I recalled that the heap lay atop a pile of old fat pine posts. When the branches made them hot, tar flowed from them, and the heap blazed into an inferno which blasted the growth back yards past the firebreak and kindled it in all directions. I fought it frenziedly, for the slave cabin is also built of heart pine, and if it caught, I felt sure the big house would burn with it—a loss no insurance could make bearable. Neighbors rushed to help, and among us we kept the fire from reaching the slave quarters, the garage, or the woods. But when it was out, I realized I had been severely burned.

Where my body was covered, my sweat-drenched clothing had protected me, but I was wearing only an undershirt, which left my arms exposed. Blisters formed on them from shoulder to wrist, some as large as fifty-cent pieces. The pain was maddening.

"I wish somebody lived near here who could 'use' for me!" I exclaimed as my daughter smeared ointment on the burns and flustered with bandages.

"I thought you knew how," she replied.

"Why, I do!" I realized. "It might work on the person who does it. Let my arms alone! I am going to try!"

I went to my room, hung a mirror on the east wall, raised my tortured arms in appeal, and gazing into the mirror tried for the first time in my own behalf.

> Lonza's bread! Christ is our consolation:
> Christ will not forget
> To remove the inflammation.
> In the name of God the Father, God the Son,
>     and God the Holy Ghost, Amen.

The image in the mirror made the Hex crosses toward the stranger in the hat. The bizarre thought came to me, "That man feels no pain." For his smudged, reddened face was rapt, detached, apart from consciousness of any kind save of the spell.

As I made the third cross, something took effect that I cannot name. I was no longer observing from the mirror but for an instant aware of my suffering body. The anguish of burning changed to a sensation of numbing cold. Gooseflesh stood up around the burns and on my whole body. When it passed, all pain had ceased.

An old Daugherty incantation for burns which Grandmother never knew in full included lines about the Angels of the Four Directions, one line of which ran:

> The one from the North brought ice and frost . . .

I felt certain that that incantation sought to procure the uncanny, blessed chill that took away my suffering—something known to the conjurers of centuries ago, but not mentioned in any psychological text I ever have read. How much, one wonders, did they know that contemporary parapsychology must rediscover? Must the scientist at last turn to the witch for knowledge? I am sure he could obtain some.

When the half hour passed, I repeated the incantation, but knew that the first had sufficed. The sticky unguent ran and the inept bandages kept trying to unwind. To my daughter's horror I took them off, washed my arms thoroughly with soap and water, and left them unbandaged. I dusted the raw spots with sulphur, hid my arms with a long-sleeved shirt, and went back to my work. At least I now had plenty of room to burn scrap safely—an acre burned bare!

Each day as I toiled, my sweat absorbed soot from a defective flue and dust from the attic. It spotted the raw flesh black, while the sulphur crusted it yellow. My arms looked gruesome. As the skin came off, I dusted finely powdered burnt alum on the flesh to keep granulation tissue from forming, and kept on working. When my wife came from Hickory, she joined my daughter in admonishing me to go to the doctor—but only halfheartedly. The burns were healing rapidly and I felt no pain—not even discomfort—so why go? She admitted that no one could expect or ask more than that.

Sometime in September a black wasp stung me, and I reacted with intolerable itching. Then I phoned the doctor, who told me to come at once, for several local people had almost died of wasp stings in the past few years. When I arrived, he told me to take off my shirt, and when he saw my arms, he gasped.

"You have had frightful burns! Who's been treating them?"

"Oh, I take care of them myself," I replied. "When I got burned back the third of July, I 'used' for them, and I dust them with sulphur and alum as they heal."

"You should have gone straight to the hospital."

"I didn't have time to fool with the hospital. I was too busy renovating the house."

"How could you stand to work with the pain?"

"After I 'used' there wasn't any pain."

He grinned an exasperated grin, then chuckled. "That's rich. You witch third-degree burns and treat them as nothing, and come running to me with a wasp sting!"

"I don't know anything to do for that. I always go to a doctor when I *need* one."

He seemed to give me a shot as a kind of personal satisfaction, inserting the needle deliberately. "A doctor should treat bad burns," he muttered.

"Don't my arms look as far along as they should?"

"July, August . . . yes. They are healing all right—and you say you felt little pain?"

"They were killing me before I treated them."

"But afterward? With your clothes rubbing the raw flesh where the skin came off, you didn't feel much?"

"I didn't feel any pain at all."

"Then I don't blame you. If you had had regular treatment, you would have felt pain—plenty of it! Before you go, I want my associate to look at your arms," he told me, and when the other doctor came in, he said, "Look at these. He uses sulphur and burnt alum on them like doctors did in the seventeenth century. He was burned back in July."

"It must have been as good a way as those we have now," the other doctor commented. "They look fine to me."

"Could a person have such burns without pain while they heal?"

"Impossible!"

"He says he 'used' for them and has felt no pain at all."

"Incredible!"

"I don't know," the older man meditated. "When I came here, I would have said so, but I have run onto some funny things around here—some damn funny things!"

I grant that the treatment may merely have disconnected my consciousness from signals which my brain would otherwise have interpreted as pain, but that is theoretical . . . over a year later, all the scars had disappeared except the three largest.

> . . . Christ will not forget
> To remove the inflammation.+ + +

Hexes do many other things besides powwow. Usually they have ordinary occupations, trades, or professions. Christopher de Witt, a great *Hexenmeister* who died in Germantown, Pennsylvania, in January 1765, was among that colony's earliest clockmakers, and was also a noted botanist, astronomer, astrologer, and philosopher. He specialized in "casting nativities"—drawing astrological horoscopes for children soon after their births—but he also raised a notable variety of medicinal and magical herbs and prepared medicines.

Other Hexes prepared amulets, drew *Anhängsel* (cryptic parchments lettered with abbreviations, figures, geometric, and mystical signs, used as talismans). Some prepared candles, burned them ritually, and applied soot from them by means of a *Petschaft*—a metal stamp which printed Hex signs on the bodies of the sick or injured, and allegedly cured according to the ingredients in the candles and the rituals and incantations used at their preparation and at the time of stamping.

Father Conrad Matthai, the last *Hexenmeister* of the Wissa-hickon Rosicrucian monastic group, had no visible means of support, and was so near—or far—out of this world that he needed little. His distinctive specialty was securing information from distant places, lying on his bunk in trance, sending out a *Doppelgänger,* and appearing and conversing with persons elsewhere, sometimes even in Europe, giving or securing messages for his clients. Before the telegraph, his was the swiftest communication service between Pennsylvania and London, and it has not been improved upon since in its field (this isn't really true). It *is* rare, though.

Since powwow is only one area of a much larger field in which parapsychological activities affect nature and call into effect laws which are inactive without such factors, it behooves a powwow to familiarize himself with the other areas: witchcraft, Christian Science, faith healing, astrology, spiritualism, hypnotism, parapsychology, and plain psychology. It will broaden his understanding of his own area, and the benefits are manifold.

When a man realizes that he is able to affect nature and alter circumstances by the power of his mind, he suddenly ceases to feel absurd or meaningless. He realizes that man is only a little lower than the angels—which the Bible says he is. "I have said ye are gods," quoth Jesus, who is regarded as authoritative by many. When man discovers his power, he *does* assume godlike ability to create, alter, or destroy. I dare not say, "Ye are gods," as Jesus did, but I do say that man is profoundly meaningful, exceedingly powerful, and sovereign over the earth and all that pertains to it.

When an individual realizes this, he cannot call existence absurd. He can integrate his personality and shape his destiny as he wishes. He can even assume his right relationship with God, which is to embody in matter the spirit in him, which is of God, and to manifest in the plane of matter what God cannot manifest without a material agent. God has mind or *is* Mind, and has consciousness, or *is* Consciousness, but God does not have hands. Man does. God does not have lips or a tongue. Man has them. God does not operate a typewriter or print books, or build schools and universities. These things man must do.

And when man does what God cannot do, but needs have done, he fills the role intended for him and assumes his right identity. Then is he godlike.

"And God said, [Let us make man] . . . in our image, after our likeness, and let them have dominion . . . over all the earth. . . ." Let everyone be reminded that God is a spirit, and the image and likeness of God must be man's *spirit*.

Merely to stop the flow of blood from a wound by uttering words from the Bible gives the Scripture a very different kind of meaning from that usually assigned it. A searcher who knows that only one verse in the Bible can be used to stop bleeding will begin searching for other secrets in it. Truth is concealed, not revealed, in the Book. It had to be so, otherwise the Bible would have been destroyed or altered by those in custody of it.

When he finds that a verse in Ruth will cause the whole Book to turn when suspended in a certain manner (when a key is tied across the verse) to answer questions, whereas no other verse in any other book will serve to move, he begins to comprehend the very strange power of this Book. If he is interested in the mystical power of numbers, he will find some very singular things when he begins studying the arrangement of the King James Version. More and more, I am convinced that this arrangement of the Bible by verse and chapter was reached by conscious—or more likely unconscious—division of the text to enable occultists to identify hidden mysteries by their numerical implications.

The secret of powwow is concealed in the first Gospel. The words are Jesus' own. One is a key number, the number of unity. Thus what the Bible says about the unity of anything should appear in a first book, a first chapter, or first verse. Three is the number of spirit, and six of creativity. So in the first book, in a location numerically suggested by three or six, should be a statement of prime importance regarding spiritual creativity, and it does. Matthew 18:18 reads, "Whatsoever ye shall bind on earth shall be bound in heaven: and whatsoever yet shall loose on earth shall be loosed in heaven." This is the secret. Jesus referred to it as "The keys to the kingdom of heaven." The same words are reiterated in another place. Repetition in the Bible is always a clue. What is said twice is worth reading twice—many times, until it is comprehended.

The Catholic Church holds that this was spoken only to St. Peter, despite the plural pronoun, and the crossed keys on the papal seal refer to it. However, Jesus said "What *ye* shall loose . . . what *ye* shall bind," and ye *is* plural. It is meant for every man. Moreover, it is not a promise to Peter to confirm his authority, but a statement of principle, of universal law.

This law makes magic, prayer, Hex, powwow, and every other activity which consciously binds anything by mental action effective. Perhaps even more important, it makes effective anything that is bound by habitual mental action, even though no conscious act of binding takes place. If one continually thinks about disease, fearing it, lo: he binds it, often upon himself.

Binding, however, implies more than idle thinking. To truly *bind*, there must be concentration and emotional intensity. In powwow, the concentration comes from remembering the odd incantations and the gestures, and the emotion is faith. In a black Hex, the concentration comes from the incantation and the ritual, and the emotion either from fear (of the devil and his demons) or from horror induced by some act of the ritual. In idle-minded hypochondria, disease is induced by the fear that one will develop the symptoms, by fear of contagion, and by some strong emotion—hate, envy, greed, or whatever—held simultaneously, though not necessarily in connection with the contemplation of disease.

All anyone needs is to know this simple truth which Jesus stated, have the power to concentrate, and the resourcefulness to surround himself with strong emotion as he binds his charm, be it faith, love, fear, fury, lust, or horror, and he can get what he wishes.

Anything more that can be said on the subject is mere elaboration. Follow these instructions, and you can be a Hex, a faith healer, a saint who works miracles, a Satanist, a Christian Science practitioner, a powwow, a witch doctor, or whatever you please. "What ye shall bind on earth . . ." is a metaphysical *law*. It does not matter in the least who does the binding, or whether what is bound is good or evil, whether in Christianity or in witchcraft. The laws of nature operate for all alike; as the lady said, "It's the same power."

If you have stopped blood, you are a Hex yourself, and there is no Hex you cannot perform if you have the faith. See? What the old woman in Dutch Fork told me was true. There is no taboo except what one taboos himself, for the taboo says a man cannot tell a man, or anyone more than three, and I have told the thousands who read *Fate* that charm. It *can* be taught publicly. Now, as one Hex to another, I say, "Let thy walk be Jesus' limp; thy speech be Jesus' stammer." It means, "You can't ever come up to His performance: but as long as you try to do good, you're doing the same things He did, so do your best." It's taken as a kind of blessing, and a hope that the Hex to whom it is said will always do good with his *Hexen*.

# 8

# Hex Death

*Joan Halifax-Grof*

*The following selection is a survey of an ancient phenomenon. The author, a meticulous researcher, provides a scholarly account of the numerous explanations of a hex death, including the possibility of psychical influences.*

• • •

The phenomenon of hex death, although widely reported in the anthropological literature, has received very little systematic attention. Hex death, sometimes referred to as voodoo death, curse death, or death by suggestion, can be defined as the demise of an individual resulting from a malign magical procedure or the breaching of a taboo. It has been described in every major culture area of the world and appears to have existed in every historical period.

Hex death, however, is usually talked about in relationship to preliterate peoples. In fact, some researchers have even postulated preliteracy as a necessary prerequisite to hex death! This, of course, is not the case. It has been frequently observed and described in both southern and northwestern Europe as well as the United States. There exist numerous anthropological, psychiatric, and popular descriptions regarding the effects of malign magic, but most of these reports are anecdotal and only a few of them include pertinent and longitudinal physiological data and adequate descriptions of events leading to and surrounding the hex death itself. Moreover, most accounts of hex death are from living informants and, therefore, secondhand. (An exception to this is Professor Gilbert Lewis's unpublished doctoral thesis, 1972.)

I would like to mention in this context that I, too, suffer from the same critical lack of data as have my forerunners and colleagues. During the years of my clinical anthropological studies, I never personally witnessed a case of actual hex death. While on the faculty of the University of Miami School of Medicine, I was, however, confronted daily with the perplexing problem of the hexing syndrome, both in the psychiatric setting and in other clinical areas. This experience has convinced me that there are some rather specific aspects of the hexing syndrome that are not adequately explained by existing psychiatric theories, which consider them manifestations of hysteria or schizophrenic psychosis. Moreover, it has become increasingly obvious to me that the conventional medical and psychiatric approaches to hexed individuals are often rather ineffective and inadequate. In staff meetings and seminars, I tried to communicate to the clinicians and other healthcare professionals that the hexing syndrome is a complex problem *sui generis* and should be seriously considered. It was not only a matter of teaching clinicians a bit of anthropology, but also of being deeply involved in the therapeutic process, including finding appropriate indigenous healers on occasion. This approach is described elsewhere (Halifax-Grof, 1972); I mention it only because of the paucity of work being done in this area (Tingling, 1967; Wintrob, Fox, O'Brien, 1972; Halifax-Grof, 1973).

In my approach to the discussion of hex death, I will, therefore, combine an intimate knowledge of the phenomenon of hexing with literary data concerning hex death *per se*. Study of the existing literature suggests that hex death is a complex multidimensional and multifactorial event. In addition to the emotional, psychological, and physiological factors operating within the individual, it involves an explicit or implicit relationship between the hexer and the hexed. It is also happening in a broader interpersonal and social context set into the larger frame of the cultural milieu. In individual cases of hexing these factors appear in different combinations; yet, for the purpose of this discussion, I have made an effort to isolate several levels of information related to hex death. Briefly, the following factors have been postulated as the direct or underlying cause or causes of hex death: (1) poisons and other physical agents; (2) the critical relationship between emotional factors and physiological processes in the organism; (3) interpersonal and social interactions in a particular cultural context: and (4) parapsychological influences.

We will consider first the most prosaic and obvious cause of hex death, namely, poisons. Barber (1961), Clune (1973), and others argue strongly that hex deaths are to a great degree attributable to poison. Ackerknecht (1925), in his "Problems of Primitive Medicine," states that about 25 percent to 50 percent of the substances found in the aboriginal pharmacopoeia are pharmacologically active. Some of these active substances have unquestionably toxic properties and could be used for the purpose of malign magic. From the hundreds of noxious drugs we could cite, only the most salient will be mentioned in this context. There are the well-known metallic poisons, such as lead, arsenic, and mercurial derivatives, all causing fatal damage to the organism. The infamous plant poison curare paralyzes the victim by interfering with neuromuscular transfer. Strychnine, another plant poison, on the other hand, increases the sensitivity of the nervous system to the point of producing tetanic spasms and ultimately death. There are numerous poisonous mushrooms with toxic alkaloids, such as muscarine and phalloidine. Venomous snakes and insects are another plausible source of fatal aboriginal poisons. The skin of the toad Bufo bufo, a favorite ingredient of witches' brews, contains powerful toxic substances, such as bufotenine and bufotoxin, which have psychoactive and cardiotropic properties. The medieval practitioners of witchcraft employed extracts and ointments made from solanaceous plants, such as the deadly nightshade (*Atropa belladonna*), thornapple (*Datura stramonium*), henbane (*Hyoscyamus niger*), and mandrake (*Mandragora officinarum*). The active substances from these plants can cause drastic mental changes when used in small dosages and are, at the same time, extremely dangerous if the dosage is increased. These or similar substances can be found in the pharmacopoeia of many different cultures.

The following tragicomic case of the "hippity-hoppity heart syndrome" can be used as an illustration of the point in discussion:

Most notorious of root doctors was Dr. Bug who for fifty dollars would guarantee anyone who didn't want to be drafted into the service that he would fail the physical. Violating the usual root doctor tenet, Bug gave his clients a potion to swallow. He had a high percentage of success. In fact, so many young men with a particular type of heart condition were seen by the physicians at Fort Jackson that they named the complaint "the hippity-hoppity heart syndrome." Dr. Bug's downfall came when one of his clients, wanting to make no mistake about escaping the draft, took a double dose. He died. An autopsy showed the potion causing the heart irregularities was a mixture of oleander leaves (digitalis), rubbing alcohol, mothballs, and lead. (Michaelson, 1972, p. 58.)

It should be obvious from this brief description of toxic plant, animal, and metallic substances that aboriginal sorcerers have powerful materials available to them to induce sickness and death in their hexed victims. There are numerous cases, however, where "poison" refers to nonmaterial principles rather than noxious brews. As we will see, poison is not necessarily implicated in all cases of hex death.

We come now to the second category of factors that have been discussed in relation to hex death, namely the *psychophysiological*. Until the early 1940's there had not been any serious scientific attempts to explain death due to fear or suggestion and relating this to hex death. In 1942, Walter B. Cannon published his classic paper on voodoo death in which he attempted to explain the physiological mechanisms by which fear can result in the rapid demise of a human being. He approached this problem unusually well prepared by his previous research on fear, rage, hunger, and pain. According to Cannon, intense fear and rage have similar effects in the body and can result in profound physiological disturbances. Both emotions serve an important function in the struggle for existence and are associated with deeply ingrained instincts. In the case of rage, it is the instinct to attack that permits survival; in the case of fear, it is the instinct to escape. The physiological reacion connected with these emotions is mediated by the so-called sympathico-adrenal system. The activation of this system produces changes in the organs and vessels of the body that prepare the organism for necessary action. If, for whatever reason, such action does not follow, the lasting and intense activation of the sympathetic system can have very destructive consequences for the organism. Cannon described a complicated chain of physiological events that could in these circumstances result in a reduction in the volume of circulating blood and a critical fall of the blood pressure leading to death (Cannon, 1958).

There exist numerous reports of unusual and puzzling deaths for which Cannon's hypothesis seems to be the most plausible explanation. They involve so-called "malignant anxiety" observed during the Spanish Civil War, where young men died without any observable causes (Mira, cited by Cannon, 1958); cases of patients who died after seemingly successful operations (Freeman, cited by Cannon, 1958); and those of unaccounted deaths after minor injuries or ingestion of sublethal doses of poison (Fisher, cited by Richter, 1957).

Richter (1957), an experimental psychologist, has offered an alternative psychophysiological explanation of the phenomenon of sudden death in man (and animals). He approached this problem through his comparative studies of stress reactions in wild and domesticated rats. In his experiments, wild rats' whiskers were trimmed and the animals were then put into a glass jar filled with water. After swimming for a brief interval, they went to the bottom of the jar and never resurfaced. In the same circumstances, only a few of the domesticated rats succumbed in this comparatively short period of time. Interpreting the results of the physiological analysis of the death of those animals, Richter concluded that they may have died a so-called vagus death due to stimulation of the parasympathetic rather than the sympathico-adrenal system. He also emphasized the element of hopelessness against that of fear. In this connection, a training exposure of the wild rats to the handling and swimming situation appeared to eliminate the dramatic fatal response. Applied to the phenomenon of hex death, this indicates, according to Richter, that human victims might die a parasympathetic rather than a sympathico-adrenal death. The hexed individual is not set for flight or fight. Rather, the hex situation is characterized as being quite hopeless.

Lester (1972) in a discussion of the hypotheses formulated by Cannon and Richter pointed out that these explanations of hex death are not necessarily mutually exclusive. According to Dynes (1969), there are two types of death occurring without significant anatomical findings at autopsy; one following prolonged excitement and violence, the other occurring instantaneously and without warning. Lester suggests that these two types might correspond with Cannon's and Richter's models and that sudden death and hex death can result from excessive stimulating of any system of the body.

Lester himself proposes an alternative conceptual framework for hex death that focuses on psychological rather than physiological factors. The basic ideas for this approach are derived from Engel's research into the circumstances surrounding the onset of illness and, in some instances, death. He observed repeatedly a pattern that he calls "the giving up——given up complex" (Engel, 1968). Its essential features are feelings of helplessness and hopelessness, of worthlessness and incompetence, inability to obtain gratification from interpersonal relationships, and reactivation of memories of earlier giving up and of situations that were not adequately resolved. According to Engel, when an individual is responding to stress with the "giving up—given up complex," the body is more prone to illness and has a reduced capability to deal with potentially pathogenic processes. Lester points out that a hexed individual meets all the criteria of Engel's complex.

Although we do not have a unified psychophysiological theory explaining the mechanism of hex death, it is certainly significant that reputable researchers have not found this phenomenon incompatible with their medical knowledge and have made valid and useful attempts to elucidate it in scientific terms.

Up to this point, we have taken into consideration in our discussion of hex death only those forces operating within the individual, forces of a physical and psychophysiological nature. The situation of a hexed individual, however, has to be considered in relationship to a social context and cultural continuity. The process of hexing is not happening in isolation between sorcerer and victim. Rather, a hexed individual lives and is hexed within a community of significant others. Ultimately, all of the individuals in the hexed victim's social network will be involved in various ways and to varying degrees in the dynamics of the hex. This brings us to the third category of factors involved in hex death, the relevance of *social and cultural determinants*.

All members of a particular culture in which hexing exists share the knowledge, beliefs, expectations, and fears regarding hexing and its outcome. This knowledge can set into motion a realignment of the social network. A hexed individual, as a result of the curse put on him, can find his role and place in the community drastically redefined; he can withdraw or be forced to the very margins of his social world. In the profound social isolation that follows, he can experience a total frustration of primary and derived needs—basic material, emotional, and spiritual needs—that are usually satisfied in interpersonal interaction. An individual in this situation usually responds very sensitively to the expectations of his community, whether the cues of the outcome of the hex are explicitly stated or mediated through metacommunication, or whether knowledge of the outcome is part of the social order and the sequence of events is so prescribed and predictable that only hopelessness and frequently helplessness can ensue on the part of the victim.

In terms of mechanisms of hex death, it is not difficult to imagine that such total isolation from, or distortion of, meaningful relationships, compounded by the threat of imminent death, could result in overwhelming anxiety of malignant proportions. The combination of prolonged intense emotional stress, social isolation, sleep deprivation, and frequent refusal of food and water can produce an unusual state of consciousness in the hexed person that is associated with heightened suggestibility. It is a well-established clinical fact that autosuggestion as well as suggestion can have a direct influence on a variety of physiological functions. Examples belonging to this category range from blisters artificially induced by means of hypnosis in the laboratory setting to instances of stigmatization and pseudocyesis. Thus, social and cultural factors involved in the hex situation contribute to a chain of events that can have very distinct and concrete biological consequences.

Isolation of the victim and withdrawal of the community is not, however, the only pattern of social realignment observed in cases of hex death. A hexed individual can also be moved to the center of the social network, either for the purpose of removing the hex or in order to complete the logical sequence of culturally determined events. In this situation, direct social pressure and even sensory overload can facilitate an unusual state of mind conducive either to healing or to the annihilation of the individual.

An interesting example of a variety of social locations in order to complete the hex state trajectory is given by W. L. Warner, who worked among the aborigines of the Northern Territory of Australia:

There are two definite movements of the social group in the process by which black magic becomes effective on the victims of sorcery. In the first movement the community contracts; all people who stand in kinship relation with him withdraw their sustaining support. This means that all his fellows—everyone he knows—completely change their attitudes toward him and place him in a new category. He is now viewed as one who is more nearly in the realm of the sacred and taboo than in the world of the ordinary where the community finds itself. The organization of his social life has collapsed, and, no longer a member of a group, he is alone and isolated. The doomed man is in a situation from which the only escape is by death. During the death-illness which ensues, the group acts with all the outreachings and complexities of its organization and with countless stimuli to suggest death positively to the victim, who is in a highly suggestible state. In addition to the social pressure upon him, the victim himself, as a rule, not only makes no effort to live and to stay a part of his group but actually, through multiple suggestions which he receives, cooperates in the withdrawal from it. He becomes what the attitude of his fellow tribesmen wills him to be. Thus he assists in committing a kind of suicide.

Before death takes place, the second movement of the community occurs, which is a return to the victim in order to subject him to the fateful ritual of mourning. The purpose of the community now, as a social unit with its ceremonial leader, who is a person of very near kin to the victim, is at last to cut him off entirely from the ordinary world and ultimately to place him in his proper position in the sacred totemic world of the dead. The victim, on his part, reciprocates this feeling. The effect of the double movement in this society, first away from the victim and then back, with all the compulsive force of one of its most powerful rituals, is obviously drastic. (Warner, cited by Cannon, 1958, p. 435.)

The frequent readiness of members of a particular community to participate in or corroborate the consummation or reversal of a hex could be related to the fact that in many cases hexing plays an important part in creating social solidarity; taboos are essential for the maintenance of the social fabric and their violation could lead to disruption of the social order. The stance of the group toward the hexed individual could possibly be explained in the following terms: if culture-bearers have an ambivalent attitude toward the taboos of their society, their relationship to the hexed victim could represent a projection of each individual's own struggle against violating the taboo that the hexed person himself has violated.

In terms of social function, most anthropologists would agree that sorcery and hexing, one of the mechanisms of witchcraft, serve as a means of social control in many communities. The fear of being hexed tends to prevent individuals from violating social rules as well as breaching religious taboos. Beatrice Whiting (1950) and Guy Swanson (1960) aptly demonstrate that witchcraft is more prevalent in those societies where higher secular authority does not exist or where this authority cannot mete out punishment for transgressions against the social or religious order. According to Swanson, the existence of witchcraft has very little to do with economic deprivation but is strongly associated with the level of social organization.

No matter how one interprets the social functions of hex and hex death, the fact remains that the community plays a vital role in the fulfillment of the curse or its reversal, depending on the specific circumstances of individual cases. In view of the paramount significance of social factors in human existence, it is not surprising that manipulation of social variables in terms of inclusion into the community or rejection by it can dramatically affect the hexed individual's emotional and physiological well-being and, ultimately, his survival.

We have now explored some of the most important physical, psychophysiological, and social variables involved in hex death. At this point in our discussion, the question arises whether there exists a sufficient basis for postulating yet another category of variables operating in death by curse, namely, parapsychological factors. Certainly, the previously discussed parameters, or a combination thereof, offer a plausible explanation for most of the cases of hex death. There are, however, aspects of certain cases of hex death and of the process of hexing reported in the literature for which such scientific interpretations would appear to be inadequate. In spite of the fact that incomplete and often unreliable reporting of these events makes it rather difficult to offer a conclusive analysis, it appears to be worthwhile to consider which characteristics of these cases do not lend themselves to explanations based on the existing scientific paradigms. In some instances, it is the striking accumulation of deaths attributed to hexing, the quite specific timing, and unusual circumstances that are difficult to account for and explain in strictly scientific terms. In other instances, it is not easy to identify or postulate the factors that could be instrumental in a causal chain of events responsible for a specific phenomenon. Finally, it is not exceptional that the performance of the sorcerer, shaman, or exorcist involves some rather unusual elements suggestive of psi phenomena.

The most famous examples of multiple and serial hex deaths are, of course, the instances of curses related to the violation of ancient tombs and relocation of sacred objects. We can cite the story of the discovery of Tutankhamen's tomb in the Valley of the Kings as an example of this particular genre. These situations are often colored by sensationalistic journalism; however, it is not difficult to discover similar examples in more sober frameworks. Thus, Melford Spiro, in *Burmese Supernaturalism,* describes an interesting case of multiple deaths attributed to witchcraft:

> The case begins with a woman who, without any previous symptoms, died while bathing at the village well. A few days later her elder daughter died of a scorpion bite and her younger daughter was smitten with a strange swelling of the body from which, shortly after, she too died. (Spiro, 1967, p. 27.)

Although these deaths were considered witch-caused by the villagers, Spiro unfortunately does not give any of the contextual details of this case.

Another example of this category is a medically well-documented case published in 1967 in the Bulletin of Johns Hopkins Hospital. On the 29th of July, 1966, a 22-year-old Afro-American woman was admitted to Baltimore City Hospital because of shortness of breath and episodes of chest pain and syncope of one month duration. After having been hospitalized for fourteen days, the patient disclosed to her physician that she had a "serious problem and only three days to solve it." She volunteered the following details:

> She had been born on Friday the thirteenth in the Okefenokee Swamp and was delivered by a midwife who delivered three children that day. The midwife told the mothers that the three children were hexed and that the first would die before her sixteenth birthday, the

second before her twenty-first birthday, and the third (the patient) before her twenty-third birthday. The patient went on to tell her physician that the first girl was killed in an automobile accident the day before her sixteenth birthday. The second girl was quite fearful of the hex and on her twenty-first birthday called a friend and insisted on going out to celebrate the end of the hex. She walked into a saloon, a stray bullet hit the girl and killed her. (Boitnott, 1967, p. 187.)

The patient was firmly convinced that she was doomed. She appeared to be terrified and manifested signs of profound anxiety. On August 12, she died—one day prior to her twenty-third birthday.

Although the clinicians and pathologist concurred on the diagnosis of primary pulmonary hypertension, the organic findings did not provide a sufficient explanation of her death and particularly its specific timing. Freisinger, assistant professor of medicine at Hopkins, made this comment in his discussion of the case:

> The other factor in this woman's death is the hex. I have no doubt that the pathologist will be able to demonstrate anatomic changes which can be held accountable for her death. However, I am equally certain that he will not be able to rule out the hex as the real cause of her death. It seems very clear that she was hexed at the time of her birth and she died precisely at the time predicted. . . . [He goes on to say] It is not a part of our society and hence we know little about it; I suspect many of us would prefer to think it did not exist. Special circumstances and beliefs in a community must exist before an individual can die by hex, but once the proper background and individual conditioning exist, there is no reason why [the described physiological processes] cannot occur and lead to death, at the proper time. (Boitnott, 1967, p. 9–10.)

In addition to the cumulative nature of this case, making a coincidence highly improbable, and the accuracy of the timing of the three deaths, one more aspect of this situation deserves attention. Only in the case of the last young woman can the death be explained from forces operating within the organism. Regarding the death of the first girl, there is insufficient information that would make it possible to assess the role she played in the automobile accident. However, where a stray bullet was the cause of death, the critical factors lie in this case outside of the hexed individual. An obvious weakness of this otherwise fascinating case is lack of information about how carefully and closely the doctors from Johns Hopkins verified the claims of the patient concerning the deaths of the other two victims.

The second aspect of hexing that might entail parapsychological dimensions has less to do with statistical probabilities than the former. Rather, it is concerned with certain elements of hexing that seem to transcend the usual limitations of the time/space continuum. Unfortunately, most of the reports mentioning these kinds of phenomena are not well documented and are often dubiously regarded by anthropologists, clinicians, and historians. Because of the rather poor quality of most of the data, we must approach this category only on a theoretical level, enriched with anecdotal material.

There are numerous reports about individuals developing knowledge that a sorcerer has conducted a hex-inducing ritual. Harner (1973, p. 21), for example, notes that one of the distinguishing characteristics of the process of hexing among the Jivaro is that the victim is given no indication that he is being bewitched, lest he take protective measures. Harner's informants say that sickness almost invariably follows an attack with a magical dart, the regurgitated tsentsak, and death is not uncommon.

In some instances, the victim of so-called simulated magic supposedly develops specific symptoms, the onset of which coincides with the sorcerer's manipulations of the individual's symbolic image, whether it is a doll, clothing of the intended victim, body exudates, nail parings or hair, dirt from the tracks of the victim, a photograph, or even an X-ray photo. It has also been said that, occasionally, a hexer is able to follow his victim's movements in his "mind's eye" or by using a special mirror and thereby monitor the consequences of the hexing procedure. Alfred Metraux (1972, p. 272) described the Haitian sorcerer who, through an incantation, attempts to lure the intended victim into a bucket of water. If his victim's image appears on the water's surface, he then stabs it. The water reddens if the sorcerer has been successful. Another variation of this type of procedure is cited by Robert Caneiro (1964, p. 10) in his work with the Amahuaca of eastern Peru. He reports that the shaman, after ingesting ayahuasco, can contact the jaguar spirit which discloses to him the whereabouts of his witchcraft victim. Although such situations seem quite fantastic, these and others like them have been so frequently reported in various parts of the world that they certainly deserve systematic exploration in the field. I emphasize field research because of the complexity of the phenomena vis-à-vis set and setting; it is highly improbable, if not absurd, to attempt to replicate such experiences in the laboratory. From this point of view, it is necessary to differentiate between so-called objective reality and the phenomenological reality of the subjective world of the sorcerer.

For the last point of our discussion of parapsychological dimensions of hexing, we will explore the display of paranormal abilities on the part of the sorcerer. It is not uncommon for such an individual to demonstrate psi ability on (at least) the first interaction with a client. This level of expertise and performance would most certainly establish the sorcerer in a position of authority in the eyes of his client and, undoubtedly, in the eyes of the community. In fact, he is not only in a position of special authority but can also be perceived as dangerous, because he is capable of penetrating and ultimately manipulating individuals and sequences of events. The sorcerer, as well as the diviner and healer, has often been characterized as a shrewd psychologist, able to elicit information from his clients in a most skillful and subtle manner. Sorcerers have also been endowed in the literature with extraordinarily long memories and sharp ears. In spite of these explanations given by social and behavioral scientists for the acumen demonstrated by such individuals, there are many reports in the literature that tell about events which intuition, memory, and access to gossip simply cannot adequately explain. Numerous accounts ascribe to sorcerers and healers the ability to make instant diagnosis of medical problems, to penetrate immediately the personalities of their clients and their basic psychological conflicts, to have access to material from the individual's past history, and to predict correctly future events.

One aspect of hexing and hex death that has been considered by some witnesses to be indicative of involvement of paranormal forces is the consistently reported helplessness of Western medicine to cope with these phenomena. The failures of experienced clinicians to prevent the consum-

mation of a hex and save the patient's life are notable.
(Examples are cited in: Cannon, 1958; Prince, 1960; Boitnott, 1967; Tingling, 1967; Watson, 1973; and others.)
This contrasts sharply with the quite dramatic therapeutic
successes of indigenous healers to remove a death curse
put on an individual. (Examples are cited in: Richter, 1957;
Cannon, 1958; Wilson, 1963; and others.) This situation,
however, is not necessarily a proof of supernatural forces
operating in hex death. It can simply suggest the lack of
understanding on the part of Western medicine of the complexity of this phenomenon and the significance of specific
psychological and sociocultural variables in the etiology of
the hex syndrome. In such instances, clinicians would benefit
from consultation with an anthropologist experienced in the
culture of the cursed individual and/or collaboration with an
indigenous healer. It seems that, because of the nature of this
problem, the effective remedy must come in a specific and
culturally appropriate form that contemporary medicine does
not usually offer.

It would be interesting in this context to approach the
problem of the relevance of parapsychological factors for hex
death from yet another perspective. It is possible to look at
the phenomena postulated and studied by parapsychology
and hypothesize which of them, if proved beyond any
doubt, could be considered instrumental in the hexing procedure. The most obvious of them, of course, would be
"telepathic control" and psychokinesis. (It was Robert Van
de Castle who suggested to me that psychokinesis might be
a relevant mechanism to explore in relation to hex death.)
In the former case, the hexer could directly influence the
emotional condition and thought processes of an individual
and produce a state of mind, such as malignant anxiety or
Engel's "giving up—given up complex," that could have
catastrophic biological consequences. In the latter case, it is
conceivable that direct psychokinetic influence could be
exerted on certain parts of the body that are crucial for
survival, such as the pacemaker in the heart and the cardiac
conduction system, or certain areas in the central nervous
system that are vitally important and crucial for survival.
Numerous instances of telepathic control and psychokinesis
have been reported in the parapsychological literature, including recent experiments in the Soviet Union (Krippner,
1972; Herbert, 1973), and experiments with Uri Geller at
Stanford Research Institute in Palo Alto (Mitchell, 1973;

O'Regan, 1973). If confirmed, the psychokinetic experiments in which the Russian psychic Kulagina succeeded in stopping a frog's heart would be of special relevance in this context (Herbert, 1973).

Three other parapsychological phenomena that have been studied both in the laboratory and in the field are telepathy, clairvoyance, and precognition. Gifts of telepathy and the ability to make an instant diagnosis of physical and psychological problems could be exploited by the sorcerer, not only for impressing the victim and his social network, and, thereby, enhancing his authority and power of suggestion, but also for identifying the physical and psychological "loci minoris resistentiae" in the individual to be hexed. Such knowledge could then be utilized for specifically destructive manipulations by other means. In terms of precognition, there exist cases of hexing and hex death that theoretically could be explained in terms of this mechanism rather than direct malign influence.

One more theoretical consideration deserves notice in this connection. Lawrence LeShan (1969), a prominent researcher in the area of psychic healing, has made an attempt to formulate a comprehensive theory of the paranormal. According to LeShan, our understanding of reality and our interaction with it is determined by our way of perceiving the world. Throughout mankind's history, reality has been perceived in a variety of ways. These perceptions oscillate widely between two extremes. One extreme could be exemplified by the Newtonian world view. It has the following set of postulates or principles: matter is real and solid: valid information about the world comes to us only through the senses; causes must precede effects in time; and objects separated by space are different objects. Our practical life and the ordinary activity of physical existence are confined by these limiting principles. This is also true for the mainstream of contemporary science. The other extreme is the mystical world view. It has an alternative set of postulates: the true nature of the world is consciousness and matter is only ephemeral: there is a better way of gaining information than through the senses (and intellectual processing of sensory data); there is no reality to time; and there is a basic unity of all things.

According to LeShan, the process of psychic healing can be explained by the fact that the healer operates on the basis of the set of postulates characterizing the mystical world view and this has practical consequences. During the healing process, the healer and the ailing individual are part of the same psychophysical field and are not separate from each other, as it appears to the Newtonian observer. This model, interestingly, can be applied without any change (except in terms of intentionality) to the situation of hexing. In this case, the manipulations in such a unified field would be used for destructive purposes rather than healing of the individual. This conceptual framework that appears so alien to our pragmatic, intersubjective, group-validated world view is, in fact, in agreement with revolutionary developments in modern physics, and, in particular, with the basic concepts of Einstein's unified field theory.

In conclusion, I hope that I have succeeded in conveying the multidimensional nature and complexity of the phenomena of hexing and hex death. As groundwork has been done by anthropologists, psychologists, and physiologists in this area, establishing hex death as a subject worthy of further scientific exploration, it seems that the way is now open to explore the parapsychological dimensions that might possibly be involved.

One of the major problems in studying hexing and hex death in the past has been the seemingly irreconcilable conflict between the ideological and epistemological superstructures that frame such events and the accepted traditional Western scientific paradigms that are employed to analyze them. One approach that might obviate to a certain degree the frequent ethnocentric bias that permeates and ultimately distorts or obscures many anthropological accounts of possible parapsychological events, would be to study separately the observable elements of an event itself and then to explore the underlying belief system. In other words, one would analyze and evaluate the processes and mechanisms involved and the outcome, and then obtain the culture-bearers' interpretations of such mechanisms and their explanation of the outcome achieved.

These two perspectives would be described by some anthropologists as "etic" and "emic." Etic, as defined by Marvin Harris (1971, p. 632) refers to "the domains or operations whose validity does not depend upon the demonstration of conscious or unconscious significance or reality in the minds of the natives"; emic indicates in this context "the domains or operations whose validity depends upon distinctions that are real or meaningful (but not necessarily conscious) to the natives themselves." In other words, the etic/emic distinction corresponds roughly to how people behave according to the judgment of a Western scientific observer in contrast to how the subjects perceive and explain their behavior themselves.

The potential heuristic value of this approach to me seems great. In the areas of psychopharmacology and psychology alone, many revolutionary pharmacologic substances as well as psychotherapeutic techniques have been garnered from ancient and aboriginal cultures. Indeed, hexing and hex death have strong implications in the area of research being done on stress in technologically developed areas of the world. In terms of parapsychological research, it should prove to be an extremely rich area as it is accessible and researchable in Baltimore as well as the bush, and its phenomenology exists in the physical world as we know it and beyond.

## REFERENCES

ACKERKNECHT, E. H.: "Primitive Medicine and Culture Pattern," *Bull. Hist. Med.,* 1942, 12:545.

BARBER, T. X.: "Death by Suggestion: A Critical Note," *Psychosom. Med.,* 1961, 23:153.

BOITNOTT, J. K.: "Clinicopathological Conference: Case Presentation," *Bull. Johns Hopkins Hosp.,* 1967, 120:186.

CARNEIRO, R. L.: "The Amahuaca and the Spirit World," *Ethnology,* 1964, 3:6.

CANNON, W. B.: "Voodoo Death," in *Reader in Comparative Religion: An Anthropological Approach,* W. Lessa and E. Vogt, eds., Harper & Row, New York, 1958.

CLUNE, F. J.: "A Comment on Voodoo Deaths," *Amer. Anthropol.,* 1973, 75:312.

DYNES, J. B.: "Sudden Death," *Dis. Nerv. Syst.,* 1969, 30:24.

ENGEL, G. L.: "A Life Setting Conducive to Illness," *Bull. Menninger Clin.,* 1968, 32:355.

HALIFAX-GROF, J. S.: *Interaction Between Indigenous Healing Systems and Contemporary Medicine.* A paper presented at the Annual Conference of the American Academy of Psychotherapists, New York City, 1972.

——— *Indigenous Healing Systems and Contemporary Medicine: Toward an Integration of Approaches.* Unpublished doctoral dissertation, Union Graduate School, 1973.

HARNER, M.: "The Sound of Rushing Water," in *Hallucinogens and Shamanism*, M. Harner, ed., Oxford University Press, London, 1973.

HARRIS, M.: *Culture, Man and Nature*, Thomas Y. Crowell, New York, 1971.

HERBERT, B.: "Spring in Leningrad: Kulagina Revisited," *J. Paraphys.*, 1973, 7:92.

KRIPPNER, S.: Presentation at the Annual Conference of the Association for Humanistic Psychology, Squaw Valley, Calif., 1972.

—— Presentation at the Conference "Psychic Healing: Myth into Science," New York, 1973.

LESHAN, L.: *Toward a General Theory of the Paranormal*, Parapsychology Foundation, New York, 1969.

LESTER. D.: "Voodoo Death—Some New Thoughts on an Old Phenomenon," *Amer. Anthropol.*, 1972, 74:386.

LEWIS, G. A.: *The Recognition of Sickness and Its Causes: A Medical Anthropological Study of the Einu, West Sepik District, New Guinea.* Unpublished doctoral dissertation, London University, 1972.

METRAUX, A.: *Voodoo in Haiti*, Schocken Books, New York, 1959.

MICHAELSON, M.: "Can a Root Doctor Actually Put a Hex On or Is It All a Great Put-On?" *Today's Health*, March, 1972.

MITCHELL, E.: Presentation at the Fifth Interdisciplinary Conference on Voluntary Control of Internal States at Council Grove, Kansas, 1973.

O'REGAN, B.: *Personal Communication*, 1973.

PRINCE, R.: "Curse Invocation and Mental Health Among the Yoruba," *Canad. Psychiat. Assoc. J.*, 1960, 5:65.

RICHTER, C. P.: "On the Phenomenon of Sudden Death in Animals and Men," *Psychosom. Med.*, 1957, 19:190.

SPIRO, M. E.: *Burmese Supernaturalism.* Prentice-Hall, Englewood Cliffs, N. J., 1967.

SWANSON, G. E.: *The Birth of the Gods: The Origin of Primitive Beliefs*, University of Michigan Press, Ann Arbor, Mich., 1960.

TINGLING, D.: "Voodoo, Rootwork and Medicine," *Psychosom. Med.*, 1967, 29:483.

WATSON, A. A.: "Death by Cursing—A Problem for Forensic Psychiatry," *Medicine, Science and the Law*, 1973, 13:192.

WHITING, B.: *Paiute Sorcery*, Viking Fund Publications in Anthropology, No. 15, New York, 1950.

WILSON, M.: *Good Company*, Beacon Press, Boston, 1963.

WINTROB, R., FOX, R. A., AND O'BRIEN, E. G.: "Rootwork Beliefs and Psychiatric Disorder among Blacks in a Northern United States City." Presentation at the Symposium on Traditional and Modern Treatments of Indigenous American People, Fifth World Congress of Psychiatry, Mexico City, 1972.

# 9

## The Power of Desuggestion

*Allen Spraggett*

*How much of our mind potential do we ignore? How do we allow ourselves to focus in almost one-dimensional fashion and exclude much of what is around us? When proper techniques are used, the mind can be activated and learning increased to such an extent that it almost seems like science fiction.*

*Allen Spraggett, well-known personality, author, and psi investigator, explores this wasteland we call "mind" and describes an important technique developed by Dr. Georgi Lozanov of Bulgaria that may eventually revolutionize learning methods as well as play an important role in modern medicine.*

● ● ●

The most potent medicine is faith.

This was the conclusion of Dr. Alfred J. Kantor, a distinguished proctologist (specialist in rectal diseases), after investigating a new drug.

Dr. Kantor, president emeritus of the Academy of Psychosomatic Medicine and one time editor of the *American Journal of Proctology*, was asked to evaluate a treatment for benign rectal diseases that had been used in Europe but was unknown in the United States. He employed what is commonly called the double-blind method.

The physicians doing the clinical tests under Dr. Kantor's direction were sent two medications that looked exactly alike, the ingredients of which were unknown both to them and their patients. One contained the new drug; the other was a placebo—dummy medication—and contained only milk sugar.

"The interesting fact," reported Dr. Kantor in the January 1959 issue of *Science of Mind,* "was that the placebo proved to be even more effective than the supposedly active combination of drugs!"

Indeed, one of the doctors said that his sister had suffered from rectal disease for many years and this was the first medication to give her relief. He was eager to know the nature of the drug.

"It was my duty to write and tell him that the medication was only milk sugar," recounted Dr. Kantor. "It was purely a placebo effect."

The milk sugar had no inherent medicinal properties; the woman had been healed by her own belief.

Actually, noted Dr. Kantor, no medication—not even the most pharmacologically potent—can be separated from the placebo effect, which may be negative as well as positive.

"The most 'active' drugs can become relatively inactive in the hands of a physician who is not held in sufficient esteem by the patient," he observed, "and a relatively 'inactive' or even inert preparation may become highly potent when administered by a very authoritative physician."

Data on the placebo effect were summarized by Dr. Bernard Grad, a biologist in the psychiatry department at McGill University, Montreal, in *Corrective Psychiatry and Journal of Social Therapy,* Volume 12, 1966.

"A recent comprehensive review . . . reported that 40.6 percent of 14,177 patients with illnesses ranging from simple headache to multiple sclerosis obtained relief from placebo pills," said Dr. Grad.

He cited a case in which the placebo effect reversed the normal pharmacological action of a drug. A man was given atropine sulfate, believing it to be the same drug he had previously received. The previous drug was prostigmin which, as expected, had induced abdominal cramps, diarrhea, and extreme stomach acidity. The atropine sulfate had exactly the same effect on the man, although it normally has the opposite effect!

Even more puzzling, in a way, is the influence of the investigator's personality when he has no bias about the drug being tested.

Grad cited the case of two investigators who were asked to

measure gastric secretions in healthy humans in response to pill X. It was a placebo but the investigators weren't told this: nor were they told how to expect the pill to act.

Curiously, their results differed wildly. One investigator reported that his subjects showed a 12 percent increase in gastric acidity; the other measured an 18 percent *decrease* in his subjects. The differing results were consistent whenever these particular experimenters were used.

Stranger still was the case in which a doctor's mistaken faith apparently made a placebo effective and a pharmacologically active drug ineffective.

The patient in this case had suffered from intractable asthma for twenty-seven years. During this time he built up a tolerance to epinephrine, a drug commonly used to relieve acute bronchial spasms. In his desperation to find another remedy, the patient made himself readily available as a guinea pig to test new drugs.

Finally, one just-on-the-market pharmaceutical product provided dramatic relief. When he was given this drug, he was asthma-free; when it was stopped, the symptoms promptly returned. The patient's doctor wanted to test the placebo effect, so he substituted sugar pills, which the pharmaceutical company had also sent, without the man's knowledge. Immediately, as the doctor had expected, the asthmatic symptoms returned.

There were several switches from drug to placebo and back again—all yielding results consistent with the doctor's expectations. Finally, he was satisfied that the objective value of the drug to his patient had been demonstrated beyond doubt.

Then he reported to the pharmaceutical company and found, to his bewilderment, that inadvertently he had confused the drug with the placebo. The patient all along had been responding to the sugar pill.

What happened here?

The doctor had been careful not to reveal to the patient anything about the medication he was receiving. As far as the patient was concerned, all the pills were the same. Yet the placebo, which the doctor mistakenly believed was the real drug, worked consistently and the drug didn't.

The doctor's belief must have transmitted itself to the patient, suggested Bernard Grad, either directly or indirectly. Perhaps the doctor's faith adhered, as it were, to the placebo pill, in the same way that psychic impressions are claimed by clairvoyants to cling to a personal object. Or perhaps the patient picked up the doctor's faith from unconscious clues—possibly even by telepathy.

Just as the patient's faith in his physician is an important factor in his recovery, a negative transference between patient and doctor may not only slow or prevent recovery but make the patient worse. This is especially evident in psychotherapy, Grad said.

He cited studies indicating that although some mentally and emotionally ill persons showed a definite improvement with certain therapists, other patients deteriorated during therapy, ending up in poorer health than they might have been without treatment.

"While good therapists tend to produce better psychological functioning," Grad said, "bad ones tend to produce further regressive behavior."

It is not so much formal training as enthusiasm that counts in a psychotherapist, coupled with a genuine, deeply felt desire and confidence that the patient will get well. Studies have indicated that people with no training in psychotherapy, but with empathy and the capacity for involvement, have achieved better results than qualified therapists.

Group therapy was conducted with 295 institutionalized psychotics, Grad reported. One bunch was treated by undergraduate college students with no formal background in psychotherapy; the other received treatment from professionals. The results of therapy were measured by before-and-after psychological testing of the patients. The group treated by the students scored better in terms of improved mental health than the other group.

Grad speculated that possibly "the untrained personnel were taken by the novelty of the task" and this accounted for the difference. To test this theory, he suggested that the same students be used in several successive experiments of this kind.

The crucial fact about any doctor-patient relationship, Grad concluded, is that suggestion, whether overt or not, plays a dynamic part.

Someone may say here: "Well, what about it? This isn't new. Most people nowadays know about placebos. There's no mystery. Simply the power of suggestion."

The power of suggestion.

These four words are used by some scientists as a sort of incantation to conjure away many unexplained phenomena.

An unusual, totally unexpected recovery? Nothing to get excited about; it's merely the power of suggestion (or, that other stock phrase to explain away the unexplained, "spontaneous remission").

The word "suggestion" is similar to the word "gravity"; both are widely used and both are labels often mistaken for explanations.

When someone says, "What goes up must come down because of the law of gravity," all he's really saying is that it must come down because it must come down. Sheer tautology.

No one knows yet what gravity *is*; no one has observed the hypothetical particle called a graviton. The idea of gravity, therefore, although useful, does not explain anything.

The same is true with suggestion. To declare that milk-sugar ointment healed a long-standing rectal disease by the power of suggestion doesn't shed any light on the why of it. Precisely how does suggestion work? By what mechanisms? Why can sheer belief—a state of mind—relieve long-standing asthma or reverse the known action of a drug?

What really is this mysterious power of suggestion?

Hypnosis is a form of suggestion, possibly the most powerful form. In hypnosis the censor of the conscious mind is bypassed and suggestions are fed directly into the deep mind. Some of the results can be astonishing.

The *British Medical Journal* of August 1952 reported the case of a 16-year-old boy with ichthyosis—a congenital, disfiguring, incurable skin disease—who was treated by a London physician, Dr. Albert Abraham Mason, using hypnotherapy. Over several weeks of hypnotic treatment 90 percent of the boy's body affected by the ichthyosis cleared. The boy was taught self-hypnosis to maintain the improvement.

Dr. Robert W. Laidlaw, former chief of psychiatry at New York's Roosevelt Hospital, has said: "I have no way of proving this, but I have a definite feeling that there is some extrasensory or parapsychological factor in hypnosis."

In other words, when you look deeply enough into the phenomenon of suggestion, it has a large element of the unexplained.

Recently I met a Bulgarian psychiatrist, Dr. Georgi Lozanov, who has devised a spectacularly successful self-help technique which he calls suggestology, "the science of suggestion." My introduction to him came through mutual friends, Sheila

Ostrander and Lynn Schroeder, who describe suggestology in *Psychic Discoveries Behind the Iron Curtain*. Dr. Lozanov was in North America to discuss his methods with American and Canadian scholars.

According to this scientist—a handsome, charming man in his forties, with wavy, slightly receding hair—his research started with the very question I have raised: What is the power of suggestion?

He noted that many of his colleagues, when confronted with a puzzling mental or medical phenomenon, murmured the nonexplanation: "Suggestion."

"I decided to look into this so-called suggestion," he said, "to try to discover just what it is and exactly how it works."

Lozanov brought to his investigation a background of more than twenty-five years of yoga study, both in Europe and India. He reached the conclusion that suggestion, or the "suggestive state," was the key to the unusual feats of some yogis.

He said he also discovered that what releases the greatest untapped potential of the mind is "the power of *de*suggestion."

"My technique of suggestology is different from hypnosis," he said in his precise, almost unaccented English (which he told me he taught himself in six weeks, using his own methods).

"Hypnosis is a sleeplike state in which there is a limitation of perception. Suggestion, on the other hand, is a state of full connection with the environment.

"Actually, we don't suggest; we desuggest.

"All of us are bombarded constantly with limiting suggestions. We are conditioned to believe that we can only remember so much, that we are bound to be sick, that there are rigid limits so what we can achieve. The purpose of suggestology is to free people from these limitations of thinking imposed on them by the process of negative conditioning to which we're all exposed."

Using suggestology, said Dr. Lozanov, most psychosomatic diseases could be cured. The principle is not to attack specific symptoms but to saturate the unconscious with suggestions of well-being that counteract the conditioning by which most people have come to accept sickness as normal, natural, and inevitable.

As important as the healing of existing diseases, said the apostle of suggestology, is the establishment of "a prophylactic mental atmosphere" to prevent people from succumbing to new emotionally induced symptoms.

Applied to education, as "suggestopedia," the Lozanov method can speed up the learning process as much as fifty times, he claimed. An utter beginner could acquire a working knowledge of French, German, Greek, or any other European language in a month. Presumably, learning Sanskrit or Cantonese might take a little longer.

"People can learn one hundred fifty to two hundred words per lesson," Lozanov said, "once the antisuggestive barriers are removed."

These claims struck some critics as exaggerated and Lozanov was challenged. An official scientific commission was appointed by the Bulgarian government to study suggestology in its application to learning. Apparently it received a clean bill of health. In 1966 the Bulgarian Ministry of Education established a center for suggestopedia in Dr. Lozanov's state-supported Institute of Suggestology in Sofia.

The essence of suggestopedia seems to be distraction. In a typical class, as Lozanov described it, the students sit quietly while soft music—Beethoven, Brahms—is piped in. Over the music the voice of a teacher, with varying speed and intonation, repeats, say, words and phrases in French. The students don't appear to be listening to the teacher; as a matter of fact, they've been warned not to.

"Relax. Don't think about anything. Listen only to the music." This is Dr. Lozanov's formula for painless learning.

Again, he says, the secret is desuggestion. The quiet, relaxed mood and the absorption in the music eases and dissolves the tensions, stress, and anxieties which normally hamper the learning process. As people learn to enter more deeply into this "free state of consciousness"—actually, a condition of alert nonthinking—they find that their ability to absorb and retain new material is enormously increased.

Lozanov insists that human memory has an almost limitless potential and, like a sponge, constantly expands so that the more it soaks up the more it can soak up. But first the memory must be freed, by desuggestion, from the false ideas of limitation which chain it.

Suggestology has other applications. One of the most dramatic is in controlling bodily functioning. Anything that hypnosis can do, says Lozanov, suggestology can do. And, unlike hypnosis, it works with anybody and raises no legal or psychological problems.

Consider what Lozanov calls "thought anesthesia."

On August 24, 1965, the first major surgery on a patient anesthetized by suggestology took place in Bykovo, Bulgaria. It was filmed and has been seen by numerous medical scientists.

The patient was a 50-year-old gym instructor with an inguinal hernia, a condition requiring major and complex surgery. The operation was expected to take an hour. During that time the patient was to receive no anesthesia except the suggestions used by Dr. Lozanov. The two met for several conditioning sessions prior to the surgery.

As nurses wheeled the patient into the operating room, Dr. Lozanov, walking beside him, began his suggestions.

The surgeons made an incision through the skin and muscle. The patient felt nothing, was fully conscious, and talked normally to the operating team.

As the surgery progressed, Lozanov told the patient to suggest to himself that circulation to the area of the incision would decrease to control bleeding. There was very little loss of blood. The operation ended with the patient suggesting to himself that the wound would heal rapidly and without infection. This, too, transpired.

Lozanov insists that this was not hypnosis. However, without making an issue out of terminology—he agrees that hypnosis and suggestology are related phenomena—it is a fact that a subject in a state of "waking hypnosis" would behave exactly as Lozanov's patient reportedly did. Such a subject would appear to be perfectly normal—certainly not asleep—and yet have the power to reduce or cancel pain perception in part or all of his body.

Experts in hypnosis, such as Dr. George Estabrooks, former head of the psychology department at Colgate University, have pointed out that the somnambulistic subject can be trained to act as though he weren't hypnotized and defy detection by the sharpest-eyed observer.

The important point about Dr. Lozanov's report, at any rate, isn't whether suggestology or waking hypnosis was involved but that the patient, using his mind alone, was able to control pain during major surgery.

# 10

# Arigó: Psychic Surgeon

### Andrija Puharich

*This next contribution by Andrija Puharich brings him to the door of a real "sizzler" that challanges many of the basic laws of physics and modern medicine.*

*Puharich was a member of an American medical team that investigated the extraordinary drama of the late José Pedro de Freitas known as "Arigó," who has been credited with healing thousands of people in the Brazilian village of Congonhas de Campo.*

*Psychic surgery is a highly suspect ability claimed by numerous people, for example, in South America and the Philippines and without any doubt often fraudulently. Despite the hostility from the medical profession, reporters, and critics of the reality of psi, the Arigó phenomenon is only now beginning to gain increasing attention from scientists. Once "too hot to handle," it promises to challenge the very foundations of the healing process.*

*Puharich presents his views on the qualities of the "ideal" healer and ranks Arigó in these terms.*

● ● ●

I have a dream of what I call the complete healer. The complete healer is a person who has never been seen yet and may never be seen. However, to discuss it will give us some idea of what we mean by the word "healing." Now healing is used very freely in nonmedical circles. It's not so commonly used among medical men and I suppose you can understand the reason. They don't always pretend to heal! Speaking as an M.D. myself, we mostly patch things up. I think it's because we don't have a complete philosophy of medicine; we don't have a complete practice of medicine; and we don't have that model before us of the complete healer. Let me try to give you an idea of what I think the complete healer is and how much Arigó, the Brazilian healer, illustrates that such a person may indeed exist.

One of the first characteristics of the complete healer is the ability to diagnose illness. By diagnose I don't mean ordering fifty blood tests and twenty X rays, etc. I mean the ability to look at the patient, if the patient is present, and if the patient is not present, to use some intermediary contact with that individual, and make his diagnosis. Arigó had two main methods of making a medical diagnosis, and I must say that I've been extremely impressed, as well as have my research colleagues, with his accuracy in medical diagnosis. One method was to simply look at the patient and immediately give a diagnosis which was quite accurate even though the condition was invisible to the eye or inaudible to the ear. For example, he would look at a particular patient and the patient would volunteer the information that he was there because he thought he had leprosy, and Arigó would immediately say, "No, you don't have leprosy, you in fact have syphilis, and you shouldn't lie to me!" With a subsequent medical test our research team verified that indeed this man did have syphilis. In another instance, a man stepped up, and quite casually Arigó mentioned to us that we should check his blood pressure because at that instant it was 23 over 17, which in English means a blood pressure of 230 millimeters of mercury over 170 millimeters of mercury, and indeed this was found to be the case. These are the kinds of diagnosis that a complete physician should have the ability to make.

There was another aspect of Arigó's diagnostic ability which, to me, was extremely impressive and has become, for me, a paradigm of what certain types of extrasensory perception should really be like. He would hear a voice when making a diagnosis. Let us say the patient was standing in front of him so that anybody could see that something was the matter with the patient's eyes. He wouldn't say that the patient has eye trouble; rather, he would say that the patient has retinoblastoma or that the patient has retinitis pigmentosa or use other modern technical terminology. Now I was not aware nor, as far as I know, was anybody else aware of this method of diagnosis until I uncovered it during a series of some 1,000 diagnostic procedures. Arigó came up with a phenomenally correct number of diagnoses, and I was quite amazed at this in terms of the accuracy obtained and in terms of the language used. I asked him how he knew all this. He replied, "That's one of the simplest things for me to do because I simply listen to the voice, which is always in my right ear, and I repeat whatever it says."

Arigó died in his 49th year. As a boy he didn't have any education except for two years in a parochial school from which he was dismissed because he was too stupid to be allowed to continue. His subsequent career always involved doing hard labor either in the fields or mines, or later in a social security office which was more or less a clerical job. In our in-depth study of his educational background concerning how much he had read, etc., we found that, for practical purposes, he could be considered an illiterate. Nobody had ever seen him read a book or even try to read a book (based on an extensive sociological study of his background). Thus, we had to take the hypothesis very seriously that there was indeed some kind of voice presenting itself in his head. The important question was, who was the director of the program or the owner of that voice? I'll come back to that subject in a moment.

The second characteristic of the complete healer is his ability to heal by the process of laying on of hands, which I prefer to call manual healing. Manual healing is beginning to gain status, but I don't think it has quite the status that the biofeedback situation has today, even though we should have known about it several hundred years ago. (As far as manual healing is concerned, medicine should have been aware of that hundreds of years ago too.) However, thanks to the work of Bernard Grad of McGill University, and Sister Justa Smith of Rosary Hill College, we are beginning to understand some of the mechanism of the laying on of hands. For those of you who don't know their work, Berny worked with a healer by the name of Col. Estebany and a Mr. Ian. He found that when Estebany treated coded jugs of water by placing his hands on them, and the water was then poured in random fashion onto plants which were set up in a very good statistically controlled manner, the plants which had the benefit of treated water grew much more rapidly and had a greater net weight within a given period of time than those plants which received water untreated by his hands.

Sister Justa Smith extended the study to show that in using water to dilute certain enzyme systems that break down polypeptides into amino acids, the Estebany-treated water produced about a 15 percent increase in the hydrolytic activity of that enzyme.

A third criterion for the complete healer is that he be able to heal himself. It is one of the rarest phenomena to find in a healer. I've yet to find a healer who can truly heal himself and this notwithstanding extensive experience with practicing Christian Scientists, who of course do not claim to heal themselves but claim to heal through the intervention of a higher power. I've never seen this phenomenon of healing oneself in Arigó, and to my knowledge, in the twenty years in which he was a healer, he was never able to treat any organic illness in any blood relative. I think we interviewed about every living blood relative that he had. This in itself is a curious situation, which we could never rationalize.

A fourth characteristic of the complete healer is the ability to use molecular medicine. This is not too much different from that which occurs in orthodox medicine; i.e., the use of chemicals, molecules to add to the organism, whether human or animal, which affect that organism in such a way that certain functions are modulated and diseases are either mollified or disappear. A good example of that would be the taking of aspirin or insulin or other common chemical manipulations that we know about. A good healer, and I don't limit this strictly to Arigó, has the ability to somehow match, in his head, a knowledge of what is wrong with the chemical nature of an individual and fill that missing link in the chemical puzzle with the right type of chemical. In the case of Arigó, he had this ability to an extraordinary and even a superlative degree. He would prescribe every known modern pharmacological agent to patients, and he would do this in a way totally unknown to modern medicine. Namely, the voice would dictate to him what medicine to prescribe. And I must say that from a purely pharmacological point of view, those of us medical men who studied him were really quite impressed by the range of knowledge he exhibited in how to use this molecular matching problem and how to treat not only the immediate problems but also that which causes them.

Let me explain what I mean by using the following example. We all know about stomach ulcers which the modern physician will usually treat locally by giving an antacid or something else to slow down the vagus nerve and perhaps a tranquilizer if he thinks some of the problem is with one of the levels of mind or brain. Arigó did not work this way. He would in fact tend to ignore the stomach as the problem and would prescribe a series of drugs. When I say drugs, I mean modern pharmacological agents which took care of the basic cause behind that ulcer, and that may have been in the brain, or it may have been due to some parasite, or it may have been due to some problem in the liver, or some other supporting function of which the stomach was only a kind of front manifestation. For example, I think we're all familiar now with the work of Humphrey Osmond and Avery Hoffer and others in treating certain kinds of so-called organic mental problems, like schizophrenia, with massive doses of certain vitamins—the so-called megavitamin therapy. Arigó was using this some twenty years ago, and I personally witnessed many instances of his using this type of molecular preparation on cases like epilepsy and schizophrenia if he chose to treat them that way. He also treated other so-called mental illness this way. I include in this knowledge of molecular treatment, of course, all chemicals whether they be plant derived, seed derived, animal derived, or artificially derived.

The fifth area of interest that should characterize the complete healer is the ability to produce anesthesia by nonchemical means. Now I don't care to argue whether this is hypnosis or whether this is telepathy at a distance or whatever. The fact is that a good healer, like Arigó, could place a very sharp knife into a wide-awake unanesthetized patient's eye and could manipulate the knife in the eye without causing either damage to the eye or pain. Likewise, he could do surgery on that eye, such as to remove cataracts, tumors, etc. I have witnessed hundreds of operations, both major and minor, by Arigó on patients wherein he used a knife, scissors, or some such instrument, and I don't believe I have ever seen any patient complain of the smallest bit of pain during such manipulation. I can personally testify to the fact that the procedure was painless, because just as an experiment, I had Arigó operate on a lipoma which was present on my arm. This was a rather harmless condition, but, nevertheless, I wanted to see what would happen when he cut the tissue; I felt nothing and the operation went very quickly.

A sixth characteristic of the complete healer is the ability to do what I call instant surgery. Now, the kind of surgery that we carry out in hospitals today is not instant in the sense that it takes a great deal of preparation. For example, you perhaps think that a surgeon steps up to a draped patient, inserts a knife, makes an incision, manipulates, steps away, and that's instant surgery. In fact it is not, because the room had to be sterilized and much equipment had to be assembled. Anybody who has worked in an operating room can tell you how much preparation it takes to do even the most minor bit of surgery, and of course the clean-up afterward is not trivial. Arigó's instant surgery was quite different. He simply borrowed any locally available knife, usually somebody's pocketknife, and did the most fantastic and skilled surgery on the spot with that knife, and returned it to the owner after wiping it on his shirt, and went on to the next patient. That's what I call instant surgery.

There is one step beyond that type of instant surgery which you have probably heard about, particularly from the Filipino healers (some of whom, I'm sorry to say, are really fraudulent, although some are genuine). They are able, and I think we have pretty good evidence for this, to part tissue without touching the skin at all simply by pointing the finger at the site to be opened and it will open.

The seventh criterion that I have for the complete healer is what I call the bacteria stasis treatment ability, which means that a true healer violates every known surgical principle of antisepsis and does it with glee and joy. Why he does it with glee and joy is because, somehow, he seems to be able to talk to bacteria and they don't misbehave. This is, to me, one of the really great aspects of healing.

The eighth category is the treatment which I call action at a distance. Classically it's called absent healing. It literally means that the patient and the healer are separated by some distance and the patient does get well. This is the second category in which I have no clear-cut evidence that Arigó was able to manifest ability. This is quite commonly practiced by many spiritual groups and by many prayer groups in many different churches (not just Christian churches).

The ninth criterion has to do with the role in the complete

healer's practice of a so-called guide. Now this guide may be a voice as I've indicated. It may be a spirit to which the healer gives a name for identification and which is continuously with him in his work. This is one of the great frontier areas of the healing research that really should be clarified. Arigó, for example, always worked with the presence of a voice in his right ear which he identified as a Dr Fritz, and without Dr. Fritz, Arigó claimed that he couldn't work at all. It's one of the great frustrations of my life that I was never able to devise any objective research methods that would somehow clearly distinguish between Arigó's own native genius as a healer, as a physician, and the presence of an alter ego, or second personality, whom he identified as a spirit. When one gets right down to identifying the root behavior of the mind, we have great difficulty in pinning down the content, scope, and location of the mind itself.

The tenth criterion for the complete healer is the ability to regenerate tissues. Now this may be an organ, as an ear that is functionally not there because the nerves have been destroyed, or an eye, or a limb. Or in some cases that we know of from the literature, where life has been restored when all indications say that the person has definitely been dead for up to several days. I have never seen any evidence in my lifetime of any healer who could perform this function. This is included simply because this is a part of the lore and the literature of man's history in this area. However, I think it is a piece of evidence that should be actively searched for and I think it is subject to experimental inquiry, certainly in the case of lower organisms like amphibia, etc.

Of the ten criteria I have enumerated for the complete healer, Arigó, in my opinion, exhibited seven of them. The three that he lacked were (1) the ability to heal himself; (2) there is no evidence for his ability to heal at a distance; and (3) there is certainly no evidence for anything that we might call regeneration, even though that is subject to definition.

Arigó's great genius was in treating so-called incurable illnesses. Now, I can personally testify, as can my medical colleagues, that he was eminently successful with practically every type of cancer that is known to man. He would usually treat it with chemotherapy and in some extreme cases he would use surgery. I did not witness this case myself, but we have reliable testimony about a patient who had been examined by doctors, so that X-ray evidence was on hand.

He had a very advanced cancer of the stomach and was not given much time to live. The man went to see Arigó and stood in a line of people, some 300 to 400 people who were waiting to be seen. When Arigó walked up to his building where he worked, he spotted this man out of this huge crowd and said, "You, come in to see me immediately because you are really sick." He took him in and without asking him any questions said, "I know you have cancer of the stomach; there is no time to be lost; here is a prescription." He gave him a certain number of drugs to get at the drugstore and to take continuously over a twenty-four-hour period and advised him to come back the next day (all of which he did). When he returned the next day, Arigó, in this case which is rare in his practice, put his hands through the abdominal wall without using a knife and extracted a lot of bloody tissue. When the patient went back to his doctor and had subsequent X rays of the stomach, etc., the cancer had been eliminated.

Arigó, besides treating every known type of incurable illness, would also turn many patients away for a number of reasons. I've already cited one. If a patient could be healed by his own physician, he said, "Don't waste my time," or if a patient could not be treated, he also told him this. What he usually said was, "Your time has come and I cannot treat you, good-bye, God bless you." In another category of patients that he did not treat were patients who were there for some malingering cause or other. This may have had to do with faking the illness, either for their own private gain or for other reasons like being emissaries of the Brazilian Medical Association. He could quite quickly identify them and tell them they should go. He never charged, to my knowledge, during his lifetime for any treatment. He always had a full-time job to make a living.

To develop man as a complete healer, it's important that we come to know some of the inner workings of the Arigó type of phenomenon. We have Arigó's thesis before us and its claim that everything he did was programmed by a guide, by a voice, by a spirit entity. I must say that this is one of the great problems that challenge us. I, for example, cannot discount that thesis, because I cannot disprove it and, certainly, the weight of evidence, particularly in the area of medical diagnosis, leads me to believe that Arigó was working with intelligence far beyond that which one can possibly ascribe to him as an individual or even beyond that of any of the great medical diagnosticians whom I have known in my lifetime. Thus, one of the great problems that we have before us is not only to work with this kind of belief and practice, but we must try to find out whether this is indeed an aspect of mind as related to individual brain or whether this is mind unrelated to a specific brain in the true sense in which people who are spiritists teach and believe. Another possibility that arose while studying him, which we worked on most diligently, was the simple hypothesis that he was what one would call a true medical genius.

I don't know of any cases where Arigó treated animals. He treated human beings, and they are kind of invariant products of a certain type of production line. We may differ in individuality, but one has to admit that we more or less come out of the same factory, with minor flaws and imperfections which we call individuality. This invariance of biological reproduction is certainly a fact of medicine. Now, if we accept that premise, we must say that I have in me a whole blueprint of some thirty billion cells which is somehow reflected in a mental or parallel structure to the cell structure, and that you, my patient, also have this kind of thing. Somehow we get a cooperative effect between the two; you might call it resonance. But in any case it's very specific, so that if I have, as an example, a healthy heart, and I can somehow transfer my healthy field to your heart, then something is going to line up with mine and yours will get better, and so on. This, of course, can be supplemented by molecular deficiencies as I've indicated. If, for example, you do not produce a certain type of enzyme, the master plan here will somehow induce it in you. I know that's a nice hypothesis, but in the case of Arigó, it certainly didn't hold up. I think when you get to the case of manual healing that the hypothesis can be rigorously tested, and I do think it can be not only applied to work with humans but with animals, plants, etc., as has already been done.

This leads us to something suggesting that there may be common characteristics throughout all life forms. For example, water is common to all these elements. It may be that water is a very important carrier; it may, in fact, be a vehicle for this kind of blueprinting that I've indicated as occurring throughout all species that we really know; and it may be that the studying of the healing phenomena, particularly the manual aspect, will be one of the ways in which to assess the role of a substance like water in the life process.

Another hypothesis which we must consider, and I think we have to think way out in some of these things, is that other civilizations have existed elsewhere. Other civilizations may have reached this planet Earth with abilities that can direct/program/influence human beings, animals, weather cycles, etc., very much as we do with certain earthly types of telecommunication and teleaction equipment. Certainly I would not discount this and I think every effort must be made to rule this out as a possibility. The reason I bring this up is that our research team, while in Brazil, was treated by visitations of what is commonly called UFO's in current terminology. However, at least there was something we could see visually and something that we were able to photograph. The mere fact that they appeared in Arigó's proximity and that the area in which he lived was very active with this sort of thing, certainly means that we must first scientifically rule that out as a possibility or rule it in, whatever the case may be. We then come to my last hypothesis which must be considered. It is related to my first hypothesis, namely the parallel to the known genetic programing of cells that reproduces an organism and sets up all the instructions for developing it to a full-grown organism. There may be equivalent parallel genetically coded instructions which are not actual molecules but some kind of parallel mind effect, an isomorphic field, which I call psi plasma in one of my books, which may in fact give rise to the phenomena that we see in healing. I only put that out as a hypothesis, but it is something that should be tested.

I have one final general statement to make. As human beings, we're all interested in health and I think, ideally, all of us realize that, while we have to die, we would like to die in the best of health, and this really is probably the goal of medicine. Perhaps someday we'll get smart enough to determine and decide when we want to die, which I think is another goal of medicine. I don't think all these things should be left to chance. However, we cannot take the phenomena of healing in isolation from the total human scene in which we live. A sponsoring organization for this symposium is called The Academy of Parapsychology and Medicine. I, personally, would take my complete healer and place him in the category of medicine because I think perhaps medicine might have been that way if we had interpreted the ancient Egyptian records of medicine properly. We just seem to have lost sight of it and gotten off on a different track. The other word, parapsychology, gives us a whole different dimension of what is possible with humans, and here I speak particularly of telepathy, the ability of one mind to transfer information to another, and things called psychokinesis, which I believe exists, where a mind can influence or get into physical systems and do work at a distance, i.e., true action at a distance. There are many human experiences on record of people who somehow are able to perform the so-called phenomenon of astral projection, i.e., a separation of the so-called soul element from the molecular element of the body. This is the parapsychological aspect, so we have to work at all of them to prove them and bring them into our lives as we have already done with other more easily controlled things. If all these things do indeed exist, then we must take these as the matrix in which biological phenomenal feeling exists. However, I don't want anybody to think that the bounds which I have set for the complete healer by any means exhaust the possibilities. I think that some of the great religious literature of the world gives us more possibilities and, in true scientific sense, we must always keep these in mind while assessing what this phenomenon is.

# 11

## Spirit Hospitals

### Ann Dooley

*In 1966 the author, a former reporter, traveled to Brazil to investigate spiritism and psychic surgery. The result: a vivid account of an extraordinary challenge to the medical establishment in Brazil, and to the dominant Western mechanistic view of life.*

• • •

Among the many hundreds of charitable foundations established by Brazilian Spiritists, none presents a greater challenge to Western orthodoxy, particularly medicine, than the "Sanatorios Espiritas," or spirit hospitals for the mentally ill. Sometimes picturesquely described as hospitals for the healing of "illnesses of the soul," they deserve to be more widely known and studied. The work now being carried out within their confines by teams of unpaid administrators and healers may well herald the dawn of a revolutionized approach to the growing world scourge of mental illness which afflicts all societies, not least the affluent nations and the culturally proud.

Ironically, in a century technologically triumphant, when it is man's boast that even outer space is becoming increasingly submissive to their probing craft, soaring graphs of mind sickness silently mock man's empirical conquests.

Even in Britain's vaunted welfare state it is a sad fact that one woman in every nine and one man in every fourteen are likely to need hospital treatment for mental illness at some time in their lives. Indeed, mental patients occupy nearly half of all available hospital beds in the country, claiming a victim from one in every five families.

The size and complexity of the problem facing modern medicine is well exemplified in schizophrenia, commonest and one of the most tragic forms of insanity which appears to be on the increase. Its causes still baffle medical experts, yet it has been estimated that over 20 percent of all new admissions into mental hospitals come within this category and that over 50 percent of those remaining in hospital will be sufferers from one or other of the schizophrenic psychoses. Worse, it is the persecutor of youth, for some two thirds of the victims are claimed between the ages of 15 and 30— hence the term *dementia praecox* (early dementia), which was the official designation before the term "schizophrenia" became preferred.


## Porto Alegre

Against this backcloth, the medical challenge presented by Brazil's spirit hospitals is primarily reflected in the fact that orthodox medical treatments—such as electric shock, insulin comas, and tranquilizing drugs—administered by paid qualified medical staff, are supplemented with daily sessions of spiritual healing given by visiting teams of unpaid healer-mediums.

During my Brazilian visit I was privileged to visit four such hospitals, including the largest, oldest, and best known, situated in Porto Alegre, capital of Brazil's southernmost state, Rio Grande do Sul. This 42-year-old hospital, with the recent completion of a fine new seven-story wing, now boasts 600 beds.

It is a fascinating paradox that over the past century the remarkable growth of Spiritism in Brazil, a land which has often been described as "the brightest jewel in the Roman Catholic diadem," has been closely linked with the work of outstanding medical men, particularly homeopathic doctors favoring a combination of medical and spiritual therapies.

Samuel Hahnemann, founder of homeopathic medicine, was one of the first to recognize that many diseases are psychosomatic in origin, though his fame primarily rests upon his inoculation-type treatment of disease by minute doses of drugs that in a healthy person produce symptoms similar to the disease.

Although his theories have always been strongly challenged, Hahnemann, who died in 1843, was undoubtedly far ahead of his time in realizing that physical illness was all too frequently only the outward symptom of inner psychic and spiritual disease. In his introduction to *Organon* he stated: "Diseases will not cease to be spiritual dynamic derangements of our spiritual vital principle."

He believed that it was of vital importance, when seeking to cure physical ills by medical means, simultaneously to enlist the aid of spiritual therapy, aimed at making "the soul react in search of a cure." This heretical, dualistic approach to illness had a cogent appeal for Brazilians who temperamentally may be said to possess a national genius for combining mysticism and magic.

The historical accident of a friendly correspondence between Hahnemann and José Bonifácio de Andrada, a Brazilian statesman who later became revered as the "Patriarch" of his country's battle for independence from the chains of Portuguese colonialism, proved fateful.

José Bonifácio was a prominent member of one of the first groups of neo-Spiritualists in the Western world. And the fruitful consequences of his friendship with Hahnemann undoubtedly helped to shape the subsequent unique pattern and growth of Brazilian Spiritism in the ensuing century. Indeed, Pedro McGregor goes so far as to state that it was, in fact, through homeopathic medicine that Spiritism was able to penetrate so successfully in the Roman Catholic citadel of Brazil.

Certainly the views of these two disparately gifted men, particularly those of Hahnemann, strongly influenced the work of two doctors: a Portuguese, Joao Vicente Martins, and a Frenchman, Dr. Mure, who practiced in Brazil in the 1840's. McGregor tells us that these two men, who devoted their major professional efforts to treating the poor free of charge, supplemented their homeopathic medicine with "magnetic treatment." This consisted of passing their outstretched hands over the patient at a distance of three to four inches, as they prayed for God's help in the cure.

Hahnemann himself had privately recommended the use of the healing "pass" as an auxiliary aid to effecting cures. Such healing passes, of course, remain a basic feature of spiritual healing today in many countries.

And as the cornerstone of its astonishing success, Brazilian Spiritism also eventually adopted a slogan originally coined by Martins and Mure: God, Christ, and Charity.

During this period of the nineteenth century another medical doctor, later destined to become president of Brazil's State Assembly in 1880, was growing up. Widely admired for his courage, talents, and idealism, Dr. Adolfo Bezerra de Menezes, who has been dubbed the "Paul" of Brazilian Spiritism, also became president of the Brazilian Spiritist Federation.

Of his own chosen profession he wrote:

A true doctor does not have the right to finish his meal, to choose the time, to ask whether the call comes from near or far, on the hill or in the suburbs. The man who does not answer because he has visitors, because it is late at night, or because a client cannot pay, is not a doctor but a dealer in medicine, someone who works to collect interest on the capital invested in his schooling.

Appalled both by the social neglect in his day of the mentally ill and the medical ignorance concerning the causes of such illnesses, he was the first man in Brazil publicly to advocate a controversial alliance between spiritual and medical therapies in this field. He strongly held the view that the statement of the Nazarene that men could cure lunatics by casting out "the demons that possessed them," was no mere figure of speech.

Many years later the views of this good doctor were courageously translated into practice by the seven dedicated founders of Brazil's first Spiritist hospital in Porto Alegre.

Meanwhile Menezes, like many other of his colleagues, was decisively influenced by the theories of another famous nineteenth-century Frenchman, Léon Denizarth Hippolyte Rivail, better known to millions of readers today of his best-selling book *The Spirits' Book*—bible of Brazilian Spiritism —under his pen name "Allan Kardec."

Rivail, like Hahnemann and Menezes, was another pioneer bridge builder who refused to accept the increasing schism separating men of science and men of religion. He believed the time had come for the teaching of Christ to be complemented by science. In his book *Genesis* he affirmed: "Science and religion are two levers of human intelligence: one reveals the law of the material world and the other of the moral world. But both having the same principle—God— they cannot contradict one another."

Born in Lyons, but educated in Protestant Switzerland, Rivail, a successful schoolmaster and author of many educational textbooks still used in French schools, became an ardent psychic researcher. At heart a religious reformer who cherished a deep desire to create a greater degree of unity between the various Christian sects, he embarked upon a protracted experiment with two young amateur mediums, daughters of a friend. Through their mediumship, expressed in table-rapping and planchette-writing, he sought answers to a series of linked questions relating to fundamental problems of human life and the universe.

When these two-world communications had been going on twice a week for nearly two years, he confessed to his wife: "It is a curious thing, my conversations with the invisible intelligences have completely revolutionized my ideas and convictions."

His first issue of *The Spirits' Book* brought immediate success and Rivail founded the Parisian Society of Psychological Studies for the purpose of obtaining further information through a much wider circle of mediums. Weekly meetings were held in his home.

Similar associations were formed in other countries and eventually, from an extraordinary mass of spirit teachings culled from an ever-widening variety of sources over a period of fifteen years, Kardec collated, coordinated, and cross-checked an enlarged, revised edition. Published in 1857 it is this edition which became the recognized textbook of the school of Spiritualist philosophy which today counts its Spiritist followers in millions, particularly in Brazil.

The word "Spiritist" was coined by Kardec. He wrote:

Strictly speaking, everyone is a Spiritualist who believes that there is in him something more than matter, but it does not follow that he believes in the existence of spirits, or in their communication with the visible world. Instead, therefore, of the words Spiritual, Spiritualism, we employ to designate this latter belief by the words Spiritist, Spiritism, which by their form indicate their origin and radical meaning. We say, then, that the fundamental principle of the Spiritist theory, or Spiritism, is the relation of the material world with spirits, or the beings of the invisible world: and we designate the adherents of the Spiritist theory as Spiritists.

A convinced believer in reincarnation as a necessary road to eventual perfection, Rivail summed up the "moral teaching of the higher spirits" in the words of Christ: "Do unto others as you would that others should do unto you."

Four years after Rivail's death at his desk on March 31, 1869, a Brazilian group predominantly consisting of homeopathic doctors was founded under the name "Group Confucius." They published the first Portuguese translation of Kardec's main works: *The Spirits' Book, The Book of Mediums,* and the *Gospels According to Spiritism.* Their sales are estimated to have exceeded a million and a half copies. Members of the Confucius Group, inspired, like their forerunners, by a spirit of compassion and service, adopted the "Kardec" slogan: "Without Charity There Is No Salvation."

McGregor, himself a gifted spiritual healer, in his historical analysis of Brazilian Spiritism,* tells us:

> Charity, indeed, was to become the driving force behind Spiritism in Brazil. It took two main forms: spiritual healing and social assistance to the poor. . . . The spiritual healing practiced in Brazil took on an entirely different form to that known in England and the United States of America. In the first place, Brazilian mediums actually receive medical prescriptions which are dictated to them through a spirit guide. The medium is known as a healing-medium and the prescriptions are mostly homeopathic. The *Group Confucius* was the first to establish an organization dispensing a free service of homeopathic prescriptions given through healing-mediums on certain days of the week.
>
> Secondly, and perhaps more important, mediumship was exercised under the evangelical motto *Give freely what you have received freely* (Matthew 10:8, "Heal the sick, cleanse the lepers, raise the dead, cast out devils: freely ye have received, freely give."
>
> Here were no entrance fees, subscriptions, silver collections, or requests for financial help to defray costs. The majority of the practitioners were well-to-do pro-

* *The Moon and Two Mountains* by Pedro McGregor.

fessional people and the prescriptions really were fulfilled without any charge whatever.

These two factors, total and genuine lack of cost to the healed and treatment by specific medicaments "prescribed" by spirits rather than generalized healing through their aid, are the main differences between Brazilian and other branches of the movement.

He also assures us that the chief "spirit doctors" signing the prescriptions delivered through healing-mediums were believed to be none other than Doctors Bento Mure and Joao Vicente Martins, the two men who had first introduced homeopathy to Brazil.

Certainly as a pacesetter Brazilian Spiritism is unbeatable. Today the original free homeopathic service founded by the Group Confucius has burgeoned into over 1,700 social assistance establishments throughout the subcontinent. Even within the past two decades—on estimates backed both by official statistics and the dismayed numerical accounting of Roman Catholic authorities—the number of Brazilian Spiritists has increased tenfold from one million at the 1950 census to a present estimated ten million.

Official statistics also testify that while Roman Catholics numerically represent more than 90 percent of the country's population, Catholic social assistance establishments comprise only 42 percent of the total, yet Spiritists, officially listed as only 1.5 percent of the population, contribute no less than 36 percent of all such establishments. In the state of São Paulo alone, economically and industrially the most advanced in Brazil, Spiritist schools in the nine years from 1950 to 1958 increased from 9 to 43; hospitals from 1 to 13; shelters and orphanages from 11 to 47 and libraries from 59 to over 100.

### First Spirit Hospital

Resembling at night a giant jeweled starfish in concrete, sprawled over the incline of a low hill on the southern outskirts of the city, Porto Alegre's Spirit Hospital represents the impressive fulfillment of an impossible dream born in 1912—a dream shared by seven men of widely varying talents.

Members of an Allan Kardec Spiritist Society, these visionary initiators of Brazil's breakthrough in the field of mental therapy had become deeply distressed over the plight of psychopaths and the mentally ill in Brazil. Even as late as 1912 they were all too frequently condemned to a life sentence of confinement with little or no hope of cure.

Deeply impressed by the theories of Dr. Adolfo Bezerra de Menezes expressed in his treatise *Insanity from a Different Perspective*, they finally decided to put his ideas to the test.

The combined professional and practical experience of the seven men proved admirably effective for such a venture, for the group of friends comprised two medical doctors, two civil engineers, a senator, a civil servant, and an author-professor. After fourteen years of patient, arduous effort the dream eventually took shape in the modest form of a 36-bed hospital, officially opened on Christmas Day 1926 in the Avenida Cel. Lucas de Oliveira.

It was a proud moment for the seven hospital directors, especially for Dr. Oscar Pitthan, medical founder and principal instigator in 1912 of the nonprofit-making society which they had formed to back the unique project.

Dr. Pitthan's six colleagues were Dr. Henrique Inacio Domingues, a fellow physician; Dr. Augusto Pestana, a well-known civil engineer, ex-federal deputy and a former director of the State Railways; Dr. A. Verissimo de Mattos, civil engineer and a former director of the state's River Board; Col. Frederico A. Gomes da Silva, a leading official in the state's Finance Department; Algemiro Morem, a merchant; and Professor Alfonso Guerreiro Lima, author.

Generous help and encouragement was also given by Dona Maria de la Granje Mostadeiro. She not only made a gift of land and a considerable financial contribution toward the building of the first hospital, but also later became its first resident president. In 1934 the hospital had become so firmly established that the need to expand became correspondingly urgent. A larger piece of land was purchased in the suburb of Teresopolis, site of the present repeatedly enlarged building.

Building of the first wing of the present building on this site, which commands superb views of the Guaiba estuary, was started in 1940 and opened on February 2 of the following year.

The second wing was inaugurated on September 7, 1951. The third wing has now provided not only an additional 230 beds but also new workshops, service departments, and improved administrative facilities, including a modern laundry.

The hospital's visiting book contains many enthusiastic tributes, including the following testimony from Dr. Adauto Botelho, a leading psychiatrist and general director of the National Department for Assistance to the Insane, who visited the hospital on May 20, 1944. His official tribute might well be said to mark the "coming of age" of the hospital's acceptance by an important section of the medical profession.

Dr. Botelho wrote: "I have visited, with great pleasure and professional satisfaction, this spirit hospital about which I cannot conceal my praise of the medical work that is being done therein, as well as the humanitarian treatment to which it is dedicated.

"May the hospital at all times continue on these lines so that its directors may always merit the eulogies which they so justly deserve, practicing the profession of medicine in accordance with its highest precepts and exercising that charity which emanates from the heart and from true altruism."

Senhor Conrado Ferrari, septuagenarian president of the Porto Alegre Spirit Hospital, who made me warmly welcome, is unquestionably one of the busiest "retired" men in Brazil. Formerly the administrative chief of the state's Federal University in Porto Alegre, both he and his devoted wife, Ida, give so much of their time to the hospital that they not only spend most of their days in it but many nights too.

In February 1969 Senhor Ferrari told me in a letter: "Our hospital continues to progress with a daily average of 500 hospitalized patients. The two buildings that were being started when you were here are now finished, providing our hospital with a total capacity of 600 beds and extended services. A further wing is now being constructed to provide additional medical offices, dental, and administrative services."

The ever-increasing medical respect shown for the work done in this hospital is reflected in the fact that fifteen psychiatrists send their own patients to the hospital for treatment.

Senhor Ferrari told me that since the hospital does not receive a formal state subsidy, other than exemption from taxes as a registered charity and, in the past, an occasional subsidy from the government, the administrators have had to increase the provision for paying patients who now provide 75 percent of the hospital's income, the remainder being raised by individual donations, a welcome proportion of these coming from doctors.

But admittance of paying patients to meet soaring inflationary costs is *not* reflected in any special privileges for the more wealthy patients. Certainly the new wing includes additional bathroom suites, some of them also including a small sitting room, but in regard to all other aspects—medical treatment, food, and available communal amenities—there is no distinction made between paying and nonpaying patients. And Senhora Ferrari's days are largely occupied in running an extensive department, staffed by volunteer workers, to provide hospital and other clothing for needy patients.

The aims and principles of the hospital also remain unchanged:

1. The spirit hospital is the fruit of the idealism and endeavor of Rio Grande do Sul Spiritists. Its purpose is not to make profits but to shelter and to treat those who are spiritually unwell, giving them of the best at the lowest cost to themselves, welcoming and treating without payment those who cannot afford to contribute with the same tender care.
2. The personnel responsible for the maintenance of the establishment have no rights, but merely duties, and the directors are not paid for their services.
3. Neuropsychiatric patients are received without any distinction as to religion, race, or social position. All are given the same food and treatment, whether they be contributors or otherwise.
4. The Institution has its own medical staff but its doors are always open to specialists, duly authorized by the competent official department, wishing to hospitalize and attend their own patients therein.

Naturally my short stay in Porto Alegre which included visits on two successive days to the hospital provided inadequate opportunity for me to attempt to convey any analysis of its scope and significance. Neither am I qualified, as a mere laywoman, to comment upon the efficacy or otherwise of the therapies practiced within its walls. I can only tell you that the hospital facilities and amenities provided in this fine building—the treatment and patients' wards, recreation, psychotherapy facilities, and dining halls—impressed me favorably as bearing comparison with those I have seen over the years in two large mental hospitals I have had occasion to visit, one of them situated in the north of England, and the other in outer London.

On the day I lunched in Porto Alegre with members of the administrative staff in one of the hospital's spacious white-and-red-tiled dining halls, the spotless, well-equipped kitchens catered for a total of 239 resident patients and 115 hospital staff.

Our luncheon that day, as served to the patients also, consisted of a nourishing and palatable soup, a french beans and tomato salad, tasty meat stew served with well-cooked rice and the traditional Brazilian beans, a sweet from the tropical fruit mamao, and coffee.

During my tour of the hospital I garnered a mountain of statistics, ranging from patients' records to monthly hospital expenditure on psychiatric drugs—including glucose supplies, insulin injections, and neozine. But statistics alone, though apparently impressive in the case of this hospital, do not in themselves reflect the underlying importance of the work carried out in spirit hospitals.

Rather does this lie in two linked fields. The first I can best describe as a strong personal impression I gained in the four hospitals I visited, of an exceptional friendly warmth at every level—a feeling almost of a family-concern relationship linking patients and staff.

The second lies in the nature of the varied "psychic" and medical therapies used and the spiritual perspectives opened up by the achievements in this field—perspectives which would appear to challenge not only the present bounds of medical and psychiatric attitudes but also those of orthodox religion and exclusively materialist-based science.

During my visit to Porto Alegre I was privileged, with the help of my young translator, to have several long and frank conversations with the hospital president, Senhor Conrado Ferrari, a remarkable man I came both to like and respect profoundly.

Formerly a public functionary widely esteemed in varying responsible capacities—Senhor Ferrari was a former prefect of his native city—he has simultaneously also acted as unpaid president of the hospital since 1933, and edits the hospital's widely circulated monthly journal *Desobsessao*.

At the time of my visit the family links with the hospital's progress not only included Senhor Ferrari's wife, Ida, but also their son who is one of four full-time doctors employed at the hospital. Both Senhor Ferrari and his wife are modest about their own personal contribution to the hospital's astonishing success, emphasizing that this rests upon the firm foundation of team cooperation at every level combined with broad-based tolerance and acceptance of varying viewpoints and specializations.

And undoubtedly the best tribute to the work of the pioneering hospital can be found in the following frank answers given by Senhor Ferrari—and other doctors and psychiatrists associated directly and indirectly with the hospital—to a questionnaire I submitted for answers and translation.

Here are Senhor Ferrari's answers to questions I put to him.

*Q. 1. Are all kinds of mental illness treated, for example, paranoia, schizophrenia, etc.?*

*Answer:* In this hospital we treat all types of mental nervous diseases, including alcoholism and drug addiction. Regarding procedure, when a patient is admitted he is first interviewed by a psychiatrist on the day of arrival and the latter makes an initial diagnosis in his written report. The patient is also given a medical examination by the doctor in charge of the clinics and an electrocardiogram analysis. The doctor recommends suitable treatment, for example, electric shock treatment or insulin coma. An ophthalmologist carries out eye examinations and the hospital laboratory carries out all necessary tests requested by the doctor. Medical treatment commences immediately. Another psychiatrist carries out a second interview and submits a separate report, confirming or otherwise the initial diagnosis.

Similar interviews and examinations are carried out periodically during the patient's stay in the hospital, and full records of medical and psychiatric treatment are preserved in the hospital's files as well as details of daily treatment and drugs.

Simultaneously, and with the consent of the patient and relatives, healing passes are daily given by healing-mediums. There is a team of visiting mediums for every day of the week. In cases where obsession is indicated, absent healing is administered—i.e., the patient is not present—at evening seances organized twice weekly by the administration within the hospital. Absent healing is also given at separate sessions, when requested, to patients outside the hospital, sometimes in neighboring countries, for example, Argentina. Distance presents no difficulty. For absent-healing experiments we only require the name and address of the patient.

*Q. 2. Is mental illness increasing in Brazil? If so, why?*

*Answer:* In Brazil, as in the rest of the world, mental illness is increasing. Doctors say this is due to present emotional pressures such as the possibility of total war, following two world wars and worldwide economic problems. Sexual problems, alcoholism, and drug addiction are other major factors.

Spiritists, however, believe the primary cause arises from the fact that we are at present living in a difficult period of transition prior to a new era which will offer happier prospects for those who survive the impending holocaust. In other words, we are suffering the birth-pangs which precede every New Age, for I believe we are living in the apocalyptic period predicted by St. John.

*Q. 3. How do doctors regard "obsession" cases?*

*Answer:* Though some doctors accept the phenomenon of obsession, professionally they prefer to ignore it, for we believe they are afraid of criticism from their medical association, which here, as in other parts of the world, holds orthodox views. The doctors who work at our hospital are not Spiritualists, so we could not get their views on obsession. Such obsessional phenomena as clairvoyance, hearing voices, and so on are regarded by them as mere "hallucinations."

The practice of black magic, a grave problem in Brazil, is definitely a factor in obsession cases. Revenge is another prevalent Karmic cause. We treat some terrible cases of really conscienceless "obsessing" entities, but after we explain through a medium the consequences to themselves if they continue to persecute their living victims, we can make them become afraid. When this happens, more evolved spirits can take them in hand and arrange treatment in spirit hospitals on the other side.

In obsession treatments the difference in the patient can be seen by the following day. As Spiritists we are convinced that our high percentage of successful treatments at this hospital is due to this work, though the doctors, of course, naturally attribute such cures to their own medical treatments. We are content to leave it at that.

*Q. 4. Is your percentage of relapses higher or lower than the norm for Brazil?*

*Answer:* We do not have statistics on relapses. From the psychiatric standpoint every "schizophrenic" is subject to periodic returns to the hospital. Remissions in these cases are rare. As Spiritists we regard many of the patients classified by doctors as "schizophrenic" as being "obsessional" cases. These are treated mediumistically by removing the obsessors as I have already described. It must be said, however, that if the patient does not then play *his* part in consolidating the healing carried out, i.e., by developing his psychic powers if he is a budding medium, or by mending his ways if the obsession has been caused by bad habits, or learning to forgive his enemies, then he may again relapse, for the healing of obsession depends ultimately *more* upon the patient himself than those who seek to help him. We only carry out emergency treatment.

*Q. 5. Are Spiritist hospitals greatly at a disadvantage compared with orthodox mental hospitals in regard to state subsidies?*

*Answer:* Our hospital has received governmental subsidies, but not regularly. It has primarily depended on the men who are in government, though we believe there is no actual ban against us for being a Spiritist institution. Of course it is natural that in Brazil, where the majority of the population declare themselves Catholic, the hospitals headed by priests and nuns should receive larger subsidies than we do.

*Q. 6. Can you give instances of persecution of extreme prejudice (a) from doctors, (b) the state, (c) the Roman Catholic Church, past or present?*

*Answer:* We have not been subject to persecution against the hospital by any of the above-named, although doctors were prejudiced about a Spiritist organization actually building a hosptial, and priests have warned their followers against the heresy of Spiritism.

Today the spirit hospital in Porto Alegre is respected by all types of Brazilian medical institutions because of its progress and improved technical and nursing conditions, though there remains a certain dislike of the name "Spirit." Many doctors have urged the need to change this name as a means of securing better support from the medical profession. We have not done so because we have gained the respect of the public, as well as respect in medical and governmental circles, despite the title and we do not want to pander to unjust prejudice.

*Q. 7. Can present teamwork between mediums and doctors in spirit hospitals be improved?*

*Answer:* We would like to emulate the example set by Dr. Inacio Ferreira, head of the Uberaba Spirit Hospital. He is a doctor *and* a Spiritist. Young people are being prepared for such work, for we try to enlist their interest and give them the opportunity to work as interns in our hospital. We certainly hope at some future date to have a medical team who could accept medical *and* mediumistic therapeutics, both being applied by doctors. This won't be easy to achieve since the materialist and orthodox views at present held in universities and medical associations present obstacles and make doctors reluctant openly to declare themselves Spiritists. Meanwhile there are encouraging signs. Our hospital is now a big organization and the only mental hospital in this state that receives patients coming from other doctors. The other hospitals only accept patients who are treated by their own doctors. This situation inevitably causes an encouraging number of doctors to be associated with our organization.

*Q. 8. Do you think that spirit hospitals have a permanent place in (a) Brazilian medicine, (b) world medicine?*

*Answer:* Public opinion has changed very much in relation to this hospital. In the early years there was a certain prejudice which caused many people to look askance at becoming resident patients. But with the passing of time and because of the good treatment patients receive in the hospital, the situation has improved. Today there are many who *prefer* the treatment received in this hospital and indeed a considerable number seek us out just *because* of our healer-mediums. To sum up I would say that prejudice is exceptional, mainly confined to people who don't think for themselves.

I also think the hospital has won a definite place not only in Brazil but also in the world of medicine. We employ medical methods that bear comparison with those employed in any civilized country. As Spiritists we also carry out spiritual therapies, but in doing so we endeavor not to create any difficulties for the doctors, so there is perfect harmony. Our doctors do not interfere in the mediumistic service, and the mediums don't interfere in the medical area.

*Q. 9. Would you welcome visiting research teams of doctors, psychiatrists, psychic researchers, etc. from other countries?*

*Answer:* For our part, as Spiritists, medical teams or researchers coming from other countries would be welcomed to study and observe the methods used in our hospital. I cannot answer for our head doctor who is responsible to the relevant government ministry for the hospital's performance.

In regard to our work on "obsession cases" we have attended emergency cases coming from Argentina and other countries, including the United States. We have done what we could and according to information received later the effects were beneficial.

Within three months of my return to England from Brazil in 1967 Senhor Ferrari very kindly sent to me the views of four leading psychiatrists in the state of Rio Grande do Sul who had studied copies of the questionnaire I had formulated. All gave permission for publication of their views.

The men concerned are Dr. Ivo Castilhos Puignau, a specialist in psychosomatic illnesses; Dr. Nelson Aspesi, neurologist, assistant of the Chair of Neurology at the School of Medicine at the Federal University of Rio Grande do Sul (Dr. Aspesi is also president of the state's "Psychiatric Neurologist and Neurosurgery Society"); Dr. José Theobaldo Diefenthaeler, described by Senhor Ferrari as: "One of the leading psychiatrists in Porto Alegre. Not a Spiritist"; and Dr. Nelson Lemos, described as a psychiatrist of the orthodox school.

All the above had been treating their own patients at the Porto Alegre hospital over periods ranging from five to eight years.

All answered "Yes" to my question: "Has the spirit hospital given you the necessary facilities, conditions, nursing, and collaboration to enable you to treat patients admitted into the hospital?"

Dr. Puignau described the spirit hospital as "the best

hospital in the city and one of the best in Brazil, offering good conditions for work not only in respect to the atmosphere but also as regards the nursing staff."

Dr. José Theobaldo Diefenthaeler described it as "an excellent psychiatric hospital within its condition of a 'monoblock house' and large hospital."

In answer to a follow-up question: "How does it compare with similar Brazilian institutions?" Dr. Puignau replied: "It can be compared with the best ones." Dr. Aspesi said: "I have no opinion." Dr. Diefenthaeler said he had incorporated his answer in the foregoing reply quoted, while Dr. Nelson Lemos stated: "Yes. It depends on the patient's relatives' criteria. It is valuable according to the faith of relatives and patients."

Regarding spiritual assistance given to many patients by visiting teams of mediums, all four doctors said they were aware of this and did not object since it was not "imposed" by the hospital as a condition of hospitalization.

Dr. Puignau commented: "I not only know, but I constantly request spiritual assistance for those patients who need it." In regard to cases of "obsession" he declared: "In some cases, after passing through the hands of well-known colleagues I have observed that the cases were of 'obsession,' or, as they would say, to use the words of the Gospel, 'possessed,' 'mad,' and that [they] were healed by mediumistic development and by the treatment of the patient himself."

Dr. Aspesi stated he did not have "enough facts scientifically to say whether it is useful or not."

Dr. Lemos described spiritual treatment as: "Useful or harmful, depending on the relatives' disposition to accept or reject the assistance, and the same applies to patients."

Asked to comment on whether there was a favorable or unfavorable difference in the percentage of cures and positive improvements in patients, as between the spirit hospital and other mental hospitals, three of the psychiatrists said they had not enough data to pass an opinion. Two of these added the comment that they believed the results were similar.

Dr. Puignau wrote: "The percentage of healings or improvements (for the Spiritist hospital) is larger than in other similar institutions."

Asked if they would care to present a critique as to the methods followed in spirit hospitals, the psychiatrists answered as follows:

Dr. Puignau: "Methods depend on the doctor. The spirit

hospital presents good facilities, though it does not have everything that is necessary, for the building is not yet finished. [The new wing has since come into operation—author.] I think time will change for the better everything that exists.

"As to the methods employed by myself, they are different in each case, using the therapeutics described in the Gospel and the resources of the Reincarnation Law as well as the 'deobsession' processes. There are many other resources but I do not use them. It is clear that psychotherapy and hypnosis are very valuable in the cure of unbalanced human beings."

Dr. Puignau added the following comments: "I believe that the patients can be divided into two groups: those who are psychically injured, for whom nothing else can be done, and those who are partially injured or are heading for injuries. The latter group could be greatly helped by medical science if the problems of madness could be seen from a new viewpoint, say that of Dr. Bezerra de Menezes, a marvelous Brazilian who opened up new horizons in spiritual therapy.

"However, the sick man and child are considered in an isolated context, and never as they have lived. In their former lives are to be found the real causes of the major infirmities, also of their spiritual enemies.

"The 'fathers' of modern psychiatry, not realizing these facts or understanding mediumistic phenomena, could only do as they have done.

"It is necessary to open up vistas in the direction of the spiritual. Only atheists have the right to ignore the Gospel and biblical facts, from Nebuchadnezzar to Babylon. Christians must research into the prophetic dreams (clairvoyance?) of Joseph in Egypt to supernormal phenomena in the Gospels. Do not the latter speak of the 'spirit' descended upon the crowd when thousands started to speak in different languages? An atheist would say 'madness,' but why not take a fresh look at all existing theories. Not to do so is to be unscientific."

Dr. Aspesi wrote: "As a neurologist I have had opportunity to use all my knowledge, but I would like, if possible, to see more opportunities for secondary examinations." He concludes his answers with the comment: "In life and in medicine, love and security are backgrounds of basic value which should always be well cemented."

Similarly Dr. Diefenthaeler contented himself with stating: "I would only like to emphasize that mental patients are only human beings, needing, above all, help, love, comfort, and understanding."

Dr. Lemos said he would like to see: "More emphasis placed on ambient therapy with attendants skilled in talking to the patients and able to win a response."

## A Medical Prophet?

And in this highly controversial field, Brazil has found an eloquent advocate. Since it is the voice of a medically qualified "prophet," it cannot long go totally ignored, for Dr. Inacio Ferreira, author of *New Ways of Medicine* (two volumes) and *Psychiatry Face to Face with Reincarnation*, is well qualified to make his challenge. His fourteen years' medical training is backed with thirty-five years of psychiatric field experience in the treatment of mental illness.

This gentle-voiced, gray-haired, scholar-psychiatrist, who has his own modest country town practice as a specialist in nervous diseases, has at considerable cost to his own health and personal pocket been for many years the unpaid medical director of Uberaba's small 40-bed spirit hospital.

I was told that in the past fourteen years he had never had a holiday away from the town where he attends the hospital daily. Now, urgent health considerations have forced him to take Saturdays off. He generally spends them in a little cottage in the nearby countryside.

When I visited him in this remote town five hours' flying distance from Rio in midwest Brazil, he told me of the prejudice he had to surmount when he began his association with the hospital. "No doctors wanted to work in them," he told me, "because Spiritists faced much ignorant persecution. I myself wasn't keen at the commencement, but I became increasingly impressed." He has also publicly stated: "In the past I laughed at the idea of mediums with no medical training, and some of them with little education of any kind, being able to heal cases that we doctors could not. Now, after studying this subject thoroughly, I bow before these untutored healers, for I have become convinced that such people can benefit 80 percent of the mental illness that medicine fails to understand and refuses to study in a wider context."

He qualified this viewpoint by stressing that when the

cause of mental illness is spiritual, it is *not* schizophrenic. Emphasizing that it needs much experience and knowledge to be able to distinguish the spiritual from the material in mental illness, he told me: "In cases of true schizophrenia only 5 percent get cured because medicine doesn't know the cause of this illness."

In the rural districts of the vast plain which surrounds Uberaba there is much poverty, and since the kindliness of this dedicated doctor is widely known, he is sent tragic cases of the homeless and the ill picked up in desperate states by the police. Since at the time I visited him, Dr. Ferreira had no other medical help and was primarily interested in patients who could be helped by a combination of medical and spiritual therapies (he can call upon the services of twenty to thirty visiting mediums who visit the hospital in daily groups), he was providing temporary shelter to such cases. When necessary he arranges their eventual transfers to orthodox hospitals.

He told me it was only within the past few years that he had been forced to ask any hospitalized patient for any payment. He said sadly: "Now I have to take some paying patients into the hospital though I still manage to accommodate one-third of the total free of any charge, the remainder paying what they can afford."

In contrast to such outstandingly well-equipped spirit hospitals as the one I have described in Porto Alegre, Dr. Ferreira's "Sanatorio Espirita de Uberaba" was pitifully ill-equipped. Although some of the accommodation I was shown which housed the more violent inmates was disturbingly primitive, there was eloquent evidence from the patients of a reciprocal affection and trust. Wherever we went they flocked round this tired benign man like children besieging a loved father.

In the modest-sized, paint-peeling bungalow which is his home a short distance away from the hospital, the library is its chief glory, and much-loved cats the princelings. Every moment he can wrest from his onerous professional responsibilities is spent at his desk where he has embarked on the third volume of his controversial contribution to medical literature.

Dr. Ferreira believes that mental illnesses are frequently Karmic in origin, particularly cases of obsession. In his books he backs this view with an array of startling case histories. I cannot comment on their medical soundness, nor does my scant knowledge of the riddles of reincarnation enable me to pass any judgment for or against the theory. All I can tell you is that the handful of cases I have been privileged to read in translations present formidable social and philosophic implications, for they seem to indicate that we cannot hope effectively to cope even with the psychiatric problems of alcoholism or crimes of violence, unless we begin to take at least a closer look at the seemingly fantastic possibility that—in Dr. Ferreira's words—"reincarnation provides the key."

He stresses: "The basics of all life is the psychic life. In order that medicine should really fulfill its mission it must extend the battle to psychic *causes*. It must study the laws of spiritual immortality and reincarnation." He also warns that since in many cases psychic and organic illnesses are indissolubly linked, there is increasingly a need to "ally psychic treatment to organic treatment." In this view he certainly is *not* alone.

Of alcoholism he writes: "It makes a hell of everyone's life associated with the victim but science cannot give direct help because it has not found the cause *behind* alcoholism. Materialism! Materialism! They overlook *psychic* heredity with all its vices and intoxication of the spirit. They blame present environment and bad friends in this life, but the real causes lie deeper. They do not realize they can even be embedded in the past. They do not realize that psychic injuries from the past can reflect in pathological tendencies and effects."

Like his friend Senhor Conrado Ferrari, Dr. Ferreira is in possession of many tragic histories which he, too, believes point to Other Side vendettas carried out against the living by obsessing "entities" in revenge for injuries said to have been inflicted in past incarnations.

Both men would welcome visits by open-minded medical men and scientific researchers, particularly from England and the United States, to study the work now being carried out in spirit hospitals, frequently under appalling difficulties. To this I add my own insignificant plea, for no matter how wide present divergences of opinion and treatment techniques, I am convinced that such friendly interchanges would also prove mutually beneficial.

Today they are lone voices. Many would dismiss them

contemptuously as the lone voices of deluded cranks yet . . . they are not entirely alone, for even in the United States, England, and Ireland, a tiny handful of similarly courageous trailblazers have already produced significant testaments which it might be unwise to continue to ignore.

# PART TWO

❧❧❧❧❧❧❧❧❧❧❧❧

# ENERGY AND HEALING

Knowledge of our intimate relationship to cosmic energies and our universe demands a revolutionary change in attitudes about the nature of man and the basic requirements in healing.

# 12

# The Western Physician and Acupuncture

## *William A. McGarey*

*William A. McGarey, the medical director of the Association for Research and Englightenment clinic in Phoenix, in a talk given to The Academy of Parapsychology and Medicine, explores the mysteries of acupunture, the role and attitude of the physician in Chinese medicine, and discusses the Eastern impact on Western medicine.*

• • •

Many of you in this audience are of Oriental extraction and undoubtedly know more of the philosophy and background of acupuncture than I do. Born in the West and brought up under traditional Western concepts, I went to medical school at the University of Cincinnati, practiced medicine in Ohio and Arizona for twenty-five years, and I am only beginning to understand this Oriental philosophy. Perhaps, having done this, I can serve as a bridge to understanding the relationships between the East and the West. Because, you see, there is a significant difference between the manner in which we in the Western world have grown accustomed to looking at the human body and its functions and the manner in which the Oriental brought up in the traditional style has come to understand the body. . . .

In talking about the Western physician and acupuncture, I suppose it would be fair to say that since the famous postoperative needling of James Reston's distended abdomen in China and his subsequent immediate recovery,[1] acupuncture has been a highly stimulating subject in the minds and in the imaginations of both physicians and laymen here in the United States. It is indeed a very fascinating philosophical question to ask why such an event should trigger this kind of response when acupuncture has been used in the Far East for at least 5,000 years. Perhaps it can be attributed to the fact that since the great proletarian cultural revolution in China, their physicians reportedly have performed 400,000 operations under acupuncture anesthesia. That's a lot of operations!

It could be that [former] President Nixon's visit to China was a precipitating factor, but to those of us who are closely watching the events as they transpire, it seems that there were many factors operative which played a part in bringing to the American mind the reality of acupuncture therapy and acupuncture anesthesia.

One of the fascinating stories that comes to us out of mainland China deals with the way in which the acupuncturists at one point in time brought the Red Revolutionary Army out of a very serious predicament. Mao Tse-tung suddenly found that his troops in western China were coming down with malaria, and reportedly he had no Atabrine and no quinine to combat the infection. The situation was rapidly becoming critical, when some unknown but historically significant aide informed him that his acupuncturist could treat malaria. Thinking in terms of our Western tradition, it seems very strange to us that such could possibly be the case, because we don't think in terms of curing an infestation of the bloodstream, such as malaria, by puncturing the skin of the body with needles. However, Mao ordered the therapist to go to work immediately. The results are part of our recent history of the Far East. The troops were returned to full duty within three days, and the revolution progressed.

Mao subsequently ordered the restoration of this ancient folk medicine to full honor, and all doctors were directed to study it, to use it, and to try to understand it. Recent publications [2,3] from mainland China are extensive in their discussion of anesthesia, using acupuncture only as a means of anesthesia, using acupuncture only as a means of pain control. Those from the Peking Tuberculosis Research Institute, for instance, are very interesting.

The first successes in pulmonary resection using this type of anesthesia came about in 1965. The following year the cultural revolution moved things forward in a big way. An intense study toward better acupuncture anesthetic techniques was begun.

In the first procedures, there were as many as forty needles used on a patient's limbs, and four different assistants were needed to keep the needles twirling sufficiently in order to bring about the anesthesia. There was then a review of techniques and procedures, and this showed the investigators that fewer needles were actually needed. According to the story, the positive factors were gradually identified—those which were brought into play on the human organism to resist external stimuli so the pain would be alleviated or stopped altogether. A series of observations and experiments brought the number of needles down to sixteen. Results were about the same. Further work reduced them to twelve.

After six months of further work they found only two needles were necessary, both on the forearm. Next, being a rather persistent bunch—and you have to give them credit for that—the investigators explored the possibility of bringing about anesthesia in a lung operation through the use of a single needle. As it happens, there is a point a third of the way from the wrist to the elbow on the outer aspect of the forearms which, according to ancient medical literature, is effective in controlling pain. At the same level, but on the inner aspect of the forearm, there is another point which supposedly has been effective in producing sedation. Both are considered necessary in a lung operation to control the pain as well as sedation. So, they used one needle only, inserting it at one point and directing it through the arm (a so-called deep insertion) to touch the other point.

Much work and many trials later, the first operation performed with this technique came about in June of 1970. Over one hundred similar lung operations have been performed since that time. They admit to certain problems still unsolved, but they claim the major hurdles have been overcome.

These are indeed amazing stories, and they come dangerously close to uprooting many of the concepts we have held dear for many generations here in the West. In order to get things into clear perspective, I would think that we, as Western physicians, should look closely at our goals and our objectives in the practice of medicine when we consider acupuncture as a therapy or as an anesthetic agent. A therapeutic tool that has reportedly cared for 90 percent of the ills of a country as populous as mainland China is not something to be lightly discarded. The reports of therapeutic advances that have come out of China also cannot be set aside without falling short on our traditional responsibility to the one individual who makes it possible for us to practice medicine, and that is the patient himself.

What are our goals, then, and our objectives as we look at acupuncture? I suppose we could ask the same question in looking at any therapeutic technique.

Recently (1972), I heard Dr. Arthur Schwartz,[4] who is the Biological Research director at Barrow Neurological Institute in Phoenix, give a talk on the need for a research approach to acupuncture. He rather clearly pointed out the distinction between the physician who daily treats the patient and the scientist who backs up the total effort in annotating data, clarifying issues, developing new modalities of therapy and new techniques, and generally building a solid foundation under what we attempt to do. We need, however, to keep in mind continually the part that the practicing physician can play in the total research effort.

Arthur Sackler,[5] who is the international publisher of *Medical Tribune*, is a psychiatrist and a rather competent observer of the medical scene, I would think. He recently commented that good clinical observation can be as valid as experimental observations. It requires a degree of humility, he went on to say, and a sensitivity to a state of mind that Albert Einstein found very essential to his many discoveries. Einstein called this "being sympathetically in touch wih experience." Perhaps we as physicians, choosing as our goal the healing of the patient, may find our proper place in the field of medicine to be just that—being sympathetically in touch with our experience as we use our powers of observation daily, as we remain humble and open-minded, and as we accept the assistance the scientific community can offer us—whether we are working with acupuncture or any therapy that may come to our attention.

The physician, you see, is essentially a therapist if he holds to his goal of seeking to cure his patient, and all diagnostic procedures merely build a foundation under his attempt to bring the ailing body back to health. It is an interesting fact that every physician as a therapist, as an artist in his own field, is always working beyond the scientific validation. We are always seeking, exploring new ways of healing the sick, and perfecting therapies at a clinical level long before we have any scientific understanding of just how this thing really works. We don't know how aspirin works, yet we use it in a very artistic manner sometimes. We still use the bedside manner in a healing way even in these advanced days. We still instill hope in the patient and a reason for living even though we don't begin to know how to weigh either item or to know how they may be given from one person to another.

The artist in any field of endeavor must always ask questions. He must always look for answers and attempt to express himself creatively, finding himself always in the vanguard of the fact finders of his community. The physician, in my opinion, is no exception to this rule.

Perhaps, then, it is not only our responsibility but also our challenge to stay sensitive to what is bringing a healing of the body to our patients, to utilize what we find and perfect it at a clinical level utilizing what Sackler calls a good, clinical, valid observation. And, as we bring a degree of healing to our patients, we will give our colleagues in the laboratories enough puzzles to solve that the scientific aspects of medicine may once again resume alongside of, instead of in front of, the art of practicing medicine.

After a year's exposure to the bombardment of articles and books about acupuncture, with trips to the Orient by eminent physicians and their reports to the public, to the President and to the AMA about this philosophy, most physicians probably know the basics of acupuncture. I think it is valid to state that acupuncture is a philosophy rather than a science. The human being was placed in the center of things by the Oriental philosophers some 5,000 years ago. Man was considered to be a microcosm in the macrocosm so to speak—a product of the Tao, which is the originator of all things, and thus he was seen as a voyager in life. He was subject to the forces and the energies that not only surround him but are also within him.

Thus, we see why the Chinese have for thousands of years based their medical concepts, their diagnoses, and their therapy on a philosophy rather than upon scientifically derived data, as we have, in a sense, done here in the Western world. In the Orient, man is seen to be a creation in which the forces of Yin and Yang are operative, creating a constant struggle in the human organism, just as in nature, between opposing and yet unifying forces. The Oriental physician sees good health as a proper balance between these forces and bad health coming from a disturbing imbalance.

The Taoistic principle of Yin and Yang finds its counterpart in the West in the "duality" of man. We find the constant balancing processes that go on between the sympathetic and parasympathetic nervous system, the male and the female hormonal balances, the positive and the negative in our lives, the right- or left-handedness, the introvert and the extrovert, the active and the passive, the acid and the alkaline balance in the body, the assimilation of foods and the elimination of wastes. All of these, in a sense, are a manner in the West of looking at that same principle as the Yin and Yang.

It is difficult to understand the Eastern medical thought without using this principle of duality as an underlying foundation for all considerations. Thus, the twelve meridians, or lines of force, on the skin of the human body are considered to be externalizations of internal functioning organs and are classified as six Yin and six Yang meridians. I say six here, because there are six of each, and yet two of them, the so-called pericardium and the triple warmer, are not essentially reflections of organs as are the rest.

The functions that have to do with assimilation and excretion (the stomach, the gall bladder, the small and large intestines, and the bladder) are the Yang organs, while those that are constantly functioning in the body (the liver, the heart, the kidneys, spleen, and lungs) are the Yin organs. Those that are active in the Yin sense are solid organs, and in the Chinese consideration of things have their origin in the earth. The earth then becomes Yin in nature.

The other meridians are essentially hollow organs and are thought to have their beginnings in the heavens. One finds then that the heavens are Yang in nature. Yang becomes active in all of the life processes, and Yin becomes passive. The front of the body is Yin, and the back of the body is Yang.

Rules of acupuncture are numerous and are the laws that must be observed. One understands as he studies this therapeutic art that each meridian has a chronological position which it always occupies as the life force flows through the body or through the twelve meridians. In the philosophy of acupuncture, the life force, or Qi, as it is called there, flows first at one o'clock A.M. through the lung meridian for two hours and then passes on to the large intestine meridian.

It flows in order through the stomach and then through each of the remaining twelve meridians during every twenty-four hour period.

Each meridian has a point which is known as the point of tonification. Disease comes to the human body when a meridian is either choked up with energy or deficient in it. When it is deficient, the point of tonification can be stimulated, and the abnormality of that meridian can be partially or completely corrected. Likewise, when there is too much energy in a meridian, the point of sedation can be needled and the condition corrected.

There are many laws of relationship between the meridians, which, according to traditional Oriental medicine, must be observed. There is the extensive law of the five elements: wood, water, fire, earth, and metal. All of Oriental medicine, in a sense, revolves around these five elements as it involves the utilization of the concept of the flow of Qi and the balance between Yang and Yin.

Along the course of these twelve meridians, there are some 365 points traditionally distributed on each side of the body. The 365, of course, represent the number of days in the year, and we must remember that each of the laws of acupuncture follows some manifestation of life outside the body. The points have different importance and different uses, and more points are constantly being discovered, not only in mainland China but also in Russia and in some of the Western countries. I was told in Russia that Adamenko and others had identified a thousand points in the human body, and there are perhaps even more. In China, points on the nose, in the neck, and in the ear have allowed the anesthesia techniques to be more sensitively used than formerly, so that much of their anesthesia today is by stimulation of points on the nose, the face, and the ear.

Among the techniques of traditional Oriental medicine, one of the most difficult to understand and to use is that of pulse diagnosis. I understand that many of the Oriental physicians do not use this particular methodology of diagnosis; they say it takes too long to perfect. Nevertheless, it has been in use for literally thousands of years, at least since the writing of *The Yellow Emperor's Classic of Internal Medicine*.[6]

In pulse diagnosis, as it is described in ancient techniques, the index, middle, and ring fingers are used, and all three are placed on the radial artery of the left wrist with the middle finger closest to the radial styloid. One palpates with

each finger, both superficially and deeply. This gives six
positions, and thus one may determine the quality of six
meridians. Using the same procedure on the right wrist,
the other six meridians are identified and evaluated.

Since the Yang meridians reside in the heavens, the Yang
meridians are identified on the surface, because that's the
highest point. Then you feel deeply in the tissues, and you
palpate the Yin meridians.

Many different kinds of pulses have been described over
the centuries. In some texts there are twenty-eight different
kinds of pulses defined—empty pulses, full-bounding pulses,
stringy pulses, etc., but it is universally agreed that it is a
very difficult technique to learn and to use.

Having always felt my patients for their pulses and
listened to their hearts, I find it not too difficult to feel for a
pulse diagnosis. One way I have accomplished it is when the
patients sit on the end of the examining table I take their
wrists and get them to relax their forearms. Then I palpate
the radial pulse with both fingers. I am not as rapid as some
of the doctors I have observed and learned from, but I have
reached the point where I believe that occasionally, at least,
I can determine the quality of some of the pulses.

I would add here that I think a physician who has had
training in a medical or osteopathic school and who has had
a number of years of practice has a great advantage over the
beginner who goes into a school of acupuncture in the Far
East, because we are accustomed to using all our facilities in
observing and understanding the patient and in seeing what is
wrong. So to adapt ourselves to the idea of evaluating the
patient in another manner does not become too difficult.

In actual therapy, the acupuncture points are stimulated
with a needle. The needles are very fine and very sharp
(unless they are not cared for properly, in which case they
get dull and have to be thrown away), and they should be
very sensitively placed in the skin. The actual point that is
sought is found as a very small, sometimes palpable mass,
sometimes deep but more often superficially located in the
subcutaneous tissues. A deep, but rather minimal, aching
sensation is often felt when the needle is properly placed. If
you are over forty or fifty, you can examine your own bodies
and find many of the acupuncture points, and I might add
here that many of the so-called trigger points that we have
known about for years and years are also acupuncture points.
They are felt as little lymphatic nodules under the skin, and

in my research with the Cayce material, I found that Edgar Cayce said that the lymphatic tissue has a much closer relationship to the nervous system than we presently understand. It may be that this is a very factual thing, because we have not yet really understood how a needle or an electric current or pressure or heat applied to these points can bring about a healing of the human body.

Of course, it would be incomplete to talk about acupuncture without mentioning moxibustion, since in some parts of the world moxibustion is more commonly used than treatment with needles. This procedure is the burning of an herb, either on the skin or close to it, perhaps on the hilt of the needle itself. Some points of the body are not to be treated by moxibustion and must be identified by the practitioner. The herb is usually mugwort, which is known botanically as *Artemisia vulgaris*. In the United States there is a related *Artemisia absinthium* which is called wormwood, but this is not the usual herb that the acupuncturists prefer.

These two modalities of treatment are basically related, and some doctors use moxibustion at one time and acupuncture at another. But they are somewhat different in their effect on the body, and they are used according to certain rules or, I think, according to the artistic inclinations of the practitioner himself. I was talking with one of the doctors here and he said that he did not understand the treatments that were used for diarrhea the way they were explained by one of the doctors at a symposium we had in Phoenix. Then he read another description, and the points that were used for diarrhea were completely different.

If you study the suggestions in the various textbooks as to what each point may do, you come to the conclusion that there are a multitude of points that one might use. Perhaps we may find that it is the feeling of the doctor himself that adds some sort of input to the needle and brings about a healing—a sort of coupled therapeutic effect.

We talked about this at and before our meeting here at Stanford—the fact that people put out an energy, and this energy may in some way combine with the needle that is used or the moxibustion.

One of the most vital concepts to be brought to the awareness of the Western physician is that of the unity or the wholeness of the human body. The Chinese physician diagnoses the illness not as a cholecystitis or a pneumonia or a duodenal ulcer, but rather that the life energies of the body have been disturbed and are not flowing properly or in a balanced manner. His therapeutic program is designed to restore the balance of the energies once again, and in the process restore the wholeness or the unity of the entire body. This concept of the wholeness of the entire body is not really new to us in the West. It is being considered more now than it has ever been considered heretofore, but we still maintain the framework that allows us easily to fractionate our thinking, and I think that this is a danger. In other words, we remain as specialists of different parts of the body, and we still hold to the idea that there are irreversible changes that cannot be cleared up. Irreversibility is, in a very real sense, a controversial idea. There are those people who believe that nothing is irreversible.

When Christiaan Barnard,[7] for instance, transplanted a healthy heart into the body of a man who had a variety of so-called irreversible changes in his body, he was astounded that an indolent ulcer cleared up, the lungs became healthy, the kidneys started functioning again and these previously termed "irreversible" changes, in reality, did change.

Another pertinent story by Kammerer[8] tells of a sympathectomy which was done for a woman whose right hip was architecturally destroyed by a severe advanced rheumatoid arthritis. Four years later she returned to the same hospital to have a ganglion removed from her elbow, and her doctors were somewhat amazed to find that the woman had brought about a complete regeneration of the affected hip. X rays revealed normal bony structure where before there was destruction—another "irreversible change" reversing itself.

Allen Dumont[9] of New York University tells still another story which refutes the idea of irreversibility. In several cases of pulmonary edema secondary to severe heart or liver disease, the thoracic duct was vented to the outside. Within twenty-four hours central venous pressure fell toward normal, distended neck veins, peripheral edema, ascites, and liver tenderness all diminished or disappeared. The liver edges withdrew under the costal margins, and the patient felt great.

We have all seen cases of severe physical disease, which we could easily call an imbalance of the body energies if we chose to diagnose things as the Chinese do. In these instances a balance has been restored, at least temporarily, by some procedure that we have instituted in the body much like these three stories I have just told.

If we choose to interpret these stories in the concept of wholeness and body energies, and if the Chinese are correct in their statement that the body can be returned to a wholeness by the application of acupuncture needles, then we have a whole new vista stretching out in front of us in the practice of medicine. Health can be looked at as a retrievable item if we somehow manage the energies of the body so that they once again become balanced.

My own research into the Edgar Cayce psychic readings [10] and data would tend to substantiate such a point of view. Cayce time and again spoke of body energies, although he described them as moving in the form of a figure-of-eight rather than through the channels of meridians, as the Chinese have described it.

From an altered state of consciousness, Cayce spoke of the vibratory nature of the human body, relating it to the nature of the atom itself, and he described a variety of ways by which one might change the vibrations of the body, restoring a balance to the energies which he called the lifeforce.

Thelma Moss suggested that we should not talk about vibrations of atoms but rather about wavelengths. Perhaps that would be more within our own vocabulary, because in the field of medicine, for some reason, vibratory reactions or vibrations don't have the right "vibes." Cayce described methods of treating various so-called incurable conditions, which, when the directions were followed, often cleared up. In our work with this material, we have had the opportunity to repeat some of the suggested therapies and have found consistently encouraging results. This is working with an idea of the balance of the life-force or the energies of the body.

So, perhaps the time has come for us to look at the human body as a whole entity, a whole being, one that operates under the influence of numerous measurable and unmeasurable electrical and electronic impulses, one that sets up a magnetic field of its own and responds to other magnetic fields, one that repairs one portion of itself after another portion has arrived at a normal, healthy balance. Such a concept would put us into the position where we might not only accept but utilize information from the Orient to the advantage of the ultimate consumer, and this is the person we so often forget—the patient who continually shows up at our office.

Of interest to all of us, I think, is a story which really originates in Japan. Dr. Michio Tany, on his return to Tokyo after visiting us in Phoenix, remained in correspondence with us and has since sent us slides taken of EKG tracings before and after acupuncture therapy. Tany is an MD who is researching acupuncture in Tokyo. In an individual diagnosed as having angina pectoris, the first tracing that he sent shows sagging ST segments in leads one, two, and AVF; inversion of the T wave in lead three; and other indications of an electrocardiogram that is not quite normal. In a tracing taken fifteen minutes after the patient was acupunctured, a remarkably normal tracing is shown in all respects, with all the abnormalities reversed. This is the most obvious of the four sets of tracings that he sent, and those included two of acute coronary occlusion. All showed definite changes with the use of acupuncture.

This kind of result seems to be in accord with the generally accepted ideas concerning acupuncture, that is, that the nervous system is the portion of the body most directly affected and is in many instances apparently normalized.

In France in 1951, J. E. H. Niboyet [11] demonstrated electrocardiogram effects after acupuncture on auricular fibrillation, sinus tachycardia, and T-wave abnormalities. So, Tany's responses are not new or particularly unusual, but they are of considerable interest. He did not tell us if the patient has had relief of the pains of angina pectoris, but we have had experience in our office with one patient with this condition who was acupunctured and then for two and a half weeks had no pains as a result of his supposed cardiac deficiency. When pains did recur (there was no medication being given), the patient was treated once more and had a more permanent relief.

So these are not unusual responses, and yet I think they are very fascinating and very important for us to consider when we are talking about and looking at the whole field of acupuncture.

In a 1972 publication from mainland China entitled *Scaling Peaks in Medical Science,*[3] a story is told of how medical researchers inserted acupuncture needles far more deeply into the Yah-min point on the back of the neck than tradition would have one believe was safe. I have tried to isolate and identify where the Yah-min point is. I think it is either gall bladder point No. 12 or gall bladder point No. 20; but I am not sure. . . .

In any event, the instructions stated that the needle should not be placed deeper than five fen. Five fen is half a cun. A cun is the distance between the second and the third interphalangeal joints when a circle is made by touching the thumb to the tip of the middle finger. The medical team was interested in restoring hearing and speech to a group of deaf and dumb children in a school near Peking. The Yahmin point was the point recommended for deafness, and the research team felt that if the needle were penetrated deeply enough, it would cure the inability to speak as well. This followed considerable research that had been done on deep insertion of the needles, which was one of the techniques they had used previously when they acupunctured two points on one arm to give anesthesia to the chest. According to the story, one of the researchers then inserted a needle in his own neck one and a half cun, at which point his hands became numb. He stopped there, and the numbness went away. Then he continued inserting it deeper until suddenly he felt his neck to be congested, his throat burned, and his hands went numb as if by electric shock. At that point he took the needle out and found that he had inserted it two and a half cun and was still alive—contrary to the Chinese tradition, which says that you cannot insert a needle more than half a cun or you will die.

He then used this technique on one of the girls who was deaf and dumb. He inserted it for three consecutive days. They did not tell how long they left it in, whether they twirled it, whether they took it out immediately, or how the treatment was done. But for three consecutive days the girl was treated at this point. At the end of this time she suddenly recovered her ability to speak, having earlier regained her hearing.

They then treated all the pupils at the school, and again, according to the report, 157 of the 168 pupils have regained their hearing and 149 of the 168 can now speak. It is rather a dramatic story.

Now, how would this relate to the Western physician? Most of us, I am sure, cannot even find the Yah-min point. But what would it mean to us? By utilizing the information regarding certain points that are helpful for hearing, we have had the opportunity in our clinic to treat six partially deaf patients with acupuncture. Only two showed no response. Another regained some hearing temporarily after one treatment, then regressed and did not seek any further treatment. The other three had a rather remarkable response at the clinical level, hearing noises and sounds that had not been part of their awareness for fifteen or twenty years. Most of them can now hear normal conversation, where before they had to ask for repetitions. All of these were older patients, none were children; we have not tried this with any children.

In the life of the general practitioner—and that is my life —dysmenorrhea is a rather bothersome syndrome because often a good response in the patient cannot be elicited. Because of its frequency, we have had opportunity to treat a number of cases with acupuncture not associated with other therapy. Most of the time it was not associated because they had had other therapy, and it was not being effective.

These were all chronic, nonresponsive individuals. Needles were placed bilaterally in the spleen No. 6 position, which is three body inches proximal to the medical maleolus of the ankle, and the stomach No. 36 point. Almost without exception these insertions brought about a normal period without the pain that had been previously experienced. Repeated treatment seemed to bring about a permanent balance in the bodies of the individuals and produced periods without discomfort.

We have found in our experience that we could use these things and bring about some sort of understanding to the minds of our patients simply because we think of the body as being a vital living organism that has forces and energies active within it, which need to be balanced in their action. If we can balance these forces, then people instinctively know what we are talking about. We know there is a force of love and that love can't be measured but it is real, and we know that there are other forces. We know that the kidneys and the liver have to be balanced in their excretory action, and yet we pay little attention to the balancing or the coordination between these two organs.

What kind of problems generally respond to simple acupuncture treatment in the practice of medicine? Most often it has been our experience that one treats only those that have been nonresponsive to conventional therapy first. In other words, the tough cases; those for whom you are willing to do acupuncture treatments after you have learned enough about it to try it. Then there are those patients who present themselves for acupuncture treatments specifically.

Since in our clinic we have been working with the Edgar Cayce material for several years, I have written about it at length. People who are already our patients want to have treatments with acupuncture. So, we have had a lot of experiences with individual cases. From a scientific point of view, perhaps, an individual case has no validity. From the practicing physician's point of view, however, clinical observation is just as valid as laboratory observation or a group of statistics. So, one case *may* be meaningful. Thus, we have had what we think are significant responses in a number of different conditions. . . .

Finally, I should put myself on record as believing that acupuncture has a value that could be utilized by any practicing physician from the psychiatrist and the neurologist to the gynecologist, the obstetrician, the internist, and the general practitioner. Whether it will be so utilized, of course, is dependent upon those same physicians.

Perhaps time will demonstrate that the greatest service acupuncture has performed in the Western world will not be simply relief of pain or disease, but rather if we, as Western physicians, gain an understanding of the human body that is closer to the truth and find in the process a better comprehension of what is the healing process that goes on within the human body when any therapeutic modality is administered, then acupuncture will have served the Western world in a highly important context.

## REFERENCES

1. RESTON, JAMES: "Cutting Up with Reston—Surgery Yields Lowdown on Chinese Hospital," New York Times News Service, *Sacramento Bee,* July 26, 1971.
2. *Acupuncture Anaesthesia,* Foreign Languages Press, Peking, 1972.
3. *Scaling Peaks in Medical Science,* Foreign Languages Press, Peking, 1972.
4. SCHWARTZ, ARTHUR: "Acupuncture—The Need for a Research Approach." Unpublished paper presented to a symposium sponsored by The Academy of Parapsychology and Medicine, August 1972.
5. SACKLER, ARTHUR M.: "Hubris and Humility," *Medical Tribune,* August 16, 1972.

6. VEITH, ILZA: *The Yellow Emperor's Classic of Internal Medicine*, University of California Press, Berkeley, Calif., 1966.

7. BARNARD, C. and PEPPER, C. B.: *Christiaan Barnard: One Life*, The Macmillan Company, 1969.

8. KAMMERER, W. H., and JOEN, T. L.: *Arthritis & Rheumatism*, Vol. 10, 1967, p. 288.

9. DUMONT, ALLEN: "Lymphatics' Role Stressed in Cardiovascular Disease," *Medical World News*, Vol. 7, January 21, 1966, pp. 100-101.

10. Edgar Cayce Readings compiled and indexed by the Edgar Cayce Foundation, P.O. Box 595, Virginia Beach, Va.

11. NIBOYET, J. E. H., *Essai sur l'Acupuncture Chinoise Pratique*, Domique Wapler, Paris, 1951.

# 13

## Laboratory Evidence of the "Laying-on-of-Hands"

### *Bernard Grad*

*Bernard Grad is an associate professor in the Department of Psychiatry at McGill University in Montreal and a research scientist in the Gerontological Unit of the Allan Memorial Institute of Psychiatry. One of the greatest pioneers in the study of healing, he discusses his experiments in how energy from a healer can be transferred to an organism.*

• • •

I came into the field of healing quite green and new. My background is Jewish, so the stories of the healing of Jesus played no role in my consciousness.

My entry into the field came about because an Hungarian gentleman worked in my lab. We got to talking about unconventional things, and he mentioned that the wife of a friend had been healed of arthritis by an Hungarian healer, a Mr. E. Having a curious mind, I said I would like to meet this gentleman.

Because Mr. E. could not speak English, my Hungarian technician acted as interpreter. Through him, we decided to collaborate on a series of experiments with animals and later with plants. These experiments were begun as an extra activity, not part of my usual work.

The experiments were done using laying-on-of-hands. I had not really known what the procedure was, but, of course, the name itself implies that the healer places his hands on the object of the treatment. Since we were not going to be studying patients, only mice, the question was how we were going to "lay hands" on mice. I knew how to catch mice and restrain them, but that isn't really the "laying-on-of-hands" (LH). After some discussion, we decided to use a small galvanized iron box with compartments, placing one mouse in each compartment and covering the box with wire mesh. The healer positioned the box between his hands, with one hand on the top of the box and the other on the bottom.

When we first met, Mr. E. told me that in Hungary for ten years before he came to Canada he had treated many people with thyroid disease with good results. I had done studies on thyroid physiology, myself, so this seemed a natural place to start. I knew that mice could be made goitrous by feeding them a diet low in iodine; in addition, I knew that if we gave them thiouracil, we could further prevent even the small amount of iodine present in a low-iodine diet from getting into the thyroid. The combination of thiouracil and the low-iodine diet tended to produce an enlargement of the thyroid several times its normal size.

Our first experiments, then, were on thyroid enlargement. The aim of the experiment was to see whether LH could prevent normal enlargement of the thyroid gland in mice fed with a diet low in iodine and given water containing thiouracil to drink.[1]

An adult mouse thyroid weighs about 2mgms when the animal is on a diet containing a normal amount of iodine. After eleven days on an iodine-deficient diet there was a slight increase in thyroid weight. At this point, the ordinary drinking water was replaced with water containing 0.1% thiouracil. We couldn't start the mice on thiouracil and the iodine-deficient diet simultaneously, because we have found this to be too stressful for the animals and many died. Therefore, we fed the mice the diet alone for about eleven days and then gave them thiouracil to drink.

The experiment consisted of three groups of mice: two control groups and an experimental group receiving the LH treatment fifteen minutes twice daily, five days a week. The two control groups were treated in every way like the experimental group, except that they did not receive the LH treatment. One of the two control groups was given a "heat" treatment by means of an electrothermal tape which raised the temperature to that which occurred when the animals in the box were held between the hands of the healer. We wanted to make sure that if there were any effects of LH they would not be due to the heat which developed during the LH treatment.

The experiment lasted about six weeks, during which time the rate of increase in the size of the thyroid was reliably faster in both the non-heated control and the heated control than it was in the group which received the LH treatment. So there was an inhibition in the rate of development of the goitre under the conditions of the experiment. Mind you, the LH treatment did not prevent the enlargement totally, but it clearly slowed it down.

We were working here with an artificial condition, not with human goitres, which many believe develop because of psychosomatic factors. In the animal experiment, the thyroid enlargement was due only to the deficiency of iodine.

In the experiment that followed we used two groups of mice which were rendered goitrous as in the first experiment. One of the groups was a control group, while the other received the LH treatment. However, instead of LH, Mr. E. held between his hands pads made of wool and cotton. The pad was then placed in the cages with the animals for an hour in the morning and another hour in the afternoon of each day.

The results were the same as in the first experiment, that is, the rate of development of the goitre was definitely slower in the LH group than in the control group, which also had treatment with cotton-wool pads that had not been held between Mr. E.'s hands.

The third thyroid experiment was approached differently. Feeding the mice on iodine-deficient diet and 0.1% thiouracil as before, the goitres were allowed to develop for six weeks, and only then were the mice divided into two groups, one of which was given the "heat" treatment by means of electrothermal tapes and the other the LH treatment as in the first experiment. Also, at the end of the sixth week, the mice were taken off the iodine-deficient diet and fed Purina fox chow, which contains sufficient iodine. Even without LH the thyroid weight began to decrease, but with LH as well, the rate of decrease was much greater.

That comprised the series of thyroid experiments. We then asked ourselves whether LH would work on other biological processes, and for this we chose to observe the effect of LH on healing of skin wounds in mice. I know that the mouse is not the most desirable animal to use to investigate wound healing, because a mouse will heal its skin wounds very well, even in dirty conditions. However, because of its size, a mouse is inexpensive to feed and maintain. The mice were separated into three groups: a control group, a group which received LH, and a group which received the "heat" treatment described above. Each animal was put to sleep before a piece of skin the size of a quarter was removed from the back with scissors. Then the area of the wound was outlined on a piece of transparent plastic placed over the wound, and the outline was transferred to a piece of paper which was weighed and recorded. In this way a weight corresponding to the area of the wound was obtained, and the wound areas in all three groups were very similar at the beginning of the experiment.

One day after wounding there was already some evidence of healing in some of the wounds. Eleven and fourteen days afterward some of the wounds were quite small, and it was obvious that Mr. E.'s group was healing faster than the other groups. (For further details see other published reports on this study.[2,3])

Our next project was to study plants, and for two reasons. First, we wanted to know if healing worked on plants as well as animals and second, we wanted to find experiments that would give us results more quickly than the goitre experiments (which generally required six weeks) or the wound healing experiments, also very time consuming.

With the plants, we first tried germinating barley seeds on wet blotting paper to learn whether differences would occur between groups of seeds which had had LH and those which did not have such treatment. Perhaps other people might get significant differences in trying this type of experiment, but we did not. So we moved on to planting seeds in soil. There, too, we found that we had to do something to make the seeds "sick" or, more correctly, to put them in a state of lack because, as in the animal experiments, we didn't see much in the way of an effect from LH when we first started working with completely healthy animals.

In the case of the animals, we decided we were going to make the mice sick, and we did so either by making them goitrous or by producing a wound. With the plants we found it necessary to put the plants in a state of need, and we did this by pouring salt water on them. Now, salt, you know, is one of the oldest ways to inhibit the growth of plants. When Carthage was defeated by the Romans, the land around

Carthage was plowed with salt. We tested several different concentrations of salt, but for our needs, the best concentration was 1%. Even after we put the salt solution on, we found it best not to water too abundantly. We let the seeds dry out a bit—not dry enough to kill them—but again, enough to put them into a state of need. That was the underlying philosophy of our experiments. (For details of the technique used, refer to the bibliography at the end of this paper.[4])

In preliminary experiments there were no less than six pots per group with twenty seeds per pot. Mr. E. would place his hands on the seeded pots, and also treat the saline which was poured over them. The control pots and the saline were held in the hands of anyone. Later, we learned that it was not necessary to treat the plants directly, but only to treat the saline to be poured over the plants. To "treat" in this context means to hold the 1% saline solution between the hands for half an hour. To repeat, just treating the saline and pouring it over the plants was enough; it wasn't necessary to practice LH on the plants directly. Moreover, further studies showed it was necessary to treat only the initial watering, the one with the 1% salt water, and all other waterings were then made with untreated water. The saline water was first LH treated in an open beaker, but in subsequent experiments it was treated in glass-stoppered reagent bottles and still later in sealed bottles.

Barley seedlings come up through the soil looking like grass and can be counted. They started coming up about seven days after beginning the experiment under our conditions. In the experiment in which saline was treated in open beakers, the number of treated seedlings coming through the soil was higher than that of the untreated controls at the beginning of the experiment. However, the differences were especially marked in the height of the plants between LH-treated and controls. The yield of plant material was also centainly higher, the yield being simply the product of the number times the mean height.[4]

To make sure that the previous results were not obtained by chance, the entire experiment was repeated exactly as before, with the difference that nobody laid hands on the saline of either group. The question was: Would the normal biological variation yield the kind of difference observed in the previous experiment? This control experiment's answer was no.[4] So the findings of the first experiment were not due to chance. There was a real difference, and LH was able to stimulate the growth of barley seeds over that of the controls.

The subsequent series of experiments dealt with the LH treatment of saline in glass-stoppered reagent bottles. Mr. E. held the bottles between his hands for half an hour. Whatever was producing the effect was able to do so through the glass because the outcome was that the saline treated in the stoppered bottle by LH also significantly stimulated the growth of the barley seedlings over that of the controls.[5]

When the LH experiments were started, Mr. B. had no idea that he, too, was able to have an effect of this kind. By trying to use him as a control in some other experiments not reported so far, we learned that he was really not a control, and so it was decided to do a plant experiment with him. The experiment in which he participated also involved two other people, both of whom were depressed. They were patients in a hospital.

One of these was a woman who had a neurotic depression, and the other, a man, suffered from a psychotic depression. I asked these people to hold in their hands a bottle of 0.9% saline. Here, the saline was that produced commercially for hospitals for use where infusions of saline are required. Now, the saline in these bottles is sterile, non-pyrogenic and is sealed under vacuum.

Four bottles of this kind were used in this experiment. Three were held for half an hour, one by each of the three people involved. The fourth bottle was not held by anyone; it served as a control. After the initial watering with saline, untreated water was used in subsequent waterings.

The aim of the experiment was to see whether people who were in low spirits would inhibit the growth of the plants, and if a person with a positive attitude would have the opposite effect. This was a large experiment. There were four groups, eighteen pots per group, twenty seeds per pot. It was a multiblind experiment in which the information was divided among five people. We measured the mean height per pot over the period of the experiment, which was sixteen days. Mr. B.'s group grew the best. The group that grew the least was that of the person with the psychotic depression.[6]

So three of the four groups showed results in the expected direction, that is, the person who was most depressed really produced an inhibition, while Mr. B., the person who was most positive produced a stimulation with the control group in between the two. The girl with the neurotic depression gave a result which was better than that of the man with the psychotic depression (she was less depressed than he) and slightly better than the control group. The statistics of the three groups (the control group and the two depressive groups) showed there was no real difference between them. However, Mr. B.'s group was significantly above the others. But still, apart from the fact that there was no statistically significant difference between the three groups, there is a reason, I think, why the girl's group did not show an inhibition in growth compared to the control group as did the other depressed patient's.

To get at that, I must tell you what happened during the experiment. When I handed out the bottle to the man with the psychotic depression, I asked him to hold the parcel between his hands for half an hour. Each bottle had been placed in a brown paper bag as one step in the multiblind procedure, and so the man couldn't see what was in the bag but could feel that it was a bottle. He didn't know what was inside, and he really didn't care. He thought I was a doctor coming to prepare him in some way for electroshock therapy, and he kept telling me that he didn't really need it. I tried telling him I was not there for that purpose, but he refused to believe me; he seemed quite anxious, and inasmuch as he did not ask for any information about the parcel, I didn't volunteer it.

But when I came to the girl, her first question was "Why are you giving me this to hold?" I told her the idea of the experiment, saying, "We are trying to see if by holding the bottle you can have an effect on the growth of plants watered with its contents." Well, when I walked into the room, before speaking to her, she was sitting somewhat forlornly there, but when I told her about the experiment, she said, "Oh, that's a marvelous idea," and she brightened up. Now, that depressed *me,* because she had been chosen because she was depressed, not elated. Well, the die had been cast, and I didn't know whether her mood change would have an effect or not on the experiment but decided to proceed. It was too troublesome getting the patients; I had to ask permission of the doctor involved, and I didn't wish to go through that again. Half an hour later when I came back to pick up the bottle, she was holding it, almost cradling it as you would a doll or a child. The fact that her group grew faster than that of the control and not slower as did that of the other depressed group was, in my opinion, probably due to the improvement in the girl's mood while holding the bottle.

I would like to make some comments on these experiments. I don't want you to look at the experiments and draw the conclusion that LH is the final answer to all the ills that man is heir to and should therefore displace conventional healing. That would be ridiculous, because if we ever decide to look deeper into the effects of LH, we will probably find many areas where LH has little or no effect. In short, just as conventional healing methods cannot cure all diseases, the same is probably the case with LH and other unconventional methods. But that is different from the present-day attitude that won't even look into the question of whether LH works or not. And the purpose of the experiments I have described here is to draw attention to what may be very useful in medicine, as well as providing additional evidence for the existence of an energy associated with living things. If LH is found to be useful in medicine, then conventional medicine should take it under its wing and look for this ability among its own MDs. Healing in this way could bring to ailing mankind something very useful in selected cases.

Another point I would like to make concerns the fact that LH has often been called "faith" healing. Faith that a healing can occur is involved, but the first person who must have faith is the physician or healer, and this is more important than the patient having the same belief. For, if the healer has no faith, then there is really no hope of a cure. On the other hand, while it is most desirable for the patient to have faith, it is not really an essential part of the process. Of course, if the patient is absolutely negative about his possibility of being cured, then I am sure LH will not work, but if he is neutral but open in his attitude and says, "I don't know if this will work or not, but I'm ready to see if it does," then healing still has a chance.

I'll give you an example of this from our work. We found in working with mice that we had to have them sitting quietly in the boxes if they were to receive the healing. And so we went through the tedious but necessary business of getting them used to the boxes by putting them in every day for an hour or more, as described earlier, until they finally settled down. When we tried to hurry up things, the mice would be nervous and agitated, as seen by the fact they kept turning around in the space available to them in the box, biting the wire mesh, trying to get out from under these conditions, and the healing did not go well.

Another procedure which was followed to quiet the mice was to stroke their fur gently for a few minutes when putting them in or removing them from the boxes. Both this procedure and the previous one were done to all the mice before they were separated into those that were to serve as controls and those to receive LH. In other words, these procedures were done on the mice before it was known which were to be placed in the control or the treated group. Occasionally, even after following the quieting procedures for a week or more, a mouse still would not settle, and such animals were not included in our experiments, because experience showed that such mice did not respond to the LH treatment.

Experiments have been conducted on the effect of stroking the fur of animals, which is called gentling, and their ability to grow and resist stress. A review of the literature shows that the results are rather conflicting; some reports claim that gentled mice do better than the non-gentled controls, others report no difference, while still others indicate that the gentled mice do worse than the non-gentled ones. In the light of our studies, I believe that the explanation for this confusion is as follows: If the gentling is done by somebody who dislikes the animals, the results should be negative. If he loves them, the results should be positive. Similar processes must happen with plants, as found in our plant experiment with the normal and depressive subjects. You all know of the persons with the "green thumb" who love plants and can make them flourish.

How does LH work? I believe that it works by a transfer of an energy from the healer to the patient. If the healer is disturbed emotionally, or his own energy is low because of disease or other factors, then this flow may not occur. Another point about LH is this: you know that one of the most common ways to show affection is to stretch the hands out to the object of affection. This has even been symbolized by the handshake when we are introduced to someone for the first time or when we encounter a friend. The laying-on-of-hands is part of this process, during which, given the right individuals and the right set of circumstances, a transfer of energy will pass from one to the other. Some healers even claim to be able to diagnose sick areas by the resistance to the flow of energy from their hands, a resistance which they say causes a very strong heat to develop, more than is explicable on the basis of any local inflammatory process. That there is an energy involved in LH is indicated in the experiment involving the LH treatment of the saline in a stoppered or sealed bottle, for such saline still influenced the growth of plants.

Why has LH not been accepted as part of medical practice, when it has been known to exist for such a long time? Perhaps it is because the procedure itself is so simple that it can readily be abused. However, although medicine has learned to use dangerous substances and energies for the good of man, it still feels uneasy when having to deal with the energies within man himself. There may be other reasons as well. When the healer does LH, he really does not "do" anything other than place himself in the right frame of mind, part of which means placing himself in rapport with the sick person. Therefore, when a healing occurs over a shorter or longer period, but especially when it occurs quickly, he will experience awe and religious feelings, which is another part of the "right frame of mind" mentioned above. That is, the healer comes to feel that he is really not doing anything, but is a kind of transmitter of the healing force, which he feels moving or vibrating in his hands during LH. This has a kind of humbling effect, which most of us may not relish, especially when we take such great pride in our capacity to know all and master all creation. On the other side of the coin, feelings of omnipotence may well be an occupational hazard of healers. And this brings us to the character of the healer. He has to be very careful, I feel, to keep himself spiritually clean, for if he does not, he will have effects which are undesirable, even though he may still be able to continue to heal.

## REFERENCES

1. GRAD, BERNARD: "Healing by the Laying-on-of-Hands: Review of Experiments and Implications." *Pastoral Psychology* 21: 19-26, 1970.
2. GRAD, BERNARD: "Some Biological Effects of the 'Laying-on-of-hands': A Review of Experiments with Animals and Plants." *Journal of the American Society for Psychical Research* 59: 95-127, 1965.
3. GRAD, BERNARD, CADORET, REMI J. and PAUL G. I.: "An Unorthodox Method of Treatment of Wound Healing in Mice." Internal. J. Parapsych. 3: 5-24, 1961.

4. GRAD, BERNARD: "A Telekinetic Effect on Plant Growth." *Internat. J. Parapsych.* 5: 117-133, 1963.
5. GRAD, BERNARD: "A Telekinetic Effect on Plant Growth. II. Experiments Involving Treatment of Saline in Stoppered Bottles." *Internat. J. Parapsych.* 6: 473-498, 1964.
6. GRAD, BERNARD: "The 'Laying-on-of-Hands': Implications for Psychotherapy; Gentling and the Placebo Effect." *Journal of the American Society for Psychical Research* 61: 286-305, 1967.

# 14

# Wilhelm Reich, Orgone, and Cancer

## David Boadella

*The work of Wilhelm Reich, a German-born psychoanalyst, previously greatly ignored and often ridiculed, is being revived due to growing interest in vital energies in man and nature.*

*David Boadella, educator and editor of* Energy and Character: The Journal of Bioenergetic Research, *describes Reich's controversial cancer research and treatment.*

•  •  •

While working on his biological experiments in Oslo, Reich had been accused in an early stage of the Norwegian newspaper campaign of claiming a "cancer cure." At that time he had not the slightest thought of doing any research in the field of cancer. It was as though the malicious critic had unconsciously divined the connection between the derivation of the bions and the origin of cancer cells.

This connection only became clear to Reich at a later date, after he had carried out the experiments with the injection of T-bacilli into mice, and observed the transitional stages between health and the development of the cancer tumors that many of the mice died of.

Reich was actively working in the field of cancer research as his prior work interest for a period of about seven years, from 1937, when the T-bacilli were first discovered, to 1944, when the last of his findings on cancer were written up.

Reich's understanding of the cancer process falls into three clear divisions: his studies of the origin of the cancer cell, based on microscopic observations during the last two years in Norway; the clinical account of the cancer process based on a number of patients suffering from the disease, whom Reich accepted for observation and treatment free of charge; and the actual treatment process that he initiated, at first with mice and later with patients.

The cancer disease remains an unsolved problem as far as traditional medicine is concerned. Though tumors can be affected by means of X rays, surgery, and other drastic procedures, the background to the disease is not yet understood. Some of the bitterest of all the attacks that Reich received in the course of his life were over his work in the cancer field.

The failure of orthodox cancer research *until recently* to digest Reich's total organismic approach should not be taken as indicating that there was no support for his findings. Many of the individual discoveries that Reich made were independently *confirmed* by classical cancer researches. Only these findings remained, for them, isolated and their significance in the total picture was not grasped. . . .

### Healthy and Unhealthy Tissues

The first opinion Reich formed of the results of his experimental production of cancer tumors in mice was that the T-bacilli that he had injected were in some way specific tumor agents.

The questions that his research at this time had to answer were the following.

1. Is the T-bacillus in fact "specific" for cancer and only found in conjunction with the cancer disease?

2. If they were not specific, what was the connection between the T-bacilli and the cancer disease? Did they help to produce the cancer or were they the products of the cancer process?

3. The T-bacilli in Reich's mice had got there by injection. How did the T-bacilli get into the cancer tissue that Leif Kreyberg, the Norwegian cancer pathologist, had supplied?

The answers to these questions were based principally on careful microscopic observation of tissues in a live unstained state. Reich used his usual high powers where movements were visible that were invisible at lower powers. Also he took observations over a long period and filmed the development of cancer tumors by time-lapse photography over a period of eight to fourteen months.

The T-bacillus did *not* prove to be specific for cancer. Reich examined samples of *blood and of secretions* from different people and found that T-bacilli could be found in tissues which were perfectly healthy. He even found T-bacilli in a small erosion of his own tongue. T-bacilli from the blood of an assistant, produced during the course of one of the Reich blood tests to be described later, were injected into a mouse and resulted in a malignant tumor (adenocarcinoma) in the buttock. The mouse was sent to Columbia University for identification and the cancerous nature of the tumor was confirmed in the department of pathology.

How was it, then, that microorganic forms taken from a healthy person could produce disease in the mouse? This question threw Reich up against the whole question of resistance to disease, whether infectious or noninfectious. Why is it that some people are carriers of a virus and are immune to its effects, while others go down with the disease? What is the nature of immunity? Why is it that though most sufferers from lung cancer are heavy smokers, most heavy smokers do not get lung cancer? What determines the biological resistance in organic tissues to pathological processes?

Reich's observations were that T-bacilli in a healthy organism were destroyed before they could multiply or cause any damage. Normally they were destroyed by the white blood cells in the healthy blood stream. But if the organism was flooded by T-bacilli, either through some internal process of weakness and deterioration, or, as in the case of his experimental mice, through an outside agency, then a second, pathological form of defense against the T-bacilli proved to develop. The tissue weakened by the presence of T-bacilli in concentration began to decay prematurely into vesicles in a way that exactly paralleled the bionous process that Reich had already been studying in all manner of substances since 1936.

The same packet-shaped bions with amoeboid-type movements (the PA bions) were produced from the weakened tissue in the injected mice. Reich was struck by the fact that in his earlier experimental grass infusions it had always been much easier to produce bionous disintegration in old, autumnal grass than in young spring grass. Fresh materials resisted decay. Weaker and older tissues were less "cohesive," and more readily broke down into a simpler, more protozoal level of organization.

The significance of the PA bions in the ailing mouse was that Reich was able to follow every stage of development of these bions into bion-heaps that aggregated together and developed into cancer cells that were club-shaped and moved with a slow jerky action, visible at a magnification of 3,000 ×. Reich distinguished the following five stages of development:

1. The cells of the weakened tissue change shape and texture. The usual pentagonal shape of epithelial cells is lost, the cells tend to shrink in and round up. Instead of being clear and translucent, granules are visible. T-bacilli are observable within the cell and around its periphery in the adjacent fluid.

2. Granulated tissue spreads and infiltrates the neighboring tissues and leads to a chronic inflammatory area.

3. Several cells disintegrate into vesicles and coalesce to form club-shaped and spindle-shaped cells which multiply rapidly. Tissues at widely separated parts of the body may yield such cells, but in regions of particular concentration they begin to cluster.

4. The club-shaped and spindle-shaped cells mature into highly mobile amoeboid cancer cells; the cells proliferate to form a tumor.

5. The original tissue continues to disintegrate into vesicles and into T-bacilli, but the cancer cells also begin to disintegrate. A process of putrid living decay, or autointoxication, sets in, to which the organism inevitably succumbs.

Death in the cancer mouse or cancer patient is not caused necessarily by the tumor. Malignant tumors can form in nonvital parts of the body and are not fatal. Where the tumor itself does not prove fatal, death occurs due to the final blood and tissue putrefaction process in the organism. The tumor is merely the most visible symptom of an underlying tendency in the body for cells to break down and lose their cohesiveness.

### The Reich Blood Tests

As a result of his study of the reactions of the blood in healthy and diseased mice, and later in healthy and sick people, Reich devised a series of blood tests for assessing the *biological vitality* of the tissues. The blood tests were three in number:

1. *Disintegration test.* A small drop of blood is put on a slide with a concavity containing a small amount of warm physiological saline solution (0.9 percent). A number of observations are then made over a period of twenty to thirty minutes both at low- and high-power magnification. In particular, Reich was interested in the visual appearance of the red blood corpuscles and in their rate of disintegration. In unhealthy blood, disintegration set in straight away and was over in a very short time, under five minutes. In healthy blood, disintegration did not begin for three or four minutes and was not complete even at the end of half an hour. Visually the healthy blood, when it did disintegrate, broke up into large uniform granules; whereas unhealthy blood— e.g., from cancerous mice—disintegrated into shrunken granules and the red blood cells also showed characteristic spikes at the periphery, which Reich referred to as T-spikes. Many other observations were made which are too detailed to describe here. The point to grasp is that blood varied in the way in which it disintegrated in the saline solution, and the variation proved to be distinctive between healthy and unhealthy mice.

2. *The blood-culture test.* A drop of blood is inoculated into a culture medium, under sterile precautions. The culture is put in the incubator for a day or two at a temperature of 37° C. Reich used Difco's heart-infusion broth. Healthy blood left the infusion clear. Unhealthy blood yielded T-bacilli, which caused the broth to turn putrid and give off an unpleasant smell after standing for a day or two. Examination of the fluid under the microscope revealed the presence of many T-bacilli.

3. *The biological-resistance test.* Several drops of blood are put into test tubes containing equal mixture of the same broth and of 0.1 percent potassium chloride solution. The solution is then autoclaved at steam pressure for about half an hour. Healthy blood disintegrated into large brownish flakes, which settled rapidly and degenerated slowly. Unhealthy blood disintegrated into small greenish flakes, which settled slowly and degenerated rapidly.

Full particulars of all three tests are given in the manual on the subject which Reich's colleagues compiled. Their immediate importance is that they provided a crucial *diagnostic tool*. Since the cancer tumor did not appear until the fourth stage of the cancer process, there was at the time Reich developed these tests (1938) no means known of diagnosing cancer before the presence of the tumor was established. "No tumor, no cancer" followed the familiar medical doctrine that was exposed by the biologists in the Peckham health experiment as the shortsighted policy of "no symptom, no disease." Reich's blood tests, however, enabled him to detect the pretumorous cancer process at stage one.

The bion experiments at high magnification and in living preparations had led logically to the solution of the riddle of the development of the cancer cell. It remained to solve two more gigantic problems of cancer research:

1. What processes, in human beings, led to the *biological devitalization* that manifested itself in an unhealthy blood picture which in extreme forms could amount to a cancer background which would eventually culminate in tumor formation?

2. Was it possible to *revitalize* the blood and the tissues so that the tendency to produce T-bacilli, and for the tissues to decay into antithetical amoeboid vesicles as a defense reaction, could be overcome? Was it possible to assist the body to resist the biological deterioration so as to save it from such a drastic last-ditch reaction?

Before looking at the answers Reich's research provided to these two questions, it is important to see which, if any, of his cancer findings so far have received confirmation elsewhere.

### Comparison of Reich's Tissue Findings with Other Cancer Researchers

During the last ten years classical cancer research has been studying minute bodies called *Mycoplasmas*, which have a number of properties in common with Reich's T-bacilli, according to Coulson.

1. The Mycoplasmas are gram-negative. So are the T-bacilli.

2. The Mycoplasmas are very small (0.1 mu.); so are the T-bacilli (about 0.2 mu.).

3. The Mycoplasmas have the ability to absorb to the red blood cells and lead them to clump. T-bacilli in sufficient numbers lead the red blood cells to disintegrate into T-bacilli, which often agglutinate.

4. Mycoplasmas can produce leukemia in mice. T-bacilli produce adenocarcinoma and other malignancies in mice.

5. Mycoplasmas produce a lot of acid when incubated with cells. T-bacilli have a strong acid smell.

Whether what Reich called T-bacilli are identical with Mycoplasmas is not established. But very similar forms have been found to have a close association with cancer. They were first obtained directly from cancer tumors in 1964.

Reich's ability to diagnose cancer by examination of cells in the body secretions anticipated the cervical smear test of classical cancer research by at least fifteen years. The discovery that cancer cells could be detected in the sputum of cancer patients before tumors developed was not made by classical cancer pathology until 1955. Reich's discovery of cancer cells in the sputum was published in 1943.

Reich himself has quoted the research of a number of cancer researchers who observed amoeboid forms in the tissues of cancer patients, and paid no attention to them, believing that they were amoeboid *parasites:* the old idea of infection from without once again.

Enterline and Coman published a paper in 1950 in which they confirmed Reich's conclusion that the amoeboid cells were not parasites but were derivatives of the cancer process. No reference to Reich's priority in this respect was given. The authors concluded that "neoplastic cells in general are actively amoeboid."

Reich's description of what he called "T-spikes" on the biologically devitalized red-blood corpuscle—a formation that played an important diagnostic role in his blood tests—appears closely similar to what Schwartz and Motto have called a burr cell and described in the following words in 1949: "The burr cell is a mature erythrocyte about 7.5 micra or less in diameter, which has one to several spiny projections along its periphery. We have chosen to call it a burr cell because of its resemblance to the prickly envelope of a burr."

The "burr" cell was found associated with a number of pathological conditions and the authors concluded that burr cells were valuable diagnostic pointers to anemic conditions.

Lack of cohesiveness was, for Reich, one of the principal features distinguishing unhealthy blood and tissues from healthy ones. This finding was confirmed for cancer tissue though not for normal tissue by Coman in 1944, who suggested that a decrease in mutual adhesiveness that he had observed and measured between cancer cells "may constitue the physical basis for the malignancy of these cells."

Here are five specific areas where Reich clearly appears to have *anticipated* the findings of the cancer experts. If only Reich could have isolated his cancer conclusions from the bion research and from all other fields which had led him in this direction, perhaps he would have been listened to if he had been qualified in cancer research and had devoted a lifetime to it. But this kind of exclusive specialism, had he followed it, would have been precisely the kind of pursuit most likely to have blocked the perception of the crucial transdisciplinary links and functional interrelations that Reich was in fact able to make.

### The Bioenergetic Background to Cancer

Reich had been studying the cancer process in mice for four years before he accepted his first human cancer patients for observation and experimental treatment in March 1941. Reich's first cancer patient was the sister of a friend of a man who advised Reich on tax matters and who had known of Reich's mice experiments from this source. She was the first of many patients that Reich accepted. The treatment was *free,* though donations to the fund of the Orgone and Cancer Research Laboratory were encouraged, however small. The details of the therapy, its effectiveness, and its mode of action, will be explained in detail below.

But first it is necessary to describe Reich's findings on the background to the cancer disease. When he first approached these patients he was able to draw on all his earlier psychiatric and vegetotherapeutic skills in assessing the total organismic and personality picture.

When he had first got immersed in the biology of the cancer cell, Reich confessed to a secret relief that he had got away from the "cursed sexual problem" and could concentrate on organic pathology. Former friends of his work complained that Reich was trespassing outside the realm at which he had become expert. Reich himself believed that he was moving into the realm of the biology of death and decay, apparently far removed from his early Freudian studies of the libido. But such was not the case. When he came to study the life-styles of his patients, Reich found that he was again confronted, but at a much deeper level, with the "cursed sex problem."

Every one of the cancer patients he dealt with was deficient in libido. All suffered from chronic sexual stasis, in many cases of a severe form involving abstinence over a decade or more. Reich was already familiar with the detailed sexual picture of orgastic impotence. How, then, was the cancer sufferer different from the vast majority of mankind? Reich's eventual conclusion after treating many different conditions was that there are two fundamental biological responses to sexual stasis, or any other blockage to emotional functioning: one can suppress the expression of strong emotions outwardly but continue to experience them inwardly, in the form of anxiety attacks or stress due to unexploded anger; or one's emotions can be sapped of strength by a process of inner withdrawal. The study of personality in cancer patients revealed the combination of sexual stasis with characterological resignation.

Whereas the cardiovascular patient, and many other forms of psychosomatic disturbance, involved a high central energy charge (even though with a weak charge at the skin surface), the cancer patient had become relatively empty of strong emotion. He lacked the strong central vegetative excitations and presented, typically, a chronic emotional calm. Reich introduced the term "biopathy" around this time to describe any illness that had been produced by a chronic disturbance in biological pulsation. Cancer revealed itself to be such a severe disturbance that it manifested itself at the core of the life process, in the very metabolism of the cells.

Reich was studying a process which functioned in depth and involved many areas that are usually viewed separately and come under different specialists. The disturbance of biological pulsation expressed itself in the following forms:

1. Sexually, in the form of the withdrawn sexual interests, and the chronic absence of sexual satisfaction.

2. Characterologically, in the form of resignation and the feeling of emotional emptiness.

3. Muscularly, in the form of spasms and deep tensions in various areas, many of which in the cancer patient proved to be sites for tumor development as the later stages of the biopathic illness set in.

4. Vegetatively, respiration proved to be chronically deficient. Poor external respiration led to a poor internal tissue respiration in cancer patients.

5. Bioenergetically, the skin charge was always lowered. The cancer sufferer was biologically devitalized and suffered

from chronic contraction, with poor color and turgor to the skin.

6. Organically, the weakened charge of the tissues revealed itself in the lack of cohesiveness that was detected by the blood tests and the secretion examination.

The total picture was one of *shrinking* and premature dying. Reich saw this process as taking place in three typical phases. In the first phase, which he called the phase of contraction, the sex-economic, characterological, and vegetative inability to expand predominated. The second phase, which he called the phase of shrinking, produced the characteristic first four stages of cancer, from the weakened blood picture to the formation of tumors. The final phase, the phase of putrefaction, set in as the organism literally began to disintegrate as the plasma system became swamped by the toxic products of the tumors.

Reich reasoned that the rapid division in the malignant cells was parallel to an acute anxiety attack in the organism as a whole, at the level of the nucleus. It was as though the nucleus itself took over the task of discharging energy in a system which had given up the ability to radiate and to expand at all higher levels.

### Confirmations of Reich's Understanding of the Cancer Biopathy

As in the field of Reich's discovery of the origin of the cancer cell, the confirmations came in piecemeal. Many individual findings were corroborated: only the total picture was missing and avoided with the tactful silence that also traditionally descends when cancer is mentioned in society.

Reich's view of cancer as a functional psychosomatic disease was quite revolutionary. Even when other cancer researchers began to focus attention on the personality characteristics of cancer patients, they lacked the methodology to understand the chain of processes that could link emotional weakness with putrefying tissues. Nevertheless, limited though they are, these confirmations must be noted.

"In the last few years," writes Coulson, "there has been a growing wealth of evidence to indicate that cancer patients are not a random sample of the population. Emotional blockage seems to be a major characteristic of these patients, coupled with despair, resignation, loss of hope, etc. These tests, largely Rorschach inkblot and interview, can be carried out as a forecasting analysis, so any effect of the knowledge that the patient has a cancer is ruled out (although unconscious or hormonal effects of precancerous tissue cannot be). Loss of a loved one or job from six months to eight months to eight years before the diagnosis of cancer is made is as frequent as 60 percent in some surveys. The loss is seen as catastrophic to an emotional balance maintained primarily through the object lost. . . ."

Myron Sharaf has presented other evidence of sex-economic and characterological weakness in cancer patients: Stephenson and Grace found very poor sexual adjustment in patients with cancer of the cervix, as compared with other types of cancer: "Patients with cancer of the cervix were found to have a lower incidence of orgasm during sexual intercourse than patients in the control group. Dislike of sexual intercourse, amounting to actual aversion for the act, occurred far more frequently in the patients with cancer of the cervix."

Three researchers writing in *Psychosomatic Medicine* studied the personality charatceristics of forty women with breast cancers. They found typical masochistic attitudes associated with "inhibited sexuality and the inability to discharge or deal appropriately with anger, aggressiveness, or hostility covered by a facade of 'pleasantness.'"

A further trio of researchers in the same journal commented on the "polite, apologetic, almost painful acquiesence of the patients with rapidly progressing disease" and contrasted it with the more expressive personalities of those who showed greater resistance to the disease or experienced spontaneous remissions.

David Kissen, of the Psychosomatic Research Unit at the University of Glasgow, examined the emotional outlets of patients with lung cancer and formed the hypothesis that the poorer the outlet for emotional discharge, the less the exposure to smoke required to induce lung cancer.

Where Reich's findings of impaired respiration are concerned, the work of the German biochemist Otto Warburg is of importance. He reported respiratory damage in tumors in 1924 and Reich took care to refer to his findings. Warburg found a local oxygen deficiency in the cells and a surfeit of carbon dioxide with a high production of lactic acid. Although Warburg received the Nobel Prize in Physiology and Medicine in 1931 for his work in cellular respiration, his theory that cancer was due to faulty cell metabolism caused by oxygen deficiency aroused bitter controversy and has never been generally accepted. Coulson suggests that the poor respiration of the cancer cell must be due to either a metabolite released by a carcinogen that has a depressive effect on respiration (such an effect was demonstrated for the T-bacilli), or that tissue oxygen tension was chronically low (such an effect would follow from the reduced general respiration), or that both these effects operated.

Finally, Reich's view that the cell nucleus, in contrast to the depleted state of the organism as a whole, was bioenergetically overactive in the cancer tissue, was confirmed by Gurwitsch, the discoverer of the mitogenetic radiation, and by Klenitsky, both of whom found greatly increased radiation from tumor material.

The evidence makes clear that in his primary conclusion of the biopathic nature of cancer and its relationship to characterological shrinking and emotional deadness, Reich was again far ahead of traditional cancer research, which only recently, in a cautious and fragmentary way, has begun to understand some of the psychiatric implications of cancer. Far from straying from his proper field of research, Reich was eminently at home in it. It was almost uncanny the way each phase of his earlier work had equipped him with the special skills needed to understand different aspects of the cancer process. His work in the orgasm problem linked him with those researchers who found aversion to sex linked with cancer; his studies of the character resistances linked him to those who found blocked emotions were typical of cancer patients; his work on disturbed respiration linked him to Warburg's findings on cell suffocation; his work on the amoeboid movements in his bion cultures had prepared him for the amoeboid cancer cells that Enterline and Coman were to confirm were derived from within and not from parasites. Similarly, the studies of the basic antithesis of vegetative life had given Reich just that kind of understanding of the *contraction* process as a total psychosomatic shrinking that was necessary if the cancer disease was to be comprehended.

And as if all this were not enough, Reich's most recent finding, the discovery of a radiating energy, first in a bion culture and then in the organism and in the atmosphere, had provided the one avenue of approach to the biologically devitalized tissues that was necessary if there was to be a hope of affecting the cancer background therapeutically.

### Experimental Cancer Therapy

As soon as Reich had completed his move to the United States in August of 1939, he was ready to begin a series of experiments to find out if the *Sapa* bions which had shown such pronounced biological effects in Norway would have any effect on sick mice. Reich obtained a number of cancer mice from the pathology department of Columbia University. The first mouse to be injected with a solution of the culture fluid had a mammary tumor about the size of a large bean. After two days the tumor had softened and was reduced in size. This initial rapid reduction of size was followed by a slower regrowth of the tumor. By a process of trial and error Reich refined the process of injection by various methods involving prepared serums from which the bion culture had been filtered, and found that he was able to prolong the life of his mice substantially over the normal expectation for untreated cancer mice. The details are given below.

It was only after July 1940, when the atmospheric energy was first systematically concentrated, that a much superior method of treating the mice became available: the orgone accumulator. The first mouse accumulators were small boxes of sheet iron, about the size of cigar boxes, five inches square, covered with Cellotex board on the outside, and with air-holes in the lid. The mice spent half an hour a day in their therapeutic cells. The effects were far superior to the injection method: the mice improved quickly, the state of their fur changed and took on the normal sheen of health, the whole animal became lively and bright, instead of dull and contracted. The tumors ceased to grow, or receded, as in the case of the injection experiments, but this time there was no compensatory regrowth later. Reich concluded on the basis of his microscopic blood observations that both methods of treatment worked by having a charging effect on the blood, but whereas the bion injections represented a limited energy charge which was soon used up, the accumulator method involved a constant radiation effect.

The principal problem was that as the tumor softened and began to die off, it imposed a great strain on the organism which had to eliminate the dead tumor material. If the tumors were beyond a certain minimum size, the mice died regularly from the consequences of getting rid of the tumors: clogged kidneys was the most typical result of trying to excrete too much too rapidly.

In all, Reich treated 137 mice, 101 by the injection method, and 36 in the small accumulators. The results of the two series compared with a control group of 27 untreated mice are summarized in the following table:

|  | Control Group | Injection Group | Accumulator Group |
|---|---|---|---|
| Maximum life-span after detection of tumor | 11 weeks | 28 weeks | 31 weeks |
| Average life-span after tumor detection | 3.9 weeks | 9.1 weeks | 11.1 weeks |

The results were enormously encouraging and indicated a clear therapeutic influence from the orgone applications.

In March of 1941 Reich accepted his first human cancer patient, a woman in the terminal stages of cancer, whose case history fills twenty-eight pages of Reich's first published account of the cancer process. She had a tumor about the size of an apple in one breast and several metastases (secondary tumor formations) on the spine. She had been more or less inmobilized for two years due to spinal and hip pains. Two physicians pronounced her to be a hopeless case, a third thought that she would live only two weeks, and a fourth doctor gave her at most two months to live.

The physical orgone therapy involved the larger man-sized accumulator that Reich had had constructed in December 1940. They were about two feet six inches square in floor area and about five feet tall so that when a person sat down inside, he was surrounded closely on all sides by the metal walls, without actually being in direct contact with them. An aperture in the door, about one foot square, provided communication with the outside. According to the construction, the intensity of the energy-accumulation effect could be varied. Thus, building the walls of alternating layers of Cellotex and sheet iron (later, layers of glass wool and steel wool were used for additional concentration) increased the strength. The early accumulators were only a few layers, up to fivefold, though Dr. Walter Hoppe in Israel was later to pioneer the use of twentyfold accumulators.

When Reich's first cancer patient sat inside for her thirty-minute sessions, she experienced the typical subjective reactions that have already been described. She began to perspire, her skin reddened, and the blood pressure decreased. Reich's explanation for these effects was that the energy accumulated from the atmosphere stimulated the organismic energy and promoted a vagotonic, expansive, and hydrating effect on the body tissues. While cancer was a *shrinking biopathy,* the orgone accumulator provided an *expansive* therapy. The interaction was more effective the more the patient was surrounded closely by the materials. Mice responded poorly in the full-size accumulators because the organismic and atmospheric fields could not interact so readily, Reich reasoned.

However one seeks to explain the action of the accumulator, its effect on the cancer patient was astounding. The hemoglobin content of her blood climbed from 35 to 85 percent in three weeks. Her pains receded and she was able to sleep well without morphine. She was no longer bedridden, resumed her normal housework, and was able to travel to the therapy by subway, where previously she had required being supported like a cripple. X-ray photographs of the spine showed healthy bone growth in the area that had been shadowed by the metastases before. After eight orgone therapy sessions the breast tumor could no longer be palpated.

These remarkable changes, which no physician who had followed her case could explain, were not a "miracle cure." Reich was throughout his treatment of cancer patients very careful not to hold out false hopes to patients or relatives. Every patient was warned that the treatment was experimental and that the cancer disease posed many problems that could not be easily solved. One of these was the excretory problem over the tumors. A second problem was the underlying characterological fear of the very expansion process that the therapy set in motion. Although the orgone treatment of this first patient succeeded in recharging the blood and overcoming the tumor formation, it could not reverse some of the deeper organic effects of the shrinking process. There was an underlying atrophy, one of the effects of which was a characteristic thinness of the bones. A sudden accident, involving the fracture of her femur, put the patient into rapid decline, and she died four weeks later.

Her death was due to the biopathic background factors in

the disease, Reich pointed out, and not to the tumors or to the putrefaction process.

The patient had lived for ten months, five times longer than the most optimistic estimate of any physician. The treatment had freed her from tumors and from pains she had previously had to suppress with morphine.

Reich's approach to the difficulties and problems of cancer therapy resembled his approach to the difficulties of resistance analysis fifteen years earlier. Now, as then, he emphasized the disappointments and the failures.

His article on the experimental treatment with orgone therapy contains accounts of the results of treatment on a total of fifteen patients, all but two of whom were in advanced stages of cancer, and who only came to Reich because orthodox medicine had nothing further to offer them. Every one of these experienced relief from pain, so that dependence on drugs could be cut down, or dispensed with altogether. In every case the tumors reduced in size and breast tumors disappeared altogether. Four patients showed ossification in previously damaged bones on X-ray plates. Six patients who had previously been unable to work resumed their occupation. Five patients who had been dismissed by their physicians as hopeless, with inoperable cancers, responded so well that their life was prolonged by at least two years and they were still active and in good condition at the time Reich published his report.

The most important conclusion from these extraordinary results is that the cancer process is reversible if it is caught in time. The tumors can be reduced and eliminated by orgone treatment, provided they are not too advanced. The shrinking biopathy can be counteracted by a combined therapeutic program involving character therapy, vegetotherapy, and treatment in the orgone accumulator, provided it has not already led to structural changes with secondary consequences of their own. Reich was never overoptimistic about symptomatic relief. It would be a dangerous illusion, he realized, to believe that one could vanquish cancer with his orgone treatment: the only ultimate answer to the cancer misery lay in preventing the conditions that led to resignation, energy withdrawal, and devitalization. The organic pathology of the cancer biopathy led back to the fundamental *social problem* of preventing the general disturbance of functioning that set the shrinking disease into motion.

### Reception of Reich's Cancer Research

Nowhere was the irrationality that Reich's controversial discoveries provoked more intense than in the realm of cancer. To orthodox cancern research Reich was a trespasser in their territorial reserve. Let us contrast two reactions: one direct, interested, thoughtful; the other blindly resentful and hostile.

The review by Dr. Francis Regardie, of *The Cancer Biopathy*, took the view that:

"While the theories in this book may seem fantastic, they are not to be cast lightly aside. The postulates are capable of verification or the opposite, and should be studied in detail before being rejected. The riddle of cancer is not yet solved and the theory that it is a general disease with local manifestations has much in its favor.

"Reich's work might very well confirm decades of practice and empirical treatment. It appears to me that all types of therapy stand to benefit by further detailed investigations of the extraordinary concepts developed in *The Cancer Biopathy*."

Austin Smythe, the secretary of the Council on Pharmacy and Chemistry, published a scathing attack on the orgone accumulator in the journal of the American Medical Association. His concluding paragraph read: "Inquiries received concerning the 'institute' publishing this nonsense indicates that the 'theory' is promoted as a method of curing cancer. There is, of course, no evidence to indicate that this is anything more than another fraud that has been foisted on the public and medical profession."

It was attitudes such as this last one that inspired the Food and Drug Administration's prosecution of Reich in the 1950's. . . .

Ridicule is one experience; blatant misrepresentation is another. Clara Thompson, the analytic writer, could not refrain, in a reference to Reich's earlier work, from throwing into her account of the development of psychoanalysis the totally irrelevant and inaccurate information that Reich's later ideas had "not been confirmed by others." Specifically, she referred to negative results that had been obtained by T. Hauschka, senior member in charge of the Department of Experimental Zoology at the Institute for Cancer Research. Hauschka had, in fact, attempted to repeat some of Reich's bion experiments; but he had neglected to study the basic literature on the techniques of bion experimentation, and his "control" of Reich's work was of no more value than the simplistic reaction of Kreyberg in Oslo. Moreover, Hauschka, a cancer specialist, had not carried out any of Reich's experiments with orgone energy on cancer, or any of the other work described above. Most important, his paper purporting to have refuted the experiments *was never published.* . . .

Meanwhile, those of Reich's medical colleagues who carried out their own therapeutic work with the orgone accumulator in the treatment of cancer, such as Dr. Simeon Tropp of New York, and Dr. Walter Hoppe of Tel Aviv, obtained *positive* confirmations, which were published.

One of the most interesting exceptions to the apparent refusal of orthodox cancer researchers to look seriously at Reich's claims is of more recent origin. Dr. Bruno Bizzi, the vice-director of an Italian hospital, introduced a number of orgone accumulators for the treatment of physical complaints, including a few cases diagnosed as cancerous. He also obtained positive confirmations in reduction of tumors and succeeded in interesting Professor Chiurco, the director of the International Research Center on Precancer Conditions at Rome University. Professor Chiurco is one of the foremost authorities on cancer in the world, and it was on his initiative that several International Seminars on Cancer Prevention were held. At the second of these, in Rome in October 1968, Dr. Bizzi presented a paper on the Orgone Therapy of Cancer which was a milestone in that it presented Reich's conclusions factually as an approach to the treatment of cancer which merited careful scientific consideration. At an International Cancer Congress in Cassano Junio, Italy, in November 1968, Dr. Walter Hoppe presented a paper on the treatment of a malignant skin melanoma by means of the orgone accumulator and was nominated one year later as a member of the Sybaris-Magna Graecia Academy in recognition of work that by this time had been driven underground in America by the FDA prosecution.

Writing on the prejudice of orthodox medicine against Reich's cancer findings, Walter Hoppe wrote: "I only want to mention one of the hundreds of my own experiments in orgonomic medicine and orgone physics. A skin melanoma of the face, one of the most dangerous cancer forms, was treated with my orgone accumulator. The diagnosis was made by well-known specialists: a surgeon, a dermatologist, two radiologists, and by myself. The same specialists withdrew their own diagnosis and changed a cancer tumor to a harmless inflammation after orgone treatment reached decisive therapeutic success and the tumor was in a rapid disintegration. But a microscopic examination of the remainder of the tumor at the University of Jerusalem resulted in the unequivocal diagnosis of a cancerous melanoma."

It is now more than thirty years since Reich began his treatment of cancer. The amount of work done by others in extending it and building on his findings is still pitifully small, but at least a beginning has been made, with the work of Hoppe, Chiurco and Bizzi in Italy, that is already having international repercussions.

"There are today some thirty or forty men and women who constitute a sort of inner cabinet of cancerology," wrote Bernard Glemser in his survey of cancer research and progress. "They are scientists of great accomplishment and total dedication; they have immense prestige and, deservedly, considerable power; and they are involved directly or indirectly with virtually every aspect of cancer research all over the world."

That Professor Chiurco, who is one of this leading group, should be sufficiently convinced of the correctness of Reich's bioenergetic concepts to support and encourage the wider application and development of orgone therapy, may shake the confidence a little of those who, on hearsay evidence, by rumor and roundabout report, and without reference to any of the original source materials or experiments, wrote off Reich's cancer work as worthless.

# 15

# The Electrodynamic Theory of Life

*Harold Saxton Burr* and *F. S. C. Northrop*

*Interest in life energy has in turn revived interest in the "electrodynamic theory of life." Here is the classic statement, which is only now, after almost forty years, becoming recognized by many scientists as one of the most important scientific and philosophical statements of the century.*

• • •

There are several factors which suggest that living things must be viewed from the electrodynamic point of view. Certain of these factors appear in the nonbiological sciences and in general philosophical considerations; others arise in biology itself, and particularly in connection with recent evidence concerning the factors controlling the development of the nervous system.

## I.
## General Scientific and Philosophical Considerations

If one views the history of science as a whole, including its Greek as well as its modern manifestations, a certain contrast appears. Greek science was dominated largely by mathematics and astronomy, whereas since the seventeenth century physics and chemistry have been the leading disciplines. This difference in emphasis among the special sciences bespeaks a more fundamental difference in scientific outlook. Mathematics and astronomy as they appeared in

Greek times in the geometry of Euclid and in the mathematical astronomy of Eudoxus were systematic deductive sciences dealing with the entire spatial and astronomical universe as a whole. It is an obvious peculiarity of geometry as a pure science that it is concerned wholly with structure and not at all with matter. It is a more unexpected peculiarity of astronomy that it, more than any other of the natural sciences, tends to conceive of nature as a purely formal system. This was the case in Greek times and with Kepler, and is, or was, the case in our own time with Eddington and Jeans. It was not the case, however, with Galilei and Newton. They conceived of the astronomical universe as a physical system analogous to the system of earth and ball and inclined plane with which Galilei verified his profound and revolutionary reflections.

This brings us to the sharp contrast between traditional modern science and Greek science. The latter, dominated as it was by such scientists as Eudoxus, Euclid, Apollonius, and Archimedes, tended to regard mathematics as more fundamental than physics and to think of nature as a purely formal structure; the former, following Galilei and Newton, made physics primary, and hence regarded nature as an aggregate of many physical objects in motion, mathematics becoming a very necessary means, but nevertheless merely a means, of precisely formulating this physical conception. Stated in more general philosophical terms, Greek science, including biology with Aristotle, tended to conceive of nature in terms of formal causes; modern science, in terms of material causes. The two views have not been compatible in traditional scientific or philosophical theory. To maintain that nature is a system of forms, unconditioned by matter, is to maintain that nature and its systems possess a changeless structure; hence, the doctrine of the fixity of biological types in Greek biology. To maintain that nature is a collection of physical objects in motion is to regard structure as a relation between these objects, and subject to change with their motion; hence, the essentially modern character of Darwin's doctrine of the modification of biological types. In short, Greek inorganic and organic science put the emphasis on structure and the eternal constancy of forms, whereas modern science has placed the emphasis of physical and chemical and biological entities and the variability and evolution of forms.

This difference between Greek and modern science exhibits itself in one contrast which is implicit in what we have already indicated. The ancient emphasis on structure and on systematic science, such as appeared in the geometry of Euclid and the astronomy of Eudoxus, led to the conception of nature as a single system. This means that no local system can be completely understood by itself and that thoroughgoing specialization is not sound science; nothing is truly understood until nature as a whole is understood and the local part is perceived in its exact status in and connection with that whole. This was one of the major reasons why Greek science was so inherently and inescapably philosophical. The modern conception, arising with Galilei's founding of "the science of local motion," and with Newton's principle of isolation and the attendant emphasis on masses rather than structure, led naturally to the conception of nature as an aggregate of many physical objects; hence, the current notion that scientific knowledge is possible for a person only in a very narrow field, and the attendant corollary that any attempt, such as the philosopher sometimes proposes, to talk about the whole, is idle footless speculation.

This opposition expresses itself in one other distinction: Greek science, except for the atomists, who were repudiated in mathematics, for reasons which we shall show immediately, placed the emphasis on continuity; modern science, on discontinuity. The reason for the Greek point of view is to be found in the discovery of the incommensurable by the Pythagoreans. They and the atomists, like the moderns, began with a discontinuous theory. The attempt was made to build up lines and surfaces and solids out of discontinuous elements or "pebbles." In short, they tried to define the continuous in terms of the discontinuous, and to reduce geometry to arithmetic. This worked beautifully until they came upon the length of the hypotenuse of a right-angled triangle, the other two sides of which are equal. Setting the sides equal to unity the length of the hypotenuse is $\sqrt{2}$. Stated in more concrete terms, this means that any "pebble" or unit of length which goes into the length of either side a definite number of times leaving nothing over will always leave something over when the hypotenuse is measured. This convinced the Greeks that the continuous will not reduce to the discontinuous and that geometry is more fundamental than arithmetic. Modern science, on the other hand, discovered nature to be atomic, reduced geometry to arithmetic by generalizing its theory of number, and regarded discontinuity, and the many, as more fundamental than continuity, and the one.

This modern emphasis on entities, fluid forms, atomicity, and discontinuity has dominated biological thought. Galilei had no more than developed his physical and mechanical theory of the inorganic universe before Harvey proceeded to apply physical and mechanical conceptions to living creatures in the discovery of the circulation of the blood. Lavoisier revealed the chemical character of respiration and metabolism in living things at the same time that he placed chemistry upon secure foundations with the discovery of the principle of the conservation of mass. Gradually with Liebig and Wöhler, and the vast army of physiological chemists, the chemical nature of living creatures has become more and more evident. It is to be noted that this is a distinctly modern emphasis. Chemistry rests upon a discontinuous atomic conception of nature, and atomism in its traditional interpretation involves an emphasis upon entities rather than upon structure and on the constituent elements rather than upon the whole. This attitude of mind has gone all through biology even where no appeal has been made to the chemical nature of the processes or factors considered. Practically a century ago Schleiden and Schwann discovered the cellular nature of plants and animals. Here was the supposedly ultimate biological atom. More recently the emphasis has shifted from the cell to the gene, but even so the emphasis is still on entities.

It is to be noted that this entire development involves the carrying over into biology of a philosophical standpoint which was discovered and clearly formulated first in physics and chemistry. There can be no doubt of its success or validity. There is nothing to date to indicate that the biologist should hesitate to follow the lead which the more mature and exact science of physics gives him.

If this be granted, then it is clear that a slight change of emphasis must come into biological theory. For the entire modern standpoint with its emphasis on entities rather than organization, upon discontinuity rather than continuity, upon local systems rather than upon their status in the total field of nature as a whole, has been found in physics to need rather radical and thoroughgoing supplementation. The word "supplementation" is to be emphasized, for the modern standpoint has not been rejected; it is being merely amended. The amendment is so thoroughgoing, however, as to amount to the placing of the Greek upon an equal footing with the modern standpoint. Moreover, the concepts modified are so primary in the levels of importance and so general and universal in their application that every branch of human activity and even the very meaning and significance of any fact we observe or experiment we perform are affected.

The elemental and essential fact as it appears in physics can be stated very briefly; atomic physics has had to be supplemented with field physics. The point to be noted is that the particle both conditions and is conditioned by its field. Stated in more general terms this means that continuity as well as discontinuity is ultimate, that nature is both one and many. In short, any local system in part constitutes and is in part constituted in its behavior by nature as a whole and the physical field in which it is embedded. This rediscovery of the continuous field, or the one, as a causal factor conditioning the behavior of the constituent particles, or the many, is a return to the Greek standpoint. But the particles also determine the character of the field. This is the modern viewpoint. The reciprocal causal relation between field and particle amounts to a union of both viewpoints. This is the fact which anyone with an eye to first principles can see standing out amid all the complexities and confusions of current discoveries in physics.

But this mere designation of the fact is not enough. We do not possess science until our findings are formulated in terms of clear consistent principles. At this point, current scientific and philosophical thought is confronted with a serious difficulty. According to all traditional scientific and philosophical conceptions the Greek and modern views of science contradict each other. It was precisely because of this contradiction that we had to reject Plato's and Aristotle's physics, biology, and philosophy in order to accept Galilei's, Newton's, and Darwin's. The difficulty can be put very simply. The modern conception of nature as a discontinuous collection of moving particles makes all order in nature a temporary effect, renders nature as a whole a mere aggregate, and provides no meaning for continuity as a primary factor or for the field as a causal factor. The Greek conception, as formulated, either in mathematics and astronomy by Plato and Eudoxus, or in biology by Aristotle, does justice to the continuity and unity and organization, and to the field character of natural phenomena, at the cost of interpreting nature as a single substance or system and rendering change, atomicity, and the temporal origin of species meaningless. It is clear, therefore, that before the doctrine of reciprocal causal interaction between particle and field can possess meaningful, consistent theoretical formulation a new theory of the first principles of science must be developed. Moreover, this new theory must combine the Greek and modern conceptions of science which have previously been supposed to be incompatible.

It is essential that the reader sense the necessity of this theoretical formulation before going further. Otherwise the electrodynamic theory of life proposed in this paper will appear as but a new name for traditional conceptions, and its essential novelty and significance will be missed. This point may be made by referring to an experience which the authors of this paper had when the theory, proposed here, was presented to an experimental anatomist. He replied, "Yes, the field theory of life is reasonable, but what is the field except as it is determined by its physicochemical constituents?" In this query he gave expression to the fundamental presupposition of traditional modern science that the field, or nature as a whole, is a mere aggregate of the atomic parts and in no sense a primary causal factor. He was quite right also in suggesting that the field theory of life would be but a new name for old commonplaces were this all that it means. The point is, however, that the theory which we are proposing means more than this. The microscopic physicochemical constituents do determine the character of the field. No one cognizant of modern physics and physiological chemistry can deny this. But this relation between field and particle is not, as traditional modern scientific theory has assumed, an asymmetrical or one-way relation. The field both determines and is determined by the particle. But to find meaning for the field as, in this partial sense, an ultimate causal factor is the real difficulty. In the traditional modern scientific conception of nature as a collection of particles in motion and physicochemical interaction, there is no meaning to the field as anything more than a mere aggregate and effect of their compounding; in Newton's physics, given the masses with their inertial and accelerative forces, the gravitational field and the orbits are completely determined. To make sense out of the notion that the field determines the behavior of any local process or constituent within it, it is necessary to modify modern science at its very foundations by revising our theory of first principles to provide meaning for the unity of nature as a causal factor. Without this revision in our most elemental and fundamental conception of nature as conceived by science, all field theories whether in physiology or physics are mere verbiage.

It is easy enough to find meaning for the unity of nature and for the field as a causal factor providing we return to that Greek conception of science which makes continuity ultimate, regards nature as one substance, and interprets all plurality as a mere abstraction from the unity. But this is to go to the other extreme and find meaning for the causal efficacy of the field at the cost of denying all determination of the field by the particle. Clearly, modern science will not permit us to do this. It is impossible now to deny the validity of physicochemical categories. There is the particle as well as the field. It is clear, therefore, that meaning for the field and the unity of nature as a causal factor must be gained without rejecting the primacy of the atomic physicochemical categories of modern science. The only completely physical theory of the first principles of science proposed to date which accomplishes this is the macroscopic atomic theory developed by one of the authors of this paper (Northrop). It retains the kinetic atomic theory of traditional modern science, thereby providing theoretical foundations for the physicochemical categories which modern investigations have established, and providing meaning for the determination of the field by the particle. To this traditional kinetic atomic theory it adds one macroscopic atom which surrounds, and, *solely because of its relatively small fixed finite size*, compresses and congests the microscopic particles, of the whole of nature, of traditional theory, which it contains. Thus a unity of nature as a whole is impressed upon the compounding and aggregating of the microscopic particles to make complex nature one as well as many, a unity as well as an aggregate, a field which in part determines the behavior of each particle and process, as well as a complex continuum, in part constituted by the motion and interaction of the particles. Whether the macroscopic atomic theory will gain confirmation directly by further empirical investigations need not concern us here. Its mere existence as a possible theory is sufficient for our present purposes, since this demonstrates that it is possible to combine the Greek scientific conceptions of nature as a single system with the modern scientific conception of nature as an aggregate of many particles, without contradiction, and thereby gives meaningful formulation to the thesis that the particle in its behavior both determines and is determined by the field in which it is embedded.

Having demonstrated that the doctrine of the reciprocal interaction between field and particle can be given consistent meaningful theoretical formulation, it remains to designate the evidence in both physics and biology which supports it, and the modification in our attitude toward all systems in nature, which its acceptance must entail.

The first conclusive evidence in physics of the necessity of supplementing atomic physics with field physics appeared in the relativity theory. A short survey of certain developments in the history of science will make this clear. Science has always distinguished between two types of structure or relatedness in nature. The one type, most evident in space, is relatively constant through time; the other, evident in the obvious changing relations between things, is subject to change with time. Actually both types of structure of relatedness apply to the physical content of the universe, but Newtonian physics did not view the situation in this light. Instead, it separated the relatively constant spatial structure of physical nature from the physical content and turned the separated structure into an independent entity called absolute space. This space was really a field, but since it permitted matter to move through it without opposition, there was little or no meaning to the statement that the field conditioned the behavior of the particle. A similar separation and reification of the field character of physical nature occurred in the sciences of optics and electricity with the introduction of the ether. The theory of relativity has demonstrated, however, that this entire procedure is mistaken. In doing away with the independent ether, and in merging matter and space and time, Einstein has shown that the approximately constant macroscopic structure of space is the approximately constant macroscopic structure of matter itself. The field is not independent of matter but a very condition for an causal determiner of the behavior of matter. Thus Einstein replaces Newton's three laws of motion with the single law that a body moves in a path which is a geodesic of the space-time of the observer's frame of reference. But the general theory of relativity also prescribes that the distribution of matter determines the character of the metrical field, and thereby the lay of the geodesic. Thus the particle both conditions and is conditioned by the metrical field.

These considerations from the verified general theory of

elativity are sufficient to indicate that the attempt to conceive of nature entirely in terms of the pluralistic discontinuous microscopic atomic physicochemical categories of traditional scientific thought is inadequate. This does not mean that these traditional categories are invalid; they are in fact necessary, as the general theory of relativity indicates when it makes the metrical properties of space dependent upon them and their distribution, but they are nevertheless insufficient. The field also conditions the behavior of the particle.

The second evidence in physics for the theory of the reciprocal determination of particle and field appears in wave mechanics. At this point the relevance of all this for biology can be made more direct and explicit. Biologists have discovered that whatever else living creatures may be, they are in a very real and significant sense physicochemical systems. But chemists and physicists have now conclusively demonstrated that the electrodynamic theory of nature is more fundamental than the chemical theory. The reduction of the chemical atom to electrons and protons and the development of quantum theory and wave mechanics implies this. Moreover, the recent surprising tendency in wave mechanics is to put the emphasis on the field even to the point at times of attempting to derive the particle from it. This, as Darrow and G. P. Thomson have pointed out, is an error; moreover, quantum physics reveals even new evidences of discontinuity. Nevertheless, the fact still remains that the field as a distinctly causal factor is indispensable.

These established and accepted findings of contemporary physics are sufficient to indicate that the same influence from the mature science of physics, which previously drove biology with Harvey to the mechanical theory of living creatures, and with Lavoisier to the chemical theory of their nature, must now drive us to an electrodynamic theory of life. Contemporary developments in physics rest upon the discovery of the primacy of electrodynamic theory over chemical or traditional physical theory.

Moreover, and this is the crucial point, this shift involves much more than a mere shift in terms. Contemporary physics has gone very much further than the mere statement of chemical elements in terms of electrons and protons. The latter advance, while of great importance, still involves the traditional emphasis solely on entities and their motion. The current shift is much more fundamental than this, for the field as well as the particle is now revealed as a causal factor. Once this point is really grasped our whole attitude toward our scientific knowledge must change. Structure again becomes significant. It is no longer permissible to assume, as traditional modern science has done, that if the constituent chemical components are determined, the field and the structure will take care of itself.

The significance of this for biology can be made evident by a brief consideration of its most fundamental and perplexing problem—the problem of organization. It is a commonplace that living creatures, notwithstanding the modification in types in evolution, maintain a certain constancy of structure through continuous changes of material. Aristotle with his doctrine of formal as well as material causes provided a theoretical basis for this fact, but failed to account for the mutability of species. Modern science with its rediscovery of the kinetic atomic theory and its attendant doctrine of the variability of structure with motion provided meaning for Darwin's discovery, and the physicochemical nature of life, but at the cost, as Claude Bernard indicated, and as Driesch and J. S. Haldane have emphasized more recently, of failing to do adequate justice to the relative constancy of biological organization. The traditional modern doctrine that the chemical elements completely condition the structure and organization of the organism failed to explain why a certain structural constancy persisted through the chemical flux.

This obvious inadequacy led to the introduction of nonphysical factors such as *Driesch's* "entelechy," *Spemann's* "organizer," *Rignano's* "biological energy," *Child's* "physiological gradient," *Weiss's* "biological field," and *Köhler's* "Gestalten," all of which have certain validity as descriptive terms. It now appears, however, that the difficulty may have its basis not in the failure of any possible physical theory, but in the inadequacy of traditional physical theory. For the chemical view with its emphasis on entities has been demonstrated to reduce to the electrodynamic view in which the more constant structural guiding contribution of the field is found to supplement the contingent changing relatedness introduced by the motion of the particles.

If this new electrodynamic theory is correct, it follows that biological science must supplement its present emphasis on chemical analysis and on entities with a more serious study, by the experimental determination of potential distribution, of field factors and structure and organization in itself. It appears also that biology itself suggests the necessity of the particle-field theory.

## II.
## Biological and Neurological Considerations

The necessity is apparent when an attempt is made to unravel the underlying processes inherent in ontogeny. In spite of the mass of accumulated data concerning the development of the organism in general and of the nervous system in particular, no thoroughly satisfactory explanation has been given of the regulation and control of growth. Description of successive steps of development in a wide variety of forms reveals little of the relationships which exist between the steps or the factors which regulate the passage from one to the other. The very wealth of the accumulated facts tends to obscure the underlying regulation and to defy analysis. It was this difficulty which led Driesch to the repostulation of a "vital force," or entelechy. This brilliant hypothesis has never received its just due. The whole theory is a very adequate description of an extraordinarily constant control and regulation of growth. Its weakness lays in its assumption of an extrabiological agent incapable of scientific description. The field theories of Spemann, Weiss, and Gurwitsch are also valuable attempts at explanation, but like the entelechies of Driesch, scientific analysis is well-nigh impossible.

All embryologists have been impressed at one time or another with one aspect of the problem noted above. Growing systems posses an extraordinary capacity for self-regulation. Some powerful agent seems to be inherent in the system through which the progress of development from stage to stage is coordinated and regulated according to a definite plan. Each and every biological system seems to possess a dynamic "wholeness," the maintenance of whose integrity is a necessity of continued organic existence. Virtually all the theoretical analyses stress this quality, but no adequate definition of this dynamic agent or adequate explanation of its working has been offered.

Not only is the regulation in ontogeny an enigma, but we are still almost completely ignorant of the dynamic relationships in living systems. A considerable body of information is available concerning the physical and chemical structure of protoplasm, but we know little of the way in which the elements are organized into a dynamic whole. The cytoplasm of a living cell is not a formless agglomeration of chemical substances but is an integrated and coordinated system. It is impossible to conceive of cytoplasm as a haphazard arrangement of molecules. A definite pattern of relationships must exist. We possess a modicum of knowledge of these relationships at any one moment, but we have no adequate theory of the mechanism which maintains that pattern throughout the rapidly changing flux in living systems. Study of the situation in the nucleus is somewhat more advanced because of the greater definiteness of the formed elements. We possess fairly clear statements of the physical and to some extent of the chemical components of the nucleus. The dynamic activities of the formed elements, the chromosomes, have been partially unraveled by geneticists. As in cytoplasm, however, we lack any adequate hypothesis of the mechanisms involved in chromosomal aggregations or in the splitting and distribution of the component elements. The results of the processes have been widely studied and have provided an important body of information, but we still lack understanding as to how the results are accomplished. Here then, as in embryology, we find "pattern or organization" the fundamental problem.

The difficulties suggested above are no less apparent in the analysis of the development of the nervous system. The successive steps have been described by innumerable workers, but we lack any rational explanation of the appearance of local regions of growth and differentiation and of the final establishment of nuclear masses and fiber-tract pathways. Although Spemann has shown the importance of the dorsal lip of the blastopore as a concomitant of the formation of the nervous system, there is little understanding of the factors involved in this relationship. Moreover, neither fact nor theory has yet made clear the nature of the factors which give this power to the dorsal lip of the blastopore.

Careful consideration of the many facts, of which the above is but a suggestive résumé, compels us to look for a hypothesis which will cover not only the dynamics of development but also the pattern of organization of unitary biological systems. The search for such a hypothesis has intrigued many investigators. As has been shown earlier in this paper, its formulation has been hindered by reliance upon earlier physical theory. With the advent in physics of the field theory of the relationships between particulate matter, the resolution of the biological theory becomes clearer. It is believed that the theory about to be proposed satisfies this condition and, if it can be demonstrated, gives the solution to many problems of biology.

The theory is the result of many years of experimental investigation of the mechanisms involved in the development of the nervous system. In these studies it has been shown that an extremely important factor in the organization of the nervous system is the rise and fall of differential growth rates within the wall of the neural tube. Moreover, experimental work confirms the belief that the direction of growth and the end station of differentiating nerve fibers is related to these primary centers of rapid proliferation. Inasmuch as they seem to be potent factors in imparting the fiber pattern to the nervous system, it becomes necessary to inquire into the agents which could act to determine the locus of these areas and to regulate the division rates in them. If this could be settled, then it would be possible to formulate a hypothesis as to the origin of pattern in the nervous system. Conceivably this might provide a clue to the origin of pattern in developing organisms and in other living systems.

An increasing body of evidence indicates that bioelectric phenomena underlie growth as well as many other biological processes. Numerous electrometric studies compel us to believe in the presence of polar and potential differences in living systems. If this is true, it follows by definition that electrodynamic fields are also present. Their existence in the physical world is generally accepted. Moreover, the formed relations of particulate matter is to a considerable degree a function of such fields. Thus the individual characteristics of atomic matter are a result of the interdependence of fields and particles. Pattern in physics, then, is determined by the interplay of electrodynamic fields and the particular matter therein contained.

It is reasonable to extend this hypothesis into the realm of biology: potential gradients and polar differences exist in living systems. If this is so, then electrodynamic fields are also present. The following theory may therefore be formulated. The pattern or organization of any biological system is established by a complex electrodynamic field, which is in part determined by its atomic physicochemical components and which in part determines the behavior and orientation of those components. This field is electrical in the physical sense and by its properties it relates the entities of the biological system in a characteristic pattern and is itself in part a result of the existence of those entities. It determines and is determined by the components. More than establishing pattern, it must maintain pattern in the midst of a physicochemical flux. Therefore, it must regulate and control living things, it must be the mechanism the outcome of whose activity is "wholeness," organization, and continuity. The electrodynamic field then is comparable to the entelechy of Driesch, the embryonic field of Spemann, the biological field of Weiss.

The implication of the above theory for embryology yields a number of interesting points, only one of which can be considered here. An intriguing problem in chordate development is the establishment of a longitudinal axis. This is a very real structural alignment, although at early stages in development the cells which are related to it may be totipotent. Experimental rearrangement of the cellular units does not change the axis although they themselves may have their ultimate fate altered. Caudal cells may become cephalic cells, right cells may become left with little serious interference with the normal processes of growth. Yet in some way the constituent cells of the growing system have their fate determined and their behavior and orientation controlled.

At least two factors in this regulation are familiar. Embryology and genetics have given adequate evidence of the importance of the chromosomes in determining cellular fate. The investigations of Weismann, Driesch, Boveri, Hertwig, and many others attest this. The geneticists have confirmed it and we are compelled to believe that the formed elements in the nucleus partly determine the growth and differentiation of cells. But the experimental embryologists have shown that intercellular relationships are no less important. Spemann and his students have demonstrated the dependence of cells on their local environment. The induction or organization hypothesis is an expression of their findings. To genetic constitution, then, there must be added local cellular environment as an important determiner of cell fate and therefore of the organization of the growing systems.

To Driesch, however, we owe the brilliant observation that the fate of any group of cells in an embryo is not only genetically conditioned but is also a function of the position of that group in the whole biological system. The mechanism by which position could determine cellular potencies was explained by Driesch through the assumption of an extrabiological guiding principle, an entelechy. It is at this point that the electrodynamic field theory proposed above provides a significant explanation of the well-recognized facts. In the physical world the nature of an atom is dependent upon the number of entities which comprise it and the field in which they lie, the position of the electron orbits being of fundamental importance. So, on a very much more complex scale in a biological system the fate of any group of cells is determined in part by the position those cells occupy in the electrodynamic field of the embryo. It is clear that if the above be granted, three factors are present in the normal development of an organism. The cells must possess a certain genetic constitution, a certain cellular environment, and a certain position in an electrodynamic field.

This is not the place to extend the application of the theory to many other problems of embryology, for another important aspect calls for attention. The pattern of the organization of the molecular and atomic constituents of protoplasm is an even more important problem to biology than the physicochemical nature of the entities themselves. It is not enough to know the chemical formula of protoplasm. It is of vital importance to understand how the elements are related to each other, how they are gathered together in a single "whole" system. If the electrodynamic theory is sound, the characteristic relationship of the elements of any biological system is a function of the field of the system. If this be true, then the great jump from living organic matter to nonliving physical matter is no longer inexplicable. The difference between the two is to be found in all probability in more complex fields and more complex molecular structure. Life, then, is not a special creation but an expression of fundamental law operating in living and nonliving matter alike.

The theoretical considerations here presented have led us to the conclusion, reached by nearly all other investigators, that pattern or organization is a fundamental characteristic of biological systems, or of physical systems, or of the universe. The electrodynamic theory provides a working hypothesis for a direct attack upon this problem. If accepted, it opens up a wide field of study based upon electrometric methods. It should be possible, therefore, to determine by objective experiment whether or not such fields exist. In other words, this theory can be put to experimental test. Finally, the theory makes it possible to place the investigation of the organization of living systems on the same objective and physical basis as the analysis of their chemical constituents.

It appears, therefore, that a hypothesis of this type is necessary to bring biological theory into line with physical theory. Moreover, biological considerations alone affirm a similar necessity and provide a sufficient amount of data to warrant putting to nature, by experimental and electrometric methods, the questions which this theory raises. These questions fall naturally into three categories. In the first of these are to be found questions as to the presence and character of potential and polar differences in living organisms. In the second are the questions dealing with the measurement of electrodynamic fields as concomitants of the potential differences. In the third are those questions which are associated with the impact of an altered field in the environment on developing mechanisms. In all probability new technical methods will have to be devised before definite answers can be obtained. Furthermore, if the theory is established, it makes possible the application of the mathematical methods being developed for field and wave physics to biological material, thereby placing the study of biological organization on a mathematical as well as an experimental basis.

# 16

## Outwitting the Stars

### *Paramahansa Yogananda*

*The ways that we are affected by cosmic energies has become a major research interest. In more esoteric literature the influence of celestial bodies is seen as strongly affecting an individual's total personality from conception.*

*Paramahansa Yogananda, founder of The Self-Realization Fellowship in America and master of Kriya Yoga, gives a personal account of an adventure in astrology.*

• • •

"Mukunda, why don't you get an astrological armlet?"

"Should I, Master? I don't believe in astrology."

"It is not a question of *belief;* the scientific attitude one should take on any subject is whether it is *true.* The law of gravitation worked as efficiently before Newton as after him. The cosmos would be fairly chaotic if its laws could not operate without the sanction of human belief.

"Charlatans have brought the ancient stellar science to its present disrepute. Astrology is too vast, both mathematically and philosophically, to be rightly grasped except by men of profound understanding. If ignoramuses misread the heavens, and see there a scrawl instead of a script, that is to be expected in this imperfect world. One should not dismiss the wisdom with the 'wise.'

"All parts of creation are linked together and interchange their influences. The balanced rhythm of the universe is rooted in reciprocity," my guru continued. "Man, in his human aspect, has to combat two sets of forces—first, the tumults within his being, caused by admixture of earth, water, fire, air, and ethereal elements; second, the outer disintegrating powers of nature. So long as man struggles with his mortality, he is affected by the myriad mutations of heaven and earth.

"Astrology is the study of man's response to planetary stimuli. The stars have no conscious benevolence or animosity; they merely send forth positive and negative radiations. Of themselves, these do not help or harm humanity, but offer a lawful channel for the outward operation of cause-effect equilibriums that each man has set into motion in the past.

"A child is born on that day and at that hour when the celestial rays are in mathematical harmony with his individual karma. His horoscope is a challenging portrait, revealing his unalterable past and its probable future results. But the natal chart can be rightly interpreted only by men of intuitive wisdom: these are few.

"The message boldly blazoned across the heavens at the moment of birth is not meant to emphasize fate—the result of past good and evil—but to arouse man's will to escape from his universal thralldom. What he has done, he can undo. None other than himself was the instigator of the causes of whatever effects are now prevalent in his life. He can overcome any limitation, because he created it by his own actions in the first place, and because he possesses spiritual resources that are not subject to planetary pressure.

"Superstitious awe of astrology makes one an automaton, slavishly dependent on mechanical guidance. The wise man defeats his planets—which is to say, his past—by transferring his allegiance from the creation to the Creator. The more he realizes his unity with Spirit, the less he can be dominated by matter. The soul is ever free; it is deathless because birthless. It cannot be regimented by stars.

"Man *is* a soul, and *has* a body. When he properly places his sense of identity, he leaves behind all compulsive patterns. So long as he remains confused in his ordinary state of spiritual amnesia, he will know the subtle fetters of environmental law.

"God is harmony; the devotee who attunes himself will

never perform any action amiss. His activities will be correctly and naturally timed to accord with astrological law. After deep prayer and meditation he is in touch with his divine consciousness; there is no greater power than that inward protection."

"Then, dear Master, why do you want me to wear an astrological bangle?" I ventured this question after a long silence; I had tried to assimilate Sri Yukteswar's noble exposition, which contained thought very new to me.

"It is only when a traveler has reached his goal that he is justified in discarding his maps. During the journey, he takes advantage of any convenient shortcut. The ancient rishis discovered many ways to curtail the period of man's exile in delusion. There are certain mechanical features in the law of karma that can be skillfully adjusted by the fingers of wisdom.

"All human ills arise from some transgression of universal law. The scriptures point out that man must satisfy the laws of nature, while not discrediting the divine omnipotence. He should say: 'Lord, I trust in Thee, and know Thou canst help me, but I too will do my best to undo any wrong I have done.' By a number of means—by prayer, by willpower, by yoga meditation, by consultation with saints, by use of astrological bangles—the adverse effects of past wrongs can be minimized or nullified.

"Just as a house may be fitted with a copper rod to absorb the shock of lightning, so the bodily temple can be protected in certain ways.

"Electrical and magnetic radiations are ceaselessly circulating in the universe; they affect man's body for good and ill. Ages ago our rishis pondered the problem of combating the adverse effects of subtle cosmic influences. The sages discovered that pure metals emit an astral light which is powerfully counteractive to negative pulls of the planets. Certain plant combinations were also found to be helpful. Most effective of all are faultless jewels of not less than two carats.

"The practical preventive uses of astrology have seldom been seriously studied outside of India. One little-known fact is that the proper jewels, metals, and plant preparations are valueless unless the required weight is secured and unless the remedial agent is worn next to the skin."

"Sir, of course I shall take your advice and get a bangle. I am intrigued at the thought of outwitting a planet!"

"For general purposes I counsel the use of an armlet made

of gold, silver, and copper. But for a specific purpose I want you to get one of silver and lead." Sri Yukteswar added careful directions.

"Guruji, what 'specific purpose' do you mean?"

"The stars are about to take an 'unfriendly' interest in you, Mukunda. Fear not; you shall be protected. In about a month your liver will cause you much trouble. The illness is scheduled to last for six months, but your use of an astrological armlet will shorten the period to twenty-four days."

I sought out a jeweler the next day, and was soon wearing the bangle. My health was excellent: Master's prediction slipped from my mind. He left Serampore to visit Banaras. Thirty days after our conversation, I felt a sudden pain in the region of my liver. The following weeks were a nightmare of excruciating pain. Reluctant to disturb my guru, I thought I would bravely endure my trial alone.

But twenty-three days of torture weakened my resolution; I entrained for Banaras. There Sri Yukteswar greeted me with unusual warmth, but gave me no opportunity to tell him my woes in private. Many devotees visited Master that day, just for a *darshan*. Ill and neglected, I sat in a corner. It was not until after the evening meal that all guests had departed. My guru summoned me to the octagonal balcony of the house.

"You must have come about your liver disorder." Sri Yukteswar's gaze was averted; he walked to and fro, occasionally intercepting the moonlight. "Let me see, you have been ailing for twenty-four days, haven't you?"

"Yes, sir."

"Please do the stomach exercise I taught you."

"If you knew the extent of my suffering, Master, you would not ask me to exercise." Nevertheless, I made a feeble attempt to obey him.

"You say you have pain; I say you have none. How can such contradictions exist?" My guru looked at me inquiringly.

I was dazed and then overcome with joyful relief. No longer could I feel the continuous torment that had kept me nearly sleepless for weeks; at Sri Yukteswar's words the agony vanished as though it had never been.

I started to kneel at his feet in gratitude, but he quickly prevented me.

"Don't be childish. Get up and enjoy the beauty of the moon over the Ganges." But Master's eyes were twinkling happily as I stood in silence beside him. I understood by his attitude that he wanted me to feel that not he, but God, had been the healer.

I wear even now the heavy silver-and-lead bangle, a memento of that day—long past, ever cherished—when I found anew that I was living with a personage indeed superhuman. On later occasions, when I brought my friends to Sri Yukteswar for healing, he invariably recommended jewels or the bangle, extolling their use as an act of astrological wisdom.

I had been prejudiced against astrology from my childhood, partly because I observed that many people are sequaciously attached to it, and partly because of a prediction made by our family astrologer: "You will marry three times, being twice a widower." I brooded over the matter, feeling like a goat awaiting sacrifice before the temple of triple matrimony.

"You may as well be resigned to your fate," my brother Ananta had remarked. "Your written horoscope has correctly stated that you would fly from home toward the Himalayas during your early years, but would be forcibly returned. The forecast of your marriages is also bound to be true."

A clear intuition came to me one night that the prophecy was wholly false. I set fire to the horoscope scroll, placing the ashes in a paper bag on which I wrote: "Seeds of past karma cannot germinate if they are roasted in the fires of divine wisdom." I put the bag in a conspicuous spot; Ananta immediately read my defiant comment.

"You cannot destroy truth as easily as you have burned this paper scroll." My brother laughed scornfully.

It is a fact that on three occasions before I reached manhood, my family tried to arrange my betrothal. Each time I refused to fall in with the plans, knowing that my love for God was more overwhelming than any astrological persuasion from the past.

"The deeper the self-realization of a man, the more he influences the whole universe by his subtle spiritual vibrations, and the less he himself is affected by the phenomenal flux." These words of Master's often returned inspiringly to my mind.

Occasionally I told astrologers to select my worst periods, according to planetary indications, and I would still accomplish whatever task I set myself. It is true that my success at such times has been preceded by extraordinary difficulties. But my conviction has always been justified: faith in divine protection and right use of man's God-given will are forces more formidable than are influences flowing from the heavens.

The starry inscription at one's birth, I came to understand, is not that man is a puppet of his past. Its message is rather a prod to pride; the very heavens seek to arouse man's determination to be free from every limitation. God created each man as a soul, dowered with individuality, hence essential to the universal structure, whether in the temporary role of pillar or parasite. His freedom is final and immediate, if he so wills: it depends not on outer but inner victories.

Sri Yukteswar discovered the mathematical application of a 24,000-year equinoctial cycle to our present age. The cycle is divided into an ascending arc and a descending arc, each of 12,000 years. Within each arc fall four *Yugas*, or ages, called *Kali, Dwapara, Treta,* and *Satya,* corresponding to the Greek ideas of Iron, Bronze, Silver, and Golden Ages.

My guru determined by various calculations that the last *Kali Yuga,* or Iron Age, of the ascending arc started about A.D. 500. The Iron Age, 1,200 years in duration, is a span of materialism; it ended about A.D. 1700. That year ushered in *Dwapara Yuga,* a 2,400-year period of electrical and atomic-energy developments: the age of telegraphy, radio, airplanes, and other space annihilators.

The 3,600-year period of *Treta Yuga* will start in A.D. 4100; the age will be marked by common knowledge of telepathic communications and other time annihilators. During the 4,800 years of *Satya Yuga,* final age in an ascending arc, the intelligence of man will be highly developed; he will work in harmony with the divine plan.

A descending arc of 12,000 years, starting with a descending Golden Age of 4,800 years, then begins for the world (in A.D. 12,500); man gradually sinks into ignorance. These cycles are the eternal rounds of *maya,* the contrasts and relativities of the phenomenal universe.* Men, one by one,

* The Hindu scriptures place the present world age as occurring within the *Kali Yuga* of a much longer universal cycle than the simple 24,000-year equinoctial cycle with which Sri Yukteswar was concerned. The universal cycle of the scriptures is 4,300,560,000 years in extent, and measures out a day of creation. This vast figure is based on the relationship between the length of the solar year and a multiple of pi

escape from creation's prison of duality as they awaken to consciousness of their inseverable divine unity with the Creator.

Master enlarged my understanding not only of astrology but of the world's scriptures. Placing the holy texts on the spotless table of his mind, he was able to dissect them with the scalpel of intuitive reasoning and to separate errors and interpolations of scholars from the truths as originally expressed by the prophets.

"Fix one's vision on the end of the nose." This inaccurate interpretation of a Bhagavad-Gita stanza, widely accepted by Eastern pundits and Western translators, used to arouse Master's droll criticism.

"The path of a yogi is singular enough as it is," he remarked. "Why counsel him that he must also make himself cross-eyed? The true meaning of *nasikagram* is 'origin of the nose,' not 'end of the nose.' The nose originates at the point between the eyebrows, the seat of spiritual vision."

One *Sankhya* aphorism reads: *Iswar ashidha* ("A Lord of Creation cannot be deduced" or "God is not proved"). Chiefly on the basis of this sentence, most scholars call the whole philosophy atheistical.

"The verse is not atheistical," Sri Yukteswar explained. "It merely signifies that to the unenlightened man, dependent on his senses for all final judgments, proof of God must remain unknown and therefore nonexistent. True *Sankhya* followers, with unshakable insight born of meditation, understand that the Lord is both existent and knowable."

Master expounded the Christian Bible with a beautiful clarity. It was from my Hindu guru, unknown to the roll call of Christian membership, that I learned to perceive the deathless essence of the Bible, and to understand the truth in Christ's assertion—surely the most thrillingly intransigent

---

(3.1416, the ratio of the circumference to the diameter of a circle).

The life-span for a whole universe, according to the ancient seers, is 314,159,000,000,000 solar years, or "One Age of Brahma."

The Hindu scriptures declare that an earth such as ours is dissolved for one of two reasons: the inhabitants as a whole become either completely good or completely evil. The world mind thus generates a power that releases the captive atoms held together as an earth.

Dire pronouncements are occasionally published regarding an imminent "end of the world." Planetary cycles, however, proceed according to an orderly divine plan. No earthly dissolution is in sight; many ascending and descending equinoctial cycles are yet in store for our planet in its present form.

ever uttered: "Heaven and earth shall pass away, but my words shall not pass away."

The great masters of India mold their lives by the same godly ideals that animated Jesus; these men are his proclaimed kin: "Whosoever shall do the will of my Father which is in heaven, the same is my brother, and sister, and mother." "If ye continue in my word," Christ pointed out, "then are ye my disciples indeed; and ye shall know the truth, and the truth shall make you free." Freemen all, lords of themselves, the Yogi-Christs of India are part of the immortal fraternity: those that attain a liberating knowledge of the One Father.

"The Adam and Eve story is incomprehensible to me!" I observed with considerable heat one day in my early struggles with the allegory. "Why did God punish not only the guilty pair, but also the innocent unborn generations?"

Master was amused, more by my vehemence than by my ignorance. "Genesis is deeply symbolic, and cannot be grasped by a literal interpretation," he explained. "Its 'tree of life' is the human body. The spinal cord is like an upturned tree, with man's hair as its roots, and afferent and efferent nerves as branches. The tree of the nervous sytem bears many enjoyable fruits, or sensations of sight, sound, small, taste, and touch. In these, man may rightfully indulge; but he was forbidden the experience of sex, the 'apple' at the center of the body ('in the midst of the garden').

"The 'serpent' represents the coiled-up spinal energy that stimulates the sex nerves. 'Adam' is reason, and 'Eve' is feeling. When the emotion, or Eve-consciousness, in any human being is overpowered by the sex impulse, his reason, or Adam, also succumbs.

"God created the human species by materializing the bodies of man and woman through the force of His will; He endowed the new species with the power to create children in a similar 'immaculate' or divine manner. Because His manifestation in the individualized soul had hitherto been limited to animals, instinct-bound and lacking the potentialities of full reason, God made the first human bodies, symbolically called Adam and Eve. To these, for advantageous upward evolution, He transferred the souls or divine essence of two animals. In Adam, or man, reason predominated; in Eve, or woman, feeling was ascendant. Thus was expressed the duality or polarity that underlies the phenomenal worlds. Reason and feeling remain in a heaven of cooperative joy so long as the human mind is not tricked by the serpentine energy of animal propensities.

"The human body was therefore not solely a result of evolution from beasts, but was produced through an act of special creation by God. The animal forms were too crude to express full divinity: man was uniquely given the potentially omniscient 'thousand-petaled lotus' in the brain, as well as acutely awakened occult centers in the spine.

"God, or the Divine Consciousness present within the first created pair, counseled them to enjoy all human sensibilities, with one exception: sex sensations. These were banned, lest humanity enmesh itself in the inferior animal method of propagation. The warning not to revive subconsciously present bestial memories was unheeded. Resuming the way of brute procreation, Adam and Eve fell from the state of heavenly joy natural to the original perfect man. When 'they knew that they were naked,' their consciousness of immortality was lost, even as God had warned them; they had placed themselves under the physical law by which bodily birth must be followed by bodily death.

"The knowledge of 'good and evil,' promised Eve by the 'serpent,' refers to the dualistic and oppositional experiences that mortals under *maya* must undergo. Falling into delusion through misuse of his feeling and reason, or Eve- and Adam-consciousness, man relinquishes his right to enter the heavenly garden of divine self-sufficiency. The personal responsibility of every human being is to restore his 'parents,' or dual nature, to a unified harmony, or Eden."

As Sri Yukteswar ended his discourse, I glanced with new respect at the pages of Genesis.

"Dear Master," I said, "for the first time I feel a proper filial obligation toward Adam and Eve!"

## Solar Influences

### Michel Gauquelin

*From a personal astrological adventure we now turn to a scientific appraisal of the subject. Michel Gauquelin, a French psychologist and statistician, surveys some recent and controversial findings.*

• • •

Advances in medicine are achieved only through the observation of diseases and abnormal functioning of the body. The same procedure must be used to improve our knowledge of cosmic influences on life. . . . For this question must be asked: where do unforeseeable calamities come from? Could they, like the seven plagues of Egypt, be sent from heaven?

Between the two [world] wars, Dr. Maurice Faure one day made a strange assertion. He has told his story as follows: "It was at Nice, a town where there was an automatic telephone service . . . on certain days the telephones stopped working, or worked abnormally, for several hours without there being anything in the state of the apparatus to explain the disturbance. Different connections from those which had been dialed were obtained, or they were not obtained at all, or there were crossed lines, interruptions, and the like. Then the machinery would suddenly start to work normally again, without any human intervention.

"I was not particularly surprised to learn that this passing disorganization of the telephone service coincided with outbreaks of disease, and heralded serious atmospheric disturbances, which occurred immediately afterward. One day, when this unexplained disturbance of the telephone system was particularly serious, I read the news that a violent magnetic upheaval had occurred in the United States and had interrupted telegraph and telephone communications for several hours.

"I immediately got in touch with M. Vallot (an astronomer), who informed me that these disturbances were fairly frequent, and were also revealed by disorganization of compasses, appearance of *aurorae boreales,* seismic tremors, volcanic eruptions, etc. According to him, one of the most certain causes of these magnetic disturbances was the movement of an important sunspot on the meridian. We decided, together, to investigate whether the movement of sunspots coincided also with an increase in diseases afflicting people.

"Dr. Sardou was informed and lent us his assistance. This is how the first investigation was carried out. M. Vallot noted the movement of sunspots from his observatory at Mont Blanc. At the same time, Dr. Sardou recorded the incidence of ill health which he observed at Nice on the Mediterranean coast, while I recorded that which I observed at Lamalou, a place in the mountains of Cévennes, on the edge of France's central plateau. None of us revealed his observations to his colleagues: but when, after 267 consecutive days spent in taking observations, we compared results, it was a simple matter to establish that they were chronologically interconnected. Out of twenty-five movements of sunspots, twenty-one were accompanied by significant increase in the incidence of ill health. . . .

"Afterward I established as well a correlation between movement of the sunspot with successions of sudden deaths, which occur twice as frequently at such moments as at others. . . ."

In his enthusiasm, Dr. Faure expressed his opinion that sunspots were also responsible for a whole series of accidents normally attributed to failures in the nervous system or the individual's psychology: the exhaustion of an airplane pilot, a locomotive engineer, or a crossing attendant could cause serious accidents at such times; and nervous tension could drive some people to crime or suicide. He also explained accidents which had been given wide press coverage in the same way, suggesting that they were more easily interpreted as outbreaks of madness than mere unfortunate coincidences.

Is Dr. Faure right in all this, or has he let himself be

slightly carried away by his general hypothesis that everything can be explained in terms of sunspots? At any rate, he deserves the credit for having put the problem clearly. Confusion in the cosmos, which makes the barometric indicator rise and fall, could have similar effects on us too, both physically and mentally. Dr. Faure's observations were only the more spectacular symptoms of this, and they needed to be supported by numerous careful experiments.

Dr. de Rudder, a professor at the University of Frankfurt am Main, has written a considerable work, as impressive for its size as for the wealth of ideas expressed in it, investigating the cause of certain seasonal diseases which otherwise seem inexplicable. He examines epidemic diseases coming from outside (like poliomyelitis) as carefully as the sicknesses which occur within the system quite suddenly (like myocardial infarctus, angina pectoris, and pulmonary embolism). After a closely reasoned discussion of the causes which could explain them, he too advances the hypothesis of a potential meteorological influence.

Some patients are particularly sensitive to weather changes. . . . Amputees sometimes feel inexplicable twinges in the tip of their removed limb, rheumatics and arthritics suffer an increase in pain at such moments, and this happens long before metorological instruments have recorded the slightest change. The reason for this has never been explained.

De Rudder therefore put the question clearly: Do "meteorotropic" diseases exist connected with atmospheric conditions? In what way are they connected? And if they do exist, does solar activity have anything to do with them?

His question was heard, and in all the laboratories and hospitals investigators of an original turn of mind put forward their solutions to the problem.

*Heart attacks.* In a letter to the Academy of Medicine dated March 3, 1959, Doctor Poumailloux and M. Viart, meteorological engineer, wrote: "Our first findings point to a really remarkable correlation between increased frequency of myocardial infarctus at certain moments of maximum solar activity and peaks of geomagnetic disturbance. For the two years under study, 1957 and 1958, periods of slight solar disturbance are, on the contrary, almost free from heart attacks." But the writers cautiously add that "these first findings require a long-range study based on a wider sample." If their findings were confirmed, they thought that the effect of this solar and geomagnetic activity might be a sudden increase in the coagulation of the blood, thus inducing a coronary blockage through blood clots, a direct cause of infarctus.

Similar findings were reached at Sotchi, Crimea, by the health director of the region, Professor N. V. Romenski, as regards heart diseases. He established that there was a maximum of aneurisms and fatal attacks during large magnetic storms. Special precautions are now taken in the hospitals and clinics of the Crimea when these magnetic storms, which are usually preceded several days earlier by intense and violent radio static, draw near. These precautions have led to a considerable reduction in the number of deaths.

*Diseases of the lungs.* Hellmut Berg, a professor at the University of Cologne, and a merciless critic of false correlations, announced the almost certain validity of G. and B. Düll's work on the deaths of tubercular cases. At an international symposium on relations between solar and terrestrial phenomena, which took place in Brussels in 1960, Berg declared: "G. and B. Düll have plotted different curves showing the distribution of numbers of death through tuberculosis around the days marked by severe chromospheric eruptions. They may be taken as indicative of a relation between solar and terrestrial phenomena within the biological field. . . ." This work takes as its subject Hamburg in the year 1936, and it produces evidence to show that, for the time and place under consideration, serious tubercular cases were in danger of dying on days when there was a violent eruption on the sun. At about the same time another investigator, Puig, found entirely similar results. On the other hand, Lingemann found no relation between pulmonary hemorrhages in a West German hospital and geomagnetic disturbances. He was about to come to an entirely negative conclusion when he was suddenly struck by a surprising coincidence which he had not noticed until then. During the period he was studying (1948–1952), the meteorological papers had made *eighteen references* to aurorae boreales occurring in Germany. These phenomena are highly unusual in Germany, and during their appearance the incidence of hemorrhage among the patients was one hundred times higher than a statistical calculation would have predicted. Since aurorae boreales indicate that considerable solar activity is disturbing the upper atmosphere, here too the sun's disturbance brought a risk of death to tubercular patients.

*Eclampsias:* For a long time, midwives have been blaming the weather and its sudden changes for a large number of eclampsias: a serious and sometimes fatal condition which may occur in the course of a confinement, characterized by spasms and convulsions of an epileptic type on the part of the woman in labor.

Much has been written on this subject without receiving much serious attention, but in 1942 two investigators, Bach and Schluck, finally tackled the question with the requisite scientific rigor. They produced evidence for "eclampsia days." These days were precisely those which had the greatest magnetic disturbance, while on magnetically calm days few eclampsias occurred. The writers concluded: "In the last analysis the sun is responsible for eclampsia crises, since it induces magnetic disturbance." The practical effect of this conclusion is that astronomers could be of precious help to doctors by warning them of the days when, because of the sun's ill humor, women in labor need to be very closely watched.

So Professor de Rudder got his answer: there certainly are meteorotropic diseases connected to the sun's activity, as these researches have proved. However, they were a long way from clarifying all the obscurities. Each had concentrated on a different disease at different times and under conditions which were not comparable. Hence, there are some contradictory results. Some amazingly close connections between a disease and the sun did not seem to appear any longer, or as frequently, a few years later when another researcher repeated the experiment on new material.

To get rid of these discrepancies, more research, comparison, and criticism are required so that knowledge of the sun's effects may be based on firm evidence, and this work should go on without pause until all the discrepancies have been definitely ironed out.

H. Bortels, a passionate and unconventional scientist whose insights sometimes amounted to genius, was director of the Institute of Bacteriology at Berlin-Dahlem where he carried out a considerable number of experiments on the activity and virulence of microbes under particular conditions of the atmosphere and the sun. He discovered a constant factor in his test tubes and cultures of bacilli: the shift from a high to a low pressure and from a warm to a cold front in the atmosphere altered the behavior of microbes to a considerable extent. As the weather changes, the *azobacter* devours nitrogen more greedily, and therefore reproduces itself more rapidly; the *Pseudomonas tumefaciens,* in its urge to reproduce, forms magnificent stars: the *Bacterium prodigiosum* of saliva shows heightened activity, etc. In short, all the experiments were in accordance on one point: certain atmospheric conditions make microorganisms more active, and therefore much more dangerous. But Bortels wanted to know whether the atmospheric changes which transformed the microbes' virulence had their origin in the sun. The sun emitted some very penetrating radiation; would their elimination halt the microbes' reproduction?

So Bortels had a huge plated appartus constructed, the sides of which were 70 cm thick (25 cm of lead and 45 cm of iron), and put his test tubes of microbes in it. Once inside this formidable tank, the microbes ceased to respond to weather changes. However, those which had been put in an ordinary thermostat, an apparatus, that is, which kept heat and pressure at a constant level, continued to be active at recurring intervals.

Thus *Pseudomonas* behaved itself in the tank, where as the one in the laboratory continued its scandalous genetic activity; in the tank the nitrogen eater ceased to be overcome by sudden hunger pangs, etc.

All the microbes, whether in the thermostat or in the tank, were protected from atmospheric conditions; but the microbes in the thermostat were not protected from the penetrative rays of the sun. The cause of their activity therefore came directly from the sun. Bortels was preparing to carry out new experiments to confirm this when, unfortunately, the events of 1942 interrupted his work.

"How does the sound of the sea come about?" the philosopher Leibnitz has asked. Each wave, taken separately, makes a sound which is imperceptible to our ears, but millions of waves working all together make a noise like thunder. Perhaps Professor Tchijewsky was thinking of the great German philosopher when he established a connection between microbes and epidemics. It is hardly a serious matter that a microbe should be active when the cosmos is active, or that such a minor organism as a minute, isolated cell, a kind of base unit for life, should be disturbed when a sunspot moves to the meridian. But when a whole lot of microbes begin to be active, this becomes a serious matter indeed. That is how epidemics make a beginning, and in this way an epidemic is something like the sound of the sea. Tchijewsky was concerned to discover the determining cause of epidemics, those physiological crises which, often without warning, cover whole districts simultaneously and cause irreparable loss to humans. He had to find out the reason for the sudden emergence of these scourges which, even today with all our advances in preventive medicine, may appear on the least occasion. Tchijewski thought that epidemics could be connected with a cosmic determinant, a solar one, for instance, and he decided to confirm the hypothesis objectively. He went through a considerable number of old records and histories, but he also used recent statistical documents which provided him with the dates of history's great epidemics. Here he found a justification for his hypothesis and published his theory before the last [world] war: "During the years when there are most sunspots, a greater number of epidemics always emerges in history."

For instance, if his collection of dates is to be trusted, the frequency of diphtheria cases in central Europe, recurrent typhus, the great plagues, cholera in Europe, and above all, the death rate of smallpox victims in Chicago, obediently follow the eleven-year cycle of the sunspots. In the case of this last disease, the peaks of mortality were so closely correlated with the peaks of the sunspots during the three or four consecutive cycles since reliable statistics had been kept that Tchijewsky had high hopes of putting his theory on a solid foundation. . . .

Then Tchijewsky was seized with a new idea and, in order to settle the matter, collected all the statistics relating to deaths in Russia from 1867 to 1917 which he could find. He believed that he would be able to deduce from this that mortality in general, even without the help of bacterial infections, also followed the solar rhythm of eleven years.

Other investigators have turned their attention to less painful subjects. A fairly large literature even covers a happy biological event: birth. The problem here was to find out whether the number of confinements could reveal any increase or diminution in accordance with seasonal, diurnal, or cosmic conditions. Some of the results are interesting.

First of all, demographers studied the basic cosmic rhythms which split up our earthly lives: the yearly movement of the earth around the sun and its twenty-four-hour rotation on its axis. They established that births do not occur with the same frequency throughout the year. On average, there are more births during the months of May and June than in November or December. These frequencies are obviously dependent on the frequencies of conceptions nine months earlier, which means that there are more conceptions in August and September than in February and March. The reasons they give hold little mystery, but are evidently related to the movement of the earth around the sun, which causes the seasons. Summer and the holidays are more favorable to sexual relations than the end of winter, for reasons which are as much material as psychological. But doctors have recently added a biological motivation to these: the number of hormones helpful to procreative power may increase and diminish in the course of the year.

Professor de Rudder, a specialist in pediatrics, has produced an interesting statistic on this matter which would tend to support the theory of hormones and the yearly cycle of procreative power. At the time of their birth, the weight of babies born in May and June is on average higher than those born in the depths of winter. So the strongest children seem to be those who are conceived at the time when the procreative tendency is strongest. Therefore, one can say up to a point that the months when a child is born does provide some indication as to the robustness of his constitution. If you were born in, say, June, you have a better chance of having good balance and being tall and strong, and even having well developed mental faculties. Another statistic even goes so far as to show that human geniuses have most often been conceived in April, and most often died in May. Naturally, the correlation here is a weak one. . . .

In explaining the seasonal variations in reproduction and quality of newborn children, Huntington, an American, has advanced the hypothesis that this may be related to an early biological imperative bequeathed to us by our ancestors. For early man, it is said, was more directly dependent on seasonal variations and, therefore, cosmic rhythms.

Earlier statistics, like those of Quetelet, and recent ones, like those of Françoise Gauquelin, both show that as a general rule babies are in a hurry to be born at the end of night or at the beginning of the morning. The reason for these differences between the hours of the day is quite simply that the alternation of the day and night not only controls our everyday activities, which are conscious and organized, but also, and to an even greater extent, the whole of our biological system. . . . The succession of day and night is the main clock, the most powerful cosmic "timekeeper" of the neural and hormonal activity of our bodies. Now, it is a hormone factor which appears to set off the beginning of labor in a woman. It is closely linked with the universal "timekeeper" of twenty-four hours. Hormones determining the term of confinement are secreted in greater quantities during the night, and so birth generally begins toward the end of the night rather than in the middle of the day. In the last few decades, induced confinements have become fashionable, and doctors can put the normal time of the confinement forward or back by the use of drugs and injections. This has the advantage of allowing births to take place more conveniently during the day. But the hour when the baby is born may also indicate its future health. In fact, confinements which have naturally started at a time which is physiologically often the best, that is, around midnight, are quicker and easier. Hence, the saying that the child of the morning is generally more welcome than the child of the afternoon.

There are thousands and tens of thousands of them. They move forward in compact rows, annihilating everything in their path to satisfy their voracious hunger. Nothing stops them, not even the vast expanse of the sea when they meet it on their way. Then hordes of them rush forward into it and soon drown. That is a migration.

The determining factors of migrations are still very obscure. If the seasonal migrations of birds are determined by temperature conditions, how are those of locusts to be explained, or of ants, or of rats and lemmings? A frenzied desire for movement suddenly takes hold of them, for no apparent reason, and without any warning.

We are told that a migration takes place when a species of animal suddenly begins to reproduce itself in incredible quantity. But where does this burst of reproductive activity come from? The theory most widely accepted these days relates to the hormones: autopsies carried out on lemmings captured during a migration have revealed abnormal, indeed pathological, development of certain endocrine glands. But why should these hormonal glands have developed in this way? This explanation only takes us one step forward in an investigation of the phenomenon's original cause.

Some scientists have thought to examine whether cosmic factors could have justified this unhealthy reproduction of the species, for it resembles the sudden proliferation of microbes in Bortels' test tubes. Chibirnikov and Derjavin, two Russian scientists, have concentrated on this angle. The first demonstrated that locust hordes in Russia followed the eleven-year cycle of sunspots, while the second proved that sturgeon in the Caspian Sea reproduce and then die in masses following cycles of eleven and thirty-three years, both of which occur during periods of sunspots. Other studies of the same type are in progress.

But what can be said at the present time about the huge colony of microbes which is humanity? Here too we find mass reactions which are unexpected and dangerous, upheavals which are often inexplicable, revolutions, wars, or just migrations bearing a close resemblance to those of animals. Entire nations have, one day, decided to leave their country of origin to set up house elsewhere and live in a new country: warrior hordes who spread across every country like a powder trail and sowed desolation. Are demographic, economic, or other explanations always sufficient explanation for these sudden phenomena?

This question as well caught the imagination of the tireless Professor Tchijewsky. He collected the dates of a large number of recurrent social phenomena, and, as with epidemics, compared them with the fluctuations in the numbers of sunspots. In a huge study, a real panorama of history, he drew up lists of wars, revolutions, and population movements from 500 B. C. to 1900, against the curves of solar activity. By means of these historical data, Tchijewsky felt justified in concluding that out of all the "psychic epidemics" 72 percent coincided with peaks of solar activity, and only 28 percent with its low points.

Tchijewsky illustrated this conclusion with a certain number of examples, of which we print one or two of the more picturesque. The Jewish immigration into North America followed, according to him, a cosmic determining force; the succession of Liberal and Conservative governments in England did as well; between 1830 and 1930 this succession took place according to the following law: Liberals gained power during the peak years of sunspots, and Conservatives when they were at their low point. The idea behind Tchijewsky's thesis is evident: activity on the sun would tend to cause unrest among men, and this unrest might be expressed by the desire to immigrate or, more mildly, by a propensity among the English electorate to back the least traditionalist of the parties, the Liberals.

These ideas have very recently even been applied to the political economy in an effort to find a cause in the sky for major economic crises. The statement that the great crisis of 1929 coincided with a peak of solar activity was a sufficiently worrying fact to pass for proof among certain people. The work of Tchijewsky is at the back of a lot of myths; these perhaps contain a grain of truth, but it cannot be denied that there are serious lacks in the records involving mass activities. As long as there is any doubt as to their accuracy, we should be very skeptical about them.

Caution, then, is required in assuming a cosmic interpretation of social behavior patterns, but individual reactions to some effects of the cosmos are more readily examined.

A record of such occurrences has been prepared, and it includes serious and mutually supportive research. Reiter has discovered a connection between solar activity and the number of road accidents. Martini has observed a link between mining disasters and the appearance of groups of spots at the sun's central meridian. Berg is in agreement with Martini in concluding that accidents may often be put down to delayed or inaccurate human reactions, in conjunction with very violent solar activity.

Delayed reactions are not all; there are also effects inducing serious depression or morbid excitement in the nervous system. G. and B. Düll have found a correlation between the number of suicides and solar activity. To confirm it, they collected 24,739 cases of suicide at Copenhagen, Frankfurt, and Zurich from 1928 to 1932. All this material, patiently collated, enabled them to conclude that the number of suicides was not unconnected with disturbances in the cosmos. . . . Dr. Faure and Dr. Sardou had come to the same conclusion about suicide as well as criminal acts.

As for the pathological stimulation of the nervous system by the movement of large sunspots, Father Moreux wrote as long ago as 1930: "The electric flow emanating from the sun affects our nervous systems, and I have often observed that many people, and especially children, are more irritable during times of excessive solar activity. The number of punishments in schools is always higher during magnetic disturbances caused by turmoils on the solar surface. These unconscious influences are expressed, in certain cases, by attacks of nervousness causing complex effects on morbid, natures, such as dejection, attacks of gout or rheumatism, headaches, neuralgia, and even temper tantrums."

No doubt a certain naïveté is apparent to us today through Father Moreux's somewhat old-fashioned style. Tchijewsky's opinion, also, is astonishing since at about the same time he too reckoned that "The time is near when, before pronouncing sentence on the accused, the judge will ask to be provided with astronomical and meteorological data relevant to the time when the crime was committed. The nearer the crime to a time when sunspots were reaching their maximum intensity, the more diminished the responsibility of the guilty man." But the courts are a long way from acting on Tchijewsky's views.

However, Tchijewsky's idea have received unexpected support in the work of Dr. Robert O. Becker. A surgeon at the Syracuse Veterans Administration Hospital and New York's Upstate Medical Center, Dr. Becker stated in *Newsweek* on May 13, 1963: "Subtle changes in the intensity of the geomagnetic field can affect the nervous system by altering the living body's own electro-magnetic field. . . ." Dr. Becker has established a direct relation between the number of admissions to psychiatric hospitals and the earth's magnetic activity, which is generally associated with sunspots. On the other hand, when magnetic disturbances decreased, so also did the number of patients admitted.

How could the earth's magnetic activity disturb the brain of a patient, a schizophrenic, for instance? Becker showed that the human body has areas responsive to positive and negative electrical discharges, located separately. The presence of electric waves carrying a different discharge would upset these areas. In some cases the effect may cause the patient to lose consciousness.

It may be seen, therefore, that outer space makes its presence felt among living organisms in a very unpredictable way. Not only is it unpredictable, but also it is not very well understood. Not all the different studies mentioned here have equal validity. Some are impressive because of their weight of evidence, but the premature conclusions of others may raise a smile.

But the point is this: What part does the moon play on life? It would seem to be a small one, whereas the sun is responsible for a mass of strange effects which seem to influence all of life on this sphere through the weather, the atmosphere, and magnetic disturbances.

However, perhaps not all cosmic effects on earth come from the sun and the moon. There remains in the universe a huge field of influences which have yet to be explored: the influence of galactic forces, the disturbing influence of planets in the solar field, cosmic rays coming from distant space, and no doubt many other things which we know nothing about at the moment. When we do know more, we will understand better what goes on between the sky and ourselves.

And then, a fundamental question still waits to be asked: If cosmic influences affecting men do exist, how do they work? How are they imprinted on the inside of our bodies . . .?

# 18

# The New Biotechnology

### James B. Beal

*James B. Beal is an aerospace engineer whose work in "paraphysics" (an interdisciplinary synergistic science built on physics, biology, psi reseach, and electronics) has enabled him to develop a comprehensive view of man's bioelectric nature.*

•  •  •

Today, from the space program, in exploring the heavens, we see an activity that probes outward into the cosmic design to bring about an understanding of its events, its laws and principles; and inward to comprehend the basic "building blocks" of life. In the perspective of history, the objectives of the space program are as old as man himself, constituting a search into the essential nature of existense and of man's place in it.

Much of what goes on in space, especially in the earth-sun relationships, and cosmic rays from deep space, affects our environment and ecology, even our biology. It is wise and prudent to learn the mechanism of these relationships and radiation, and what trends they may be causing in the earth's evolution, climate, and ourselves.

The scientists of the Renaissance gave man an impetus toward total awareness that has carried him beyond the earth as well as toward the center of life. We are beginning to understand the basic structure of life. A new Renaissance will enable man to understand the structure of mind.

The brain and its vast web of nerves operate with electrical signals . . . a fact that has been known for decades, even to high school biology students. It would seem logical, therefore, that the artificial application of electrical impulses (or fields) could produce all kinds of potentially beneficial effects on the nervous system and the body.

This is a thesis that has been bandied about among medical researchers for many years. And with few exceptions . . . such as electroshock treatments in mental hospitals and electric pacemakers for the heart . . . this approach has been greeted by extreme skepticism and even derision from the medical community.

Today, however, there's evidence that much of the skepticism is beginning to disappear. A host of current research projects, many of them conducted with human patients, involves the application of electrical signals (and fields) to the nervous system in attempts to reduce pain, put insomniacs to sleep, relieve asthma, ulcers, and high blood pressure, and improve performance and disposition. Scientists say they are providing more than a glimmer of hope that "electromedicine" may soon emerge as a major new approach to many diseases.

The human brain is the most complicated structure in the known universe . . . but as practically nothing of the universe is known, it is probably fairly low in the scale of organic computers. Nevertheless, it contains powers and potentialities still largely untapped, and perhaps unguessed at. Probably 99 percent of human ability has been wholly wasted; even today, those of us who consider ourselves cultured and educated operate for most of our time as automatic machines, and glimpse the profounder resources of our minds only once or twice in a lifetime.

Until comparatively recently (the 1950's) biologists regarded a cell as a minute bag of fluid that was relatively simple in structure. But under the electron scanning microscope, cells were seen to be exceedingly complex. What earlier seemed to be a "simple cell wall" was likely to be folded and convoluted . . . precisely the right kind of structure to serve as a semiconductor. And components of the cell are likely to include organic semiconductors such as liquid crystals . . . a material that is hypersensitive to temperature changes, magnetic and electric fields, stress, radiation, and trace contamination. To complicate matters even more, many cells have a double outer membrane; electrically, such a membrane functions as a capacitor with the characteristics of a leaky dielectric. It should also be noted that at low frequencies the permeability of the cell membrance to ions is enhanced, thus promoting electrochemical interactions. Nerves and muscle actions are also accompanied by electrical activity involving flow of ionic currents.

It is certainly reasonable to assume that refined detection of minute magnetic and electrostatic fields that accompany biological activity may lead to interesting and useful applications in the future . . . possibly monitoring effects of mind on body physiological processes and early diagnosis of specific diseases.

Viewed as a minute but extremely elaborate electrical system, the living cell (like all electrical systems) is obviously subject to the influence of magnetic and electric fields. And these fields may induce not just one but a complex system of currents, as well as act as indicators of environmental conditions. Small wonder, therefore, that reported field effects at the cellular level are diverse and debatable; the effects will depend upon the components of the system and its organization.

A space scientist, Dr. Cone, at the NASA-Langley Research Center, has devised and demonstrated a theory that helps to explain the source of uncontrolled malignant growth and indicates shortcuts to development of chemical countermeasures against cancer. Dr. Cone specializes in the investigation of space radiation effects on the blockage of cell division. The Cone theory proposes that the division of body cells (a normal process that goes on continuously) is controlled precisely by the pattern of ion concentrations on the surface tissues of cells. The pattern is formed by the electrical voltage that normally exists across cellular surfaces and varies from one part of the body to another. This theory has provided, possibly for the first time, an explanation of the functional connection between the two major pathological features of cancer . . . uncontrolled growth of cells and the spread of the disease in the body. The theory implies that the basic deviation from normalcy producing both of these conditions lies in an alteration of the molecular structure of the cell surface. Dr. Barry Allan and Ralph Norman of U.S. Army Missile Command, Redstone Arsenal, Alabama, indicate in their description of bioelectricity and biowater that a living organism is delicately balanced, especially chemically and electrically. It seems predictable that the highly structured water (biowater) within the cell could, by the exclusion of conducting ions, form the insulation channels of the organism. Further, semiconduction and conduction phenomena might be expected if certain chemical modifications to highly pure, immobile layer of water were made by life processes. Conduction could easily occur in the less structured aqueous solutions, and any mechanism that disrupts the biological water structure will certainly disrupt the biological transfer of electrons. The need for understanding bioelectricity is most fundamental, and research in bioelectricity and biowater and their mutual dependence will yield enormous dividends.

## Electrical Field Is Basic

A tie-in here should be made with some of the work that Dr. Shafer, formerly of General Dynamics Life Sciences, has done with mice innoculated with virulent lymphatic cancer, then exposed to a high negative ion field (negative ions could be considered "supercharged" oxygen atoms with a surplus of electrons looking for chemical reactions to stimulate). Dr. Shafer noted a slowing down of cancer spread, some complete remissions, some holding constant. Life-span was greater than other mice remaining as a control group outside the charged ion environment.

It has been established that an electropower field between the earth and atmosphere exists which, relative to the earth, is normally positive. This is not a recent discovery . . . the existence of this natural electric field was discovered in 1752. The usual mean strength of this field is on the order of several hundred volts per meter positive polarity, although there are wide fluctuations due to geographical location, weather, artificially induced shielding, etc. For example, in buildings, automobiles, aircraft, and other structures which, due to their metal-containing construction, are shielded and thus have the physical qualities of a Faraday cage, this natural field does not exist. Indeed, the extensive use of plastics (almost all have a highly negative electrostatic field) inside of buildings and vehicles can provide a strong negative field which augments fatigue, irritability, and natural apathy. This statement leads to an intriguing question: Are we also electrically polluting our environment as well as our educational facilities? This seems a distinct possibility. Have you noticed how your new plastic-containing clothing sticks to your body in cold, dry weather? The body field is positive and the plastic is negative, thus creating this uncomfortable effect.

Over 150 years ago it was determined that this natural positive electric field around the earth was an important factor in the development of life and that the normal and healthy course of life, especially for vertebrates including man, is very dependent upon its presence. On the other hand, it was determined before the turn of the century that the absence of this positive electric field has a disadvantageous and negative effect on the vitality of man and influences his fertility.

Experiments and investigations which have been conducted suggest that this electric field produces electrical current in the body which excites the entire organism and its nervous system, which in turn increases the impulse rate to the wakefulness center of the brain . . . various biological clocks are also activated. Modern biological theories tend to indicate that the brain receives inputs from the nervous system by means of electrical pulse generation and transmission through the nervous system. One theory of wakefulness and sleep suggests that the number of electrical impulses reaching the brain influences the state of alertness (an increase in beta wave EEG activity occurs). Recent brain-wave experiments indicate that artificial electric fields can influence the rate of spontaneous electrical impulse generation by the nerves. Other recent tests have demonstrated that brightness discrimination improves under the influence of artificially created electric fields.

The beneficial effects of electrical fields are apparently the results of the combined action of the positive field and the suspended negative ions in the air. The electric field is the force of motion and the ions are carriers of electrical charge. This is apparently the explanation of why investigations of the effects of positive and negative ions on individuals without the presence of a proper electric field have shown negative or no effects. On the other hand, tests have been conducted to determine the effects of positive and negative ions on individuals where a natural electric field was present. The gross results were as follows:

| Item | Negative Ions | Positive Ions |
|------|---------------|---------------|
| Performance | Improved | Decreased |
| Work capacity | Increased | |
| Disposition | Cheerful | Depressed |
| Reaction time | Decreased | Decreased |
| Equilibrium | Improved | |
| Vitamin metabolism | Enhanced | |
| Pain | Relieved | |
| Allergic disorders | Relieved | |
| Burn recovery and healing | Enhanced | |

Air ions are the result of atoms, molecules, and particles which become charged by either loss or gain of electrons. The principal sources of air ions, both natural and artificial, are high-energy particles such as alpha and beta rays from radioactive sources, cosmic rays, ultraviolet rays, coronal discharges, charge separation from rapid relative movements of surfaces, and thermionic emission. Ordinarily, only about one molecule in ten is ionized or charged and these frequently clump together forming groups.

Unipolar, small air ions have been shown to be biologically active under certain conditions. Molecules and perhaps atoms of Oxygen 2 in the air have an affinity for electrons, and thus form negative ions. Only fluorine and chlorine molecules seem to have the same capacity for forming negative ions as do the Oxygen 2 molecules. Positive ions are formed primarily by $CO_2$ molecules.

Although systems for generating artificial electric fields and negative ions already exist and have successfully demonstrated beneficial physiological and psychological effect in combating fatigue, allergies, etc., such systems have not yet been employed in the classroom for extended periods of time (so far as is known by this author). Development of such a system for the classroom could perhaps minimize other problems associated with student behavior, seasonal allergies and weather changes, and even housekeeping.

Incidentally, an interesting field effect perceived by animals is the "earthquake alarm!" An earthquake causes a drastic change in the earth's magnetic and electric fields. This field change is of a characteristic "signature" pattern and propagates at the speed of light, while the earthquake travels at about the speed of sound, or slower; hence, the animals sense a sudden change in the usually stable, slowly changing environmental background electrostatic field. This is unusual, so the animal is alerted, nervous, and prepared for danger.

## Electric Tranquilizer?

Of particular environmental interest to those in Israel and pertinent to the educational environment is the khamsin wind which moves up out of the desert each spring and fall. It picks up hot air and dust as it sweeps across Africa and the Sinai Peninsula, bringing a variety of afflictions in its northerly thrust. The moistureless air causes feet to swell painfully, noses and eyes to itch, and asthmatics to gasp for breath. Automobile accidents, crime rates, and mental cases increase. Other countries suffer from such hot dry winds containing an excess of positive ions. Italy has the sirocco, Southern Europe has the foehn, France has the mistral and the United States has the chinook and Santa Ana winds. Young people become tense, irritable, and occasionally violent; older persons become fatigued, apathetic, depressed, and sometimes faint. Professor Felix Gad Sulman of the Hebrew University's Department of Applied Pharmacology in Jerusalem has conducted a nine-year study involving 500 people using drugs such as monoamine oxidase (MAO) and negative ion generators, which readily bring relief to khamsin victims. Tests made on animals eighty years ago showed that a negative electric field markedly reduced vitality and fertility of animals, whereas a positive field stimulates respiration, digestion, and metabolism in general. Forty years ago, European research revealed the effect of the absence of a positive field on plant growth and on human performance. The author of this paper also performed some experiments with plants using equipment radiating 10,000 volts per meter. A four-day earlier germination resulted for the bean plants 15 cm from the antenna, compared to the control group. The same equipment was in use on a child with recurrent monthly asthma attacks requiring hospitalization. In the two months since the equipment flat plate antenna was installed 1.5 meters over his bed, there had been no further attacks.

Since Jerusalem has up to 150 days of khamsin wind a year, and there will be deficit of natural negative ions in the air, the optimum environment for well-being would involve use of a negative ion generator in combination with a positive field device to keep the ions moving and distributed, as in the natural earth environment. Recent tests on airplane pilots showed that introducing a strong positive field into the cockpit improved brightness discrimination. Typing efficiency, mental/light mechanical tasks, auto driving response, all showed improvement in efficiency and delay in onset of fatigue. As a note of interest, Dr. Kornblueh of the American Institute of Medical Climatology studied brain-wave patterns and found evidence that negative ions tranquilized persons in severe pain. Northeastern Hospital in Philadelphia has a windowless ion-conditioned room for burn patients. In 85 percent of the cases no pain-deading narcotics are needed, and the burns dry and heal faster with less scarring, plus the patient is more optimistic. Dr. Albert P. Krueger at the University of California predicts that we shall someday regulate the ion level indoors much as we now regulate temperature and humidity. Ironically, many of today's air-conditioned buildings, trains, and planes frequently become supercharged with harmful positive ions because the metal blowers, filters, and ducts strip the air of negative ions. This explains why so many people in air-conditioned spots feel depressed and have an urge to throw open a window. The recent advent of solid-state physics and field-effect transistors have made possible inexpensive portable instruments (electric field intensity meters or scanners) which can now monitor the environment and keep it optimum for physiological and mental tasks. The availability and sensitivity of these instruments has led to some interesting spin-offs. For example, it has been known since at least 1949 that intensities of biological electrostatic field could be detected by suitable instruments, but the equipment and technology was not sufficiently advanced for economical study. Detection and interpretation of biological electrical field radiation is reported to be under intensive investigation in Russia for biomed applications. Equipment described has the same charatceristics as laboratory field effect electrometers equipped with a field mill "chopper." The equipment will detect and amplify minute electrical and electrostatic fields inherent in nonconductors (plastic and insulators) and traveling through conductors (metals). The fields can be detected, the field strength determined in volts per meter, and the polarity of positive or negative established. The equipment output can be fed into a conventional "XY" area scanning system and then into a facsimile recorder to produce a two-dimensional plan view of the electrostatic field potentials around the object or person. Variations in the shades of gray or color indicate the intensity of the field in volts meter. It should be noted here that the recent application of infrared equipment and heat-sensitive liquid crystals to the analysis of body pathological conditions have yielded color readouts of much value to the medical profession.

## New Diagnostic Methods

Preliminary investigations into body field variations indicate that the natural body field is positive, while certain types of malignancies are negative: other pathological conditions produce drastic changes in body potential of a peculiar "signature" nature. Further work remains to be done toward interpretation of received data. Recording and control of environmental factors to constant levels are also required so that the very minute signals of interest can be sifted from all the internal, external, and emotional "noise" present. Please note the tie-in of body electrostatic field potential variations mentioned above with Dr. Cone's discoveries of cellular bioelectric characteristics discussed earlier.

There is no doubt that a need exists to obtain physiological data without the necessity of restraining the individual either by sensors, wires, or rigid confinement. A means of detecting heartbeat (EKG) noncontact has also been developed by Dr. Shafer, who was mentioned earlier. Known as the Field Effect Monitor (now on the market), this equipment consists of a copperplate sensing antenna, an isolation amplifier (using FET electronics), filter systems, main amplifier section, and readout devices. Acceptable EKG signals have been received at a distance of two to three feet. Recent improvements in antenna design have neutralized local field effects (60 cycle components) and improved signal-to-noise ratio by over twenty-times. Dr. Shafer feels confident that he can also monitor brain waves (EEG) noncontact by changing a few elements of his filter circuit. EKG tracings have been made through intact space helmets or pressure suits. Use of Dr. Shafer's EKG equipment in the school clinic, for example, would provide more freedom of movement and comfort for the student, avoid anxiety, and save time, since clothing does not have to be removed or student even aware of equipment use. You can build and experiment with a somewhat similar instrument know as the "Amazing People

Detector." This is basically a very sensitive electrometer, or "rate meter," which measures a changing or varying field. In order to detect electrostatic fields, an additional device is needed which rotates, reciprocates, or swings so that the field is interrupted periodically (chopped) into a form of alternating current which can be transformed and amplified. This basic instrument, however, is extremely sensitive to moving electric charges and can give a "feel" for effects in this area around TV sets, rugs, clothing, people, animals, plants, etc.

## Deafness, Hearing, Magnetism

The magnetic field of the earth averages about 0.5 gauss and has a particular configuration, intensity, and mode of behavior. It is subject to continuous pulsations of low magnitude at frequencies ranging from 0.1 to 100 cycles per second, with the major components at about 8 to 16 cycles per second, peaking around 10 cycles per second. It is interesting to note that the average frequencies of brain waves as manifested by the typical 8 to 14 cycle alpha pattern recorded on electroencephalograms (EEG) fall precisely in this range, and, indeed, a relationship between these phenomena has been more than once suggested. This falls into the area of biological entrainment of the human brain by low-frequency radiation. Note that certain light and sound frequencies can trigger epileptic fits, induce hypnosis, and cause nausea. The step from external sensory stimuli to subconscious electromagnetic stimuli in entraining cerebral rhythms is not a radical concept. It's fast approaching reality with such items as medical equipment for treatment of nerve deafness now in the developmental stages by two U.S. companies. The type of equipment being developed stimulates hearing electrically (first discovered by Volta in 1800). Put the disk-shaped radio frequency radiating antenna plates near the central nervous system and hear! Antenna is placed near spinal column or on head. The device usually contacts the skin, but can transmit into body from a short distance. With two disks, one on each side of the head, you can get stereo that's out of this world! For more than a century there have been sporadic reports of "hearing" aurora displays and meteors entering the atmosphere. Since meteors travel far faster than sound, and other persons present did not hear any sounds, these reports have until recently been dismissed as unfounded.

## Sensory Perception Affected

With discovery that certain individuals are extremely sensitive to the sounds and other as yet undefined effects of electrical and electromagnetic fields to which they are exposed, studies have been made by many members of the scientific community to determine the source of these effects, how they are generated, and how the effects are manifested in man.

The ability of many individuals to "hear" radar waves has been well documented and is generally described as a "buzzing like bees." In other examples individuals have been forced to relocate their homes because of "noise" which was beyond the normally audible range. The development of portable, highly sensitive detection devices provided the capability to verify the existence of these electric field and radio frequency noises and to pinpoint their source. Nurses who work in mental institutions describe patients who were always complaining and trying to get away from "the terrible noise." Cotton in the ears did no good, but certain rooms or areas were more quiet for them (an electrical field null point?). How many people are now in mental institutions or psychologically affected because they are afflicted with hypersensitivity to electric fields and hear voices, buzzing sounds, and strange signals? This is a vital thing to consider in this age of increasing mental tensions. Testing by the Russians indicates that the most sensitive area of the brain to field effects is the hypothalamus. Damage to the hypothalamus can increase the sensitivity to field changes many times.

Here's another one: a bar magnet at 60 cycles and 8,700 gauss magnetic flux density held to the temple gives rise to a light sensation in perfect darkness as well as in a brightly lit room. This is known as the "phosphene" effect and can also be induced by electrical, chemical, fasting, meditation, or fatigue means. No one has a reasonable explanation why, but it is known that a person under hypnosis or in a state of mescaline intoxication can often perceive a static magnetic field . . . through modification of visual images. A flicker effect is associated with a varying field. Patterns, such as spirals and geometric shapes, are often observed which are strikingly similar to the pictographs left by ancient man in all parts of the world. It appears there may be some potential clues for electronic stimulation (or simulation) of vision in the above areas.

Research has established that some aspects of the human brain's electrical activity are related to intelligence. Sensory stimulation . . . such as audio or visual signals . . . cause nonrandom change (evoked response) in this electrical activity (EEG). An instrument called the Neural Efficiency Analyzer measures the ability to learn, as indicated by the efficiency (speed) of information transmission within the brain due to a flashing light stimulus. The neural efficiency "score" is the average time delay in milliseconds between the flash and each of two particular electrical responses of the brain. The lower the number you score, the higher your neural efficiency. Tests of thousands of children and adults reveal a significant correlation between neural efficiency and intelligence quotient with high neural efficiency a factor in high intelligence. Now in production after a dozen years of research and development, the Neural Efficiency Analyzer is the invention of Dr. John Ertl, director of the Center of Cybernetic Studies at the University of Ottawa. Some day, this five-minute electronic test of the ability to learn may be in general use in our schools . . . perhaps even replacing traditional pencil-and-paper IQ tests. Unlike standard intelligence tests with their built-in cultural bias, the Analyzer doesn't penalize so-called "culturally deprived" children. The subject doesn't have to read, write, or even speak to take this test, which also makes it ideal for testing handicapped persons. This is a culture-free technique which can be used for identification of youngsters with learning or primary reading problems; motivational factors are not important and potential high or low achievers can be identified immediately and put in special classes.

Additional aspects of brain-wave-evoked response in the audio stimulus area are being investigated for early detection of hearing loss or total deafness in children before serious learning difficulties are encountered. The electrical stimulation of hearing (or electrophonics) technique, mentioned earlier, may have some interesting application potential here, since it may work if hearing loss or deafness is indicated with the normal audio-stimulation techniques.

## Using Technology in Learning

To enhance the learning process we have many promising new tools or methods we can use, such as computers, educational closed circuit and satellite TV, perceptual test and enhancement equipment (advanced simulators), random access audio and visual retrieval and recording systems, and programmed instruction, to name just a few. We can talk all we want about these important learning methods, equipment, and capabilities we are creating—capabilities which are basic to much of what the public wants done in education, and it means exactly nothing to most of them. We are a world with the greatest total awareness potential ever known. We have reached goals formerly considered unattainable—in spirit and in fact . . . new worlds! Unfortunately, people seldom relate science and technology to the everyday business of living, fighting the daily traffic, getting the kids off to school, and buying the groceries. If they do, they are apt to curse it, particularly when it comes to new ideas to improve education quality, quantity, and environment. Far too many do not understand or care little what education their children get (except when the kids bring it home to threaten parental authority with a little "future shock" item that upsets the cultural status quo).

## Systems Approach Needed

We can point in vain to communications and weather satellites which are revolutionizing worldwide telephone, television, education, and weather forecasting techniques. People simply yawn. They rarely phone overseas, they can still catch their favorite games shows on TV, and they still get caught in sand or snowstorms.

So, who needs any more science and technology? We've got too much already . . . look at the shape the world is in!

Few seem to realize that civilized man cannot long survive on this planet without increased creation of new knowledge and its enlightened use to handle the fantastically complex interrelated and synergistic challenges of the future.

Our difficulty is that as a world of short-term pragmatists we are not geared mentally to long-range planning and some of the cultural changes and benefits resulting from advanced science and technology programs.

Concepts of man and the universe and man in the universe motivate our thinking and actions on earth. Are contributions to such concepts unimportant to the quality of life we strive for today? On the contrary, I think they are basic to definition of what we mean about quality in life. Without a growing precision of our definition of the universe, external and internal, objective and subjective, material and spiritual, and the elements involved, we cannot hope to improve more than the physical aspects of day-to-day living.

The *total human being* must be considered. We can't just sum up the inputs and say this is all there is to this or that person. It's how the inputs are combined that counts, and how the combinations act in symbiosis with the environment. Consciousness itself appears to be a kind of synergistic physical process devolving from the nature of mind. It will not be understood by studying the individual sensing systems, conscious and unconscious, i.e., putting each body input in its own "little black box" and specializing in a narrow range of view. The general systems approach is necessary.

The potentialities of the individual human being are far greater, in extent and diversity, than we ordinarily imagine them to be, and far greater than currently negative in-vogue models of man would lead us to think possible. We are finally beginning to discover some of these potentialities through the newly emerging Science of Subjective Experience which involves monitoring of unconscious processes, through bio-feedback and increasing our awareness of external and internal effects on our mind and body, so we can become optimum persons; thus, understanding ourselves and others better. The broadest possible overview of our effects on our environment, environmental feedback, and the mental physical result is needed for realization of our potential as a total human being. Thus, as a product of the cosmos we are all "tuned in" and our biorhythms react accordingly (though subtle in effect) to electromagnetic and electrostatic fields, low-frequency-radiation, ions, and perhaps other unknown factors.

There are many systems, natural and man-made, which are synergistic in nature, i.e., the total effect is greater (or different) from the sum of the effects from individual components. The end effect cannot be ascertained by a study of the discrete components. The brain may be the highest form of synergistic structure now known to exist. The phenomenon of the consciousness (and learning processes) needs more objective study. However, this may prove a tough objective, since the consciousness or mind has only itself to study itself with! When the sum of all sense-acquired data has been ordered and formulated, the picture which is presented can never be more than one confined to a particular grade of significance. Higher significant data can only be acquired by going into ourselves—for we are the observers and the interpreters of the world.

Man used to say that man the scientist brought order out of chaos.

The scientists are rapidly discovering that all that was chaotic was in man's illiterate and bewildered imagination and fearful ignorance.

# 19

# Do the French Have a Cure
# for Cancer?

*David M. Rorvik*

*Science and medicine are very wary of "black boxes" which generate strange healing energies. For the most part, this skepticism appears warranted. This report by science writer David M. Rorvik looks at one of the more dramatic claims of late that has involved many of France's most highly respected medical scientists. In light of the bioelectric nature of man, "l'affaire Prioré" perhaps is not quite as mysterious today as it would have been twenty years ago.*

•   •   •

France: For the moment it didn't matter to me that the country that gave us shoes with taillights, the musical typewriter and a machine that pulls on your socks might also have produced an apparatus that, by some electromagnetic magic, cures cancer, lowers cholesterol and vanquishes sleeping sickness. Air Inter's flight from Paris to Bordeaux was packed to its gills, and the little girl sitting next to me was green around hers. She just managed not to throw up on my new Italian shoes.

But once outside the terminal, in the city noted for its wines and, more recently, its wine adulterations, I was again enthusiastic about the prospects of seeing, at last, the machine that has been called the Second Coming. A thirty-minute taxi ride through a pouring rain delivered me to the *Institut National de la Santé et de la Recherche Médicale,* a bureaucratic huddle of buildings surrounded by mud. The little waiting room to which I was directed was in near darkness at midday: the energy crisis in the process of being paid heed. A friend of mine in Paris had said angrily, "All they're doing in Bordeaux is burning electricity in that imbecile machine at the rate of one thousand francs per day." In light of the darkness, this seemed unlikely; but such, I reflected, as a glass window slid open and a voice announced, "Dr. Pautrizel will be with you shortly," were the irrational passions of what has come to be known as *l'affaire Prioré,* a controversy of the first water that, for more than a decade now, has galvanized with excitement and often divided with suspicion, bitterness and envy the elite of the French scientific establishment. As a direct consequence of the *affaire,* some of the most august reputations in continental science stand soon to be tarnished, perhaps beyond recovery, or to be imbued with new, possibly everlasting, luster. Critical events, of the next few months, played off against those of the past decade, may well be the making, or breaking, of Nobel Prize winners. *L'affaire* is coming to a head.

For two years I had been consumed with curiosity about the affair, named after its principal character, Antoine Prioré, an Italian-born inventor noted by his enemies for his lack of formal education and by his friends for his intuitive genius. Prioré, I knew, had been tinkering with odd, complex electromagnetic contraptions of his own design for twenty-six years—since his days as a radar technician in the Italian navy. What education he received was of the trade-school variety: a diploma, in 1930, from the Alessandro Volta Technical Institute for Industry in Trieste and another, later on, from an electronics school in Bologna.

Prioré would later tell me that he had serendipitously discovered that certain ultrahigh-frequency electromagnetic waves, presumably somewhat akin to those utilized in the radar devices with which he was so familiar, had the power of preserving fruit. An orange that had inadvertently been exposed to the radiation, he noticed, remained unspoiled much longer than it should have. Assuming that the radiation must somehow have been responsible, he decided to experiment, soon verifying, he said, that the shelf life of various fruits and vegetables could be significantly extended by exposing them to certain electromagnetic waves.

Imprisoned by the Germans during World War II, Prioré had ample time to devise and reflect upon his electromagnetic theories. But whatever he devised he kept to himself. He escaped from the Germans and, in 1943, made his way to Bordeaux where he became active in and eventually a dec- orated hero of the French Resistance. He adopted the city, and the city warmly embraced him in return. With nearly every franc he could earn or borrow from his expanding coterie of admirers, Prioré purchased old generators and other electrical components set adrift by the U.S. war surplus. Out of these, he constructed a machine so bafflingly complex in appearance that it would, even today, do justice to a set for a high-budget mad-scientist movie. It filled a good-size room, its panels of knobs, dials, lights and energy units banked against the four walls so that there remained only a small space in the center of the room for a table, *over* which was suspended a huge nozzle, *through* which emanated the output of the machine, the ray itself. Just what the invisible ray consisted of, Prioré steadfastly refused to say, other than to characterize it as "an electromagnetic wave in a magnetic field," which is on a par with an ornithologist describing the aboriginal-sloe-eyed-puce-breasted-tawny-tanager as a bird.

Prioré's instincts were then, as now, those of the lone in- ventor for whom to give up the secret is to give up life. It's all he's got. But as far as Science is concerned, excusing for the moment that segment of Science that labors in the service of private, competitive industry, concealment of any sort is the prime symptom of fraud. And, thus, had it not been for the inventor's "patriotic connections," I had been told over and over, no one would ever have heard the name "Prioré" uttered, let alone uttered favorably, in the rarefied air of the French Academy of Sciences. Principal among those "connections" was Jacques Chaban-Delmas, a fellow alumnus of the Resistance and, beginning in 1947, the mayor of Bordeaux. Not so curiously, perhaps, many French scientists have been more interested in trying to establish a positive correlation between the amount of government fund- ing accorded Antoine Prioré and the various levels of political power to which Chaban-Delmas has attained than in verifying the correlation between Prioré's mystery radia- tion and cancer cures in laboratory animals.

When the French government, not long ago, decided to spend about one million dollars for the construction of a new "super machine" designed by Prioré, many pointed out that Chaban-Delmas was then premier. A couple of years earlier, when the military had offered more modest funding, some had even made a point of the fact that Chaban-Delmas, quite suspiciously, had been minister of defense in 1958! One wondered why Prioré and his machine didn't disintegrate into a puff of smoke the morning, in 1974, when Chaban-Delmas awoke to discover that he had been soundly defeated in his bid for president.

Prioré himself is the first to acknowledge that the Bordeaux politician was a help. Chaban-Delmas helped him obtain better equipment, provided him with laboratory animals on which to conduct some of his experiments and, no doubt, encouraged, with his considerable prestige, a few scientists to pay heed to some of the inventor's claims, which, if substantiated, presaged a development of tremendous import. It was through the chief veterinary officer of the city of Bordeaux that Prioré was persuaded, in 1960, to permit two members of the university of Bordeaux Faculty of Medicine to expose rats grafted with cancerous tumors to the radiation of the machine. To the amazement of the two—Professor J. Biraben and Dr. G. Delmon—all tumor growth was halted. The researchers were so startled, and so convinced that they would be accused of hallucinating or worse, that they waited until 1966, when others were also reporting spectacular results with the Prioré appartus, to publish their findings in a leading medical journal.

Reports of their results had spread by word of mouth well before that, however, and soon two eminent cancerologists from the Institute for Cancer Research at Villejuif, Professors Marcel Rivière and Maurice Guérin, were collaborating with Prioré and two other researchers, Maurice Fournier and Francis Berlureau. The results they attained seemed to one Robert Courrier so convincing and of such significance that he decided to put his immense prestige directly behind their work by personally presenting their results to the French Academy of Sciences on December 21, 1964. Professor Courrier, an internationally known biologist and the *secrétaire-perpétuel* of the Academy of Sciences, began cautiously. He pointed out that just as a great number of different chemicals had been tested on cancer so, over the years, had a variety of rays. He was mindful, no doubt, that the bad odor "biomagnetics" had accumulated over the centuries, at the hands of quacks and charlatans, persisted still. The Prioré machine, he continued, at last provided an opportunity for *scientific* evaluation of the biological effects of "radiation in an electromagnetic field." The field was

defined only as having an intensity in the neighborhood of
620 gauss—about 1240 times the power of the natural earth
field. The frequency of these waves was said to be approaching that of gamma radiation.

Some forty-eight rats of the same heritage, age and health
had been selected for the experiment that Professor Courrier
related. All had fragments of the same uterine T8 cancer
tumor grafted beneath the skins of their backs. Previous experiments had proved that this breed of rat, grafted with T8,
would die within three to five weeks if untreated in any way.
Half of the rats were controls—set aside and given no treatment. They were, however, fed and housed in exactly the
same manner and environment as the twenty-four experimentals, all of which were exposed to the radiation of the
Prioré apparatus. Exposure was effected simply by placing
their cages under the nozzle of the machine. Twelve of the
experimentals were given treatments commencing the same
day as the grafting. In the remaining twelve experimentals,
treatment was delayed for several days in order to permit
the cancer to metastasize (spread) throughout their bodies.

The results: Among those experimentals which were given
immediate treatment, the tumors were quickly and totally
absorbed. Where treatment was delayed, exposure had to be
prolonged in order to obliterate the cancer. But obliterated it
was—until all of these animals, as well, were in perfect
health, with no trace of cancer. The experimentals were observed for several months, and there was no recurrence of
the disease. All of the controls, meanwhile, died between the
twenty-second and thirtieth days after grafting.

The report was met with stunning and perhaps stunned
silence. In light of criticisms that were to erupt later it is clear
that many in the audience simply did not believe the report;
others, no doubt because they couldn't explain the phenomena
that had just been related, hoped that if they were quiet long
enough it would all go away. A Nobel Prize winner, asking
not to be quoted by name, once observed, "Cancer is not a
disease for which we will suffer a cure lightly or joyfully."
Too many competing investments of both ego and money
for that.

The Bordeaux researchers were, of course, irate over the
apparent indifference with which their labors were greeted.
But they already had new experiments under way, and, in
February, 1965, Professor Courrier presented a second paper

at the Academy on behalf of the same group. In this experiment, it was revealed, leukemia and another form of cancer had similarly been overwhelmed by the machine's radiation. Again, all the experimentals had lived; all the controls had died. If science chose to ignore all of this, the press did not. Newsmen descended on the humble Prioré abode in mass—only to find the inventor unwilling ("Isn't the word *'unable'*?" some asked) to explain the inner workings of his machine.

It was not until the next month, however, that the matter was to erupt into *l'affaire Prioré,* so noted by the French press, so called by the droves of French scientists who gossiped of little else in their laboratories, lounges, meeting room. Professor Courrier, intent upon dispelling the innuendos of fraud, told the now visibly startled Academy in March that he had personally sent one of his most trusted assistants to Bordeaux with eighteen rats, all of which had been grafted, under his own direction, with cancerous tissue.

The assistant had been instructed to watch the rats at all times and to keep them, at night, in a laboratory some distance from Prioré's house, so that no one could reasonably charge that healthy animals had been substituted for those with cancer. Ten of the rats served as controls, eight as experimentals. Professor Courrier specified that four of the experimentals be treated for one hour daily and that the remaining four be exposed for two hours daily. All of the controls, he said, had died within fifteen days of the grafting. The four experimentals that were treated for one hour each day also died. The four treated for two hours daily recovered and were in excellent health in Professor Courrier's Paris laboratory.

At the conclusion of his address, the secretary indulged in the extraordinary exercise of counseling both sides of the controversy. Noting that "science does not hold with black boxes, with apparatus shrouded in mystery," the professor advised Prioré to elucidate the inner mechanism of his machine, or, at least, to permit competent physicists to examine it without hindrance. Then he proceeded to chastise those who, through the unfounded suggestion of fraud, would impugn the integrity of scientists whose work had attested for years or even decades, to their competence, honesty and fidelity to scientific method.

It was, as some who were there recall, a moment of great theater, a moment that was heightened when, as Lord Solly Zuckerman, himself a leading biologist and former chief scientific adviser to the British government, wrote in *The Times of London,* "Professor Antoine Lacassagne, one of the most respected radiobiologists of the century, stood up to indicate his total disbelief and insisted that the printed record of the meeting include a note of his regret that conclusions had been drawn too hastily from the observations that had been reported. . . . I can well imagine," Lord Zuckerman added, "how Professor Courrier and Professor Lacassagne felt in this confrontation. I had known the two from the early thirties. Lascassagne's scientific authority was equal to that of Courrier, and he spoke with a lifelong background of work in the Radium Institute of Paris. Yet, apart from uttering his warning, he provided no word of explanation for the results which Professor Courrier had reported, even though they related to grafts which should have proved fatal. Professor Lacassagne has since died in his eighties, mortally affected by cancer."

In the meantime, Prioré had been constructing a new, more powerful machine, one capable of producing a magnetic field of about 1240 gauss. The researchers at Villejuif lost little time in making use of it, this time to see whether the animals that had been cured of their cancers in previous experiments could withstand new grafts without once again being exposed to the Prioré radiation, in short, whether they had developed immunity to cancer. Animals that had been tested two, six and ten months earlier were grafted a second time with the same type of cancer they had been exposed to before. The grafts were uniformly rejected; the immunity appeared unmistakable.

A story began circulating about this time to the effect that British scientists, seeking to verify some of the Bordeaux findings, had sent a group of diseased animals to France for treatment. The animals that came back to Britain were indisputably healthy but, unfortunately, or so the story went, they were not the same ones that had been sent in the first place! The story that still circulates among the anti-Prioré forces is that the director of the British study, feeling that he had been made a fool of, was not eager to broadcast his "mistake," and that, supposedly, is why he will not give his name for publication. A document confirming the "fraud" has been sent by the "duped" Briton to the director of a French laboratory who will show the document to reporters— on the condition that his name not be used either. Apart from the bad smell of the not-for-attribution accusation, can a reasonable individual fail to wonder why the British investigator considered himself made a fool of if, indeed, he discovered the fraud that so many others would give their best beakers and retorts to prove?

In 1966 the research in Bordeaux took a critical turn even as new accusations of "irresponsibility" were being heaped on Prioré. Some observers think the resistance to Prioré was based on fear: a Prioré cure would not only be a cure from outside the familiar areas of cancer research (chemotherapy, viral studies and the like) but worse, would be a cure from outside the club, from outside, as one doctor put it, "the cancer cartel." How could science explain to the world that a mere "handyman" as Prioré was characterized in one French publication, had succeeded, alone and with limited funds, where the best doctors and scientists at the best universities and medical schools with millions of dollars in funding had failed? It could not and it would not—not, at least, without thinking it over for a good long while.

Perceiving all of this was one Professor Raymond Pautrizel, head of the Department of Immunology and Parasitology at the University of Bordeaux and an international authority on the trypanosome, the blood parasite that causes sleeping sickness and tens of thousands of deaths each year. Professor Pautrizel had become fascinated with the Prioré apparatus when researchers began using the university's laboratory facilities to house animals they were subjecting to the radiation at Prioré's house on the other side of town.

The experiments reported on in 1966 suggested to Professor Pautrizel that the radiation, whatever its nature, might not be attacking the cancer cells directly but, instead, could be stimulating the natural immune-response mechanisms of the animals, potentiating them to the point where they were able to overwhelm and reject the cancerous grafts. If this were so, then something greater—*far greater*—than a possible cure for cancer had been found. For if this were so then the radiation might prove equally effective against any number of other diseases in which the body's immunological responses often prove inadequate. If, for example, the Prioré radiation could reverse the normally fatal course of laboratory-induced trypanosomiasis in animals, then the immunity-stimulating properties of the radiation would be substantially proved.

And, not to be overlooked, Pautrizel reasoned, an extraordinary scientific development would be permitted to cut its teeth and perhaps even grow to maturity, using, for nourishment, a disease whose cure would save primarily Third World lives and thus, to be cynical and very likely accurate, threaten fewer important First World scientific reputations. One could always attack cancer again later—when one was better established. And in the meantime, of course, Professor Pautrizel, aware that *his* competitors around the world were working hard to develop a trypanosome vaccine, would welcome the opportunity to zap the parasite. He must have been persuasive, for, abruptly, all the Bordeaux cancer research was suspended and the barrel of the machine was henceforth aimed at a new target: *Trypanosoma equiperdum.*

It was in order to interview Professor Pautrizel, the man who, next to the inventor himself, has loomed largest in *l'affaire Prioré,* that I had journeyed to Bordeaux. The professor I found to be an affable, compact man with a ready smile, precise manner and keen wit. Through the good translative offices of his secretary and assistant, Colette Cauchois, I asked the professor, who is both a doctor in medicine and a doctor of science in chemistry, how he felt collaborating with a man unschooled in either of those fields, or in, from a strictly academic point of view, *any* field. "Honored," he answered unhesitatingly. And, in any event, he added, Prioré may soon have an earned doctorate attached to his name. The inventor has completed all the doctoral requirements of the University of Bordeaux, including his dissertation, "Healing of Acute and Chronic Experimental Trypanosomiasis by the Combined Action of Magnetic and Electromagnetic Modules."

The experiments of eight years are detailed in this booklength study. From it, our conversation, interviews with others and papers published in various scientific journals, I was able to construct the following events: in 1966, the first of the trypanosome results were presented to the Academy. Mice had been injected with twenty thousand virulent trypanosomes each, enough to kill the animals within five days (at which time the prolific parasite would have multiplied to one million per cubic millimeter of blood). The experimentals were subjected to the radiation of the first Prioré machine, the one that generated 620 gauss, beginning within one hour of exposure to the parasite and were kept there for twelve hours each day for twelve consecutive days. Eighty-two percent of them survived, fully recovering their health. When the researchers used the more powerful second machine, *all* of the experimentals survived. All of the controls, meanwhile, died as expected within five days.

Over the next few years it was demonstrated that these experimental mice, along with dozens of rats and rabbits also exposed to the radiation, developed a specific immunity to trypanosomiasis. As long as two years after they had first been exposed to and healed of the disease, they could be injected with dosages of two hundred million live trypanosomes and never develop any sign of the affliction. This immunity, moreover, was shown to be transferable. Mice exposed to the disease were treated and cured with the radiation, then portions of their blood were injected into other mice. These recipient mice, none of which ever had benefit of the Prioré radiation, were then inoculated with what would normally have been lethal numbers of parasites. Those that had received highly diluted blood fractions with low antibody counts died. Those that received blood with more highly concentrated antibody content lived. Professor Pautrizel had apparently been right; the machine seemed to work by stimulating of the organism. The possibilities now seemed potentially unlimited.

Next, the researchers wanted to know whether the radiation could vanquish trypanosomiasis after it had become entrenched. Rabbits were used in these experiments because the disease produces in them a chronic malaise in which they decline toward death far more slowly than mice. Infected rabbits that were still living at the end of three weeks were exposed to the radiation; improvement began to manifest itself almost immediately, but the treatments, when initiated at this advanced stage in the evolution of the disease, had to continue for twelve hours each day for about twenty consecutive days on average before healing was complete.

In the course of one of the rabbit studies, Prioré gained another powerful supporter in the person of Gaston Mayer, a well-respected reproductive scientist. In collaboration with Professor Pautrizel, Professor Mayer found that the normally irreversible testicular degeneration caused by trypanosomiasis could be overcome with the radiation. Spermatogenesis and hormone production were restored to normal levels in rabbits, the testicles of which were already badly afflicted when first exposed to the radiation. Male rabbits thus treated fathered normal offspring.

Despite the fact that by 1969 hundreds of irradiated

animals had been tested by diverse researchers, skepticism and even the occasional suggestion of fraud were still being heard. Exasperated, Professor Courrier proposed a course of action almost unheard of in scientific research. A large committee, including individuals professionally trained in security techniques, would be formed to supervise and validate a series of experiments with the Prioré machine. Apart from ten professors of science and medicine, the committee would include a number of "pillars of the community"—an air force general, the chief legal officer of the city of Bordeaux, the prefect of the province, an electronics expert, the dean of the University of Bordeaux Law School and those security experts knowledgeable in the ways of fraud.

Elaborate precautions were taken to mark and identify control and experimental substitution of animals without resort to magic. Special seals were placed over laboratory doors; these were broken twice a day to permit the researchers to treat and examine the animals. All manipulations of the animals were witnessed by other officials, all movements of the animals dutifully charted.

At the conclusion of this exercise, the results were much as before—of the thirty mice inoculated with the parasite and then treated with the machine, twenty-nine lived. Twenty-six of the thirty mice inoculated with the trypanosome but left untreated died within a few days. An additional thirty mice, both uninfected and untreated, but housed, fed and handled in a fashion identical to that accorded the diseased mice, all continued to exhibit normal health and behavior. The committee unanimously affirmed the authenticity of the experiments.

New supporters were attracted, among them André Lwoff, the 1965 Nobel Prize winner for medicine and previously director of the Institute for Cancer Research at Villejuif. It was Professor Lwoff, not ex-Minister Chaban-Delmas, who was instrumental in persuading the research arm of the French military to give Professor Pautrizel money to continue the biological studies. At the same time, two physicists were provided funds for the purpose of making a study of the machine itself. The World Health Organization also began giving funds in 1969 and has continued to do so to the present time.

With this fresh infusion of money and support, Professor Pautrizel, satisfied now that the machine could be effective against autoimmune maladies like cancer and infectious maladies like trypanosome, decided to press his luck and see whether a third class of diseases, the metabolic maladies like atherosclerosis, might also be vulnerable to the radiation.

"But how could the machine have such diverse actions?" I asked.

"How could aspirin?" Professor Pautrizel responded. In any event, here was the evidence. He shot a 1972 paper across his desk at me. It was entitled "Action of Electromagnetic Waves and of Magnetic Fields on Lipid Modification Provoked in the Rabbit by Administration of a High-Cholesterol Dietary Regime." It was authored by Professor Pautrizel, Prioré, Modeste Dallochio and René Crockett and presented to the Academy by Professor Courrier. Sure enough, the results indicated that the radiation might make a significant contribution in the fight against heart and vessel disease.

Dozens of rabbits had been fed in identical fashion on a high-cholesterol diet which, base studies had shown, quickly resulted in a state of hypercholesterolemia followed by the extensive deposition of fatty, lipidic material in the aortic vessels of the animals. In the first experiment, six of the hypercholesteremic rabbits were given daily treatments of ninety minutes' duration under the Prioré mechine. Six hypercholesteremic control rabbits received no radiation. By the third week, all of the lipidic components (cholesterol in particular) of the irradiated rabbits were substantially lower than those of the untreated animals.

Subsequent experiments using greater numbers of animals confirmed these initial findings and, in addition, revealed that the cholesterol-suppressing quality of the radiation persisted for weeks after radiation treatment was halted, despite the fact that the animals continued to be maintained on the high-cholesterol diet. At the end of two months on the high-cholesterol diet, irradiated animals were found to have nearly normal lipid levels while the untreated controls had levels roughly three times normal, with lipid desposits covering fifty percent of their aortic surfaces. Finally, it was established that animals exposed to the radiation in advance of being made hyperlipemic could more quickly cope with the high-cholesterol diet once it was introduced.

Studies like these seemed to clinch it. Even the most hidebound of critics had to concede that it was better to give "them" the money for the "definitive experiments" than endure cries of outrage over an "imaginary" conspiracy to suppress what one Prioré opponent sarcastically called the "Second Coming." Some of the critics still spoke of "statistical flukes" and the like and reckoned that the "definitive experiment," if ever performed to their satisfaction, would only vindicate their skepticism. So, yes, go ahead; give them a million dollars for a new, more powerful, more finely tunable machine. But, and here the critics surely argued fairly, give the money only on the condition that Prioré permit both the results and his new machine to be scrutinized by teams of government-appointed experts.

And so it was done. The *Délégation Générale à la Recherche Scientifique et Technique* (D.G.R.S.T.), one of the top French government scientific agencies, drew up a contract providing $700,000 for construction of the new machine. (There are unofficial reports, confirmed by Prioré, that the actual final bill for the machine now nearing completion will be closer to $3,000,000, proving that Americans are not the only ones capable of sizable cost overruns.) The director of D.G.R.S.T. at the time the money was awarded was Pierre Aigrain, a physicist who received some of his training in the United States and who, recently, was conducting research at M.I.T. Dr. Aigrain, who has held various high government posts and is noted for his work in the complex physics of semiconductors, was at a loss to explain the underlying principles of the Prioré apparatus, despite the fact that he has personally examined the machine. "None of the possibilities of resonance appear to answer to the known laws of physics," he was quoted as saying at the conclusion of that examination.

One of the more rational skeptics, Dr. Aigrain had long maintained that even if nothing came of those "definitive" tests, they should nonethless be performed in light of the very great benefits that would accrue if something *did* come of them. In a conversation with me, he said that while "it is possible that the machine's actions represent something quite revolutionary, it is also possible that its effects accrue from something quite ordinary." He is disturbed by the "busy-ness" of the machine and wonders whether its complexity does not mask "some rather simple element" that is, alone, having the crucial effect. Could the rest all be window dressing designed to persuade where the unadorned, seemingly too simple, "bare facts" of biomagnetics had failed to have much impact so many times before?

Because there *have* been isolated reports in the literature of seemingly miraculous events occurring under the apparent influence of electromagnetic fields. In fact, if one begins looking one finds that there is quite a lot of evidence to suggest that magnetic fields have profound effects on biological organisms, but Dr. Alexander Kolin, a U.C.L.A. biophysicist writing in *Physics Today*, cautions that there has been exasperatingly little progress made in compounding these results and in bringing them into the full light of day.

Some of the experiments indicated that exposure to magnetic fields of certain intensities could *reduce* resistance to cancer. At first blush, one such report, published in the prestigious journal *Nature* thirteen years ago, might seem to contradict the French findings. But, in fact, since the intensity of the radiation was quite different from that used by the French, it perhaps, if anything, lends support by showing that such fields *do* have effects on cancerous tissues and the immunological response systems of animals.

There is no universally accepted theory to explain the effects of magnetism on life. (Some might still question whether there *are* any such effects; others with a scientific bent are sometimes quick to accept the likelihood of magnetically induced climatic changes and the effects of these fields on plant growth, but are, at the same time, quite irrationally, I submit, loathe to admit to any possibility of a magnetic effect on cancer.) It is now beyond theory, however, that electrically charged atoms and molecules called ions exist in the cells and quite naturally interact (though just how, we still do not fully understand) with magnetic fields, whether natural or man-made. In this connection, the work of Dr. Andrew Bassett and his associates at Columbia University's College of Physicians and Surgeons is instructive. They recently reported that broken bones exposed to certain electromagnetic fields heal substantially faster than fractures that do not have benefit of this stimulative treatment. In one of Dr. Bassett's studies, "fracture disability time" was reduced by 50 percent. The healing probably takes place as a result of voltage-induced changes at the site of the cell membrane. Dr. Bassett believes, *New Scientist* notes, "that electromagnetic stimulation has the effect of changing the membranes' ability to bind such ions as calcium, magnesium and sodium."

A number of other recent findings suggest that electromagnetism may have a profound impact on enzymes, the essential catalysts of metabolism. In one study, for example, magnetically deprived mice (those placed in extremely low magnetic fields) suffered shortened life-spans, unfavorable, tissue alterations, infertility and "drastic changes in enzyme activity" that were said to be "potentially lethal." A recently developed Navy study demonstrated that low-frequency fields could, at a level of statistical significance *increase* the blood triglyceride levels of man. (Triglycerides are lipids which, along with cholesterol, have been implicated in atherosclerosis.) The Navy research suggested that low-frequency fields effect a *decrease* in the activity of an enzyme that helps suppress blood triglyceride levels. It is not illogical to assume that certain high-frequency fields might affect the magnetically vulnerable lipids and enzymes in another, perhaps opposite, direction.

Nevertheless, the work in biomagnetics has never attracted widespread attention, and the possibility remained that Prioré, having taken note of how little heed had been paid biomagnetic researchers despite their sometimes spectacular findings, had reasoned that no one in this realm would be listened to until he or she constructed an apparatus as big and as impressive as the results it obtained. It was bad enough that cancer might be cured with "magnetism" (Gad! Wasn't that the stuff Mesmer fooled around with?), but to do it with a few simple horseshoe magnets would be inelegant beyond redemption. Not that anyone is suggesting that it *can* be done with simple horseshoe magnets, only that it *might* be possible with something considerably less complex than what Prioré has puzzled together "by feeling," as he puts it. This is what Pierre Aigrain seemed to be suggesting. It was what had occurred to me many months before as I read the biomagnetic literature. But while Dr. Aigrain and I shared the belief that some simpler devices might be capable of some remarkable results, neither of us, finally, believed that Prioré had knowingly added useless parts to *his* machine.

Dr. Aigrain said that Prioré, "not being a scientist," simply does not know which components are critical and which are not, that he is using what amounts to a "shotgun approach," channeling a great many energies through the machine, secure in the knowledge that something in there—but what? —works. This theory may be comforting—especially for a highly credentialed physicist who is at pains to explain a machine, constructed by a self-made engineer—and while I sympathize with it I have come to believe that it probably is not correct.

Prioré has stated that he has experimented with some of the separate outputs of his various machines, and while some of the emanations work solo to effect certain changes, none *alone* gives the results obtained in the cancer, trypanosome and cholesterol studies. The biomagnetic research of others, while very important, he would argue, only helps to reinforce the idea that there is something powerfully real coming out of his machine. Just because bones can be healed with an apparatus simple in comparison to his own does not mean that much of his machine is superfluous, there for show, or, as I once imagined, there to institute a huge mechanical placebo effect. He would defy those who are using their simpler devices to achieve isloated healings or alterations in tissues to replicate his results. Prioré is confident that while others may have bits and pieces of it only he has the *whole* secret.

Dr. Aigrain stressed that "a number of top scientists" have more faith in "this thing" than he has. "The machine does seem to have an effect; I don't deny that," he said, "but none of the tests, as far as I was concerned, were completely adequate. Only when you have a careful biological study proceeding *concurrently* with one that measures the radiation coming out of the machine, so that you know precisely what radiation has had what effect at what moment, can you call the tests definitive. We funded the new machine under the condition that just such tests be conducted." Dr. Aigrain insisted that the machine be built by a reputable electronics firm selected by the French government. He also wanted the machine constructed at a university but finally gave in to Prioré's insistence that it be built in the same building that housed its predecessors—Prioré's own home. And Prioré could not be forced to tell the technicians how the machine worked, merely how to build it. Further provisions of the contract stipulate that, once the machine is finished, D.G.R.S.T. will be permitted to test it, both from a physicist's and a biologist's point of view. Finally, the contract provides for the government to repossess the components of the machine if it fails to work. "All but about one hundred thousand dollars' worth of equipment would be reusable in other more conventional devices," Dr. Aigrain explained.

As far as he could determine from his own examination of the Prioré apparatus he looked at, the machine featured, among other things, a vacuum tube containing a plasma of mercury and neon gas. This plasma was apparently subjected to the simultaneous action of a pulsed 9.4 gigahertz electromagnetic wave (one oscilating at 9.4 billion cycles per second, a very short radio wave, indeed) modulated on a high-frequency wave of 17 megahertz (17,000,000 cycles per second). These waves, Dr. Aigrain said, were produced by radio emitters and magnetrons in the presence of a 1000-gauss magnetic field. The experimental animals were maintained during their treatments in this magnetic field through which the radiation had to pass, perhaps becoming mixed or altered in some fashion in the process. He doesn't doubt that there are many other things coming out of the machine as well.

The two physicists who examined the machine under the military contract were described by one French publication as being "absolutely stupefied" by the apparatus, which may safely be interpreted to mean that they understood very little of it. The two, A. J. Berteaud and A. M. Bottreau, were said to have "hovered over" the machine for several months. Bottreau was reported to be "irritated" on occasion by Prioré's smug silence, at other times forgiving. "If he divulged his plans he would have nothing left but to hang himself," Bottreau said on one occasion. Of what significance was the 9.4 GHz wave, whether modulated or not? The two physicists agreed with Prioré's statement: "If it were only that, it would be child's play." Observed Berteaud: "The wave is necessary but not sufficient. It is the base vehicle of something which is still unknown to us." (Indeed, in one experiment where only the 9.4 GHz wave was used, lab animals infected with the trypanosome all died despite prolonged exposure to the radiation. Yet, in another experiment the preponderance of this wave, in proportion to the other, unknown outputs of the machine, was seen to have a critical effect on the speed with which the trypanosomes were overwhelmed by the organism's immunological response mechanisms. And when the wave was omitted entirely from the machine's output no healing could take place.)

At last the time had come to see the machine. The Bordeaux rain was still pouring as Professor Pautrizel and I drove for what seemed miles through late afternoon traffic. As we crept along we communicated as best we could. He said that he believed Prioré was justified in keeping the secret of the machine, that several large concerns were already interested in manufacturing it. How would the new machine differ from the old? There would be much greater leeway, he said, in "adjusting parameters," and its magnetic field would be ten times stronger than that of the one it replaced. Prioré believed that with the new machine researchers could accomplish "in minutes what had taken hours before." Would new diseases be subjected to the more powerful radiation of the machine? "I hope; but first we must see if it works on the diseases we are already familiar with."

We came to a stop outside a building that appeared to be in need of urban renewal. We rang the bell, and a small child answered. Then another and then a young woman. Was this the right place, I wondered? But of course. These were the inventor's children and his new wife. We stepped inside and the ambience was immediately and radically altered. Everything that wasn't glass and steel and chrome was gleaming white procelain, white wood, and white plastic. Outside, an ancient, crumbling sector of the city; inside, the space age, as Madison Avenue or Antonioni would have conceived it.

I had seen pictures of Prioré and so recognized him immediately when, smiling broadly, he joined us—a short, heavyset man with close-cropped hair and a suit under his lab smock. He took me by the arm and quickly led me down a corridor, with Professor Pautrizel and Madame Cauchois, the translator, who had arrived in her own vehicle, following. The whining of unidentified and still unseen machinery grew more intense with each step. It couldn't be long now. We passed room after gleaming room—all empty. Prioré said something, and Madame Cauchois translated: "That's were the animals will be kept when the new experiments begin. Others will be offices and labs for the doctors." I was instructed to take off my watch; then we stepped down into the very heart of the complex, the lowest level, in which the ray emanates from a five-ton bell-shaped dome suspended from a very high ceiling. What could I say of it, now that I was actually viewing it? There it was. Huge. Inscrutable. Orange. Yes, the dome was painted bright orange. I felt as I approached the eye of it as if I were being tugged by a magnetic wind. My tape recorder gave every indication of wanting to leap from my hands.

"Is it safe?" I shouted. "Oui, oui." I looked straight up the barrel, a glass-lined tube that appeared to be about a foot across. Meanwhile, Prioré was shouting bits of information at me and others, and Madame Cauchois was gamely trying to translate. This piece cost $5,000, that one $10,000. It was the best equipment that money could buy. Prioré himself had made trips to the United States to pick up some of what was needed; he couldn't trust others and besides it took too long. On one trip he spent $300,000. Yes, the machine would cost $3,000,000, anyway. "Those tubes there," Prioré said, "they're for the oil that cools the machine." We wandered up a flight of stairs; corridors and entryways seemed to beckon in all directions; there were at least three distinct levels and no windows at all. There—that was from Boston. Here—this came from New York.

There were three large generators, banks of computerlike instruments, exotic switches, the glass tube that penetrated the massive magnetic nozzle below. There was a "lamp," as Madame Cauchois called it, in which *seventeen* radiations of unspecified nature joined the 9.4 GHz wave. The energy produced by the machine, the entrails of which were everywhere on display—around corners, upstairs, inside closets— Prioré shouted, existed nowhere "in nature," could be produced by no other machine "on earth." "When will it be done?" I shouted back. "Soon, I hope. In a few months anyway."

By all appearances, the inventor seemed aglow with confidence, goodwill and good health. I asked him how much time he spent under the machine's radiation. "A third of my life," he said. Had he ever been sick? "Never!" He then told me the story I have related of his early experiences with the orange that was, by chance, preserved by the radiation of one of his much earlier apparatuses.

How had he arrived at this seemingly magical mixture of rays? "Only twenty-six years of work," he responded. Was it X rays? No, no. Could it be harmful? No, there had never been any adverse side effects, and many of the one thousand mice, one hundred rabbits and four hundred rats had been observed for years after treatment. Many had been bred and had given birth to normal offspring which, in turn, were capable of reproducing normally. What about a simple heat effect? Some skeptics, with more faith in the therapeutic value of heat than I've ever been able to muster, had guessed that some of the results might be attributable to thermal outputs of the machine. But no. Extensive tests had been carried out, measuring the temperature both inside and outside the animals. Nothing. What about the electric bill? "It runs to about four hundred dollars a month."

Had people ever been treated with any of the machines? "A few," Prioré admitted, smiling. Not with the new machine, however; there was a proscription against that. Professor Pautrizel himself had sprained his wrist some time past. It was inflamed sufficiently that it impaired his ability to drive. After ten minutes under the machine, he said, it was normal again. Would the new machine ever be used to treat people? Prioré was confident that the government would permit this, once sufficient animal testing had been concluded.

He was not anticipating having to dismantle the machine, then, of having to give back the various components that he had so lovingly assembled? The inventor's eyes swept over *la machine Prioré* and betrayed not the slightest doubt.

"It will not happen," he said. "The machine is here to stay."

# For Further Reading

OSCAR BAGNALL: *The Origin and Properties of the Human Aura,* University Books, 1970.

GEORGE BEAU: *Chinese Medicine,* Avon Books, 1972.

ALAN RALPH BLEICH: *The Story of X Rays: From Röntgen to Isotopes,* Dover Publications, 1960.

DOUG BOYD: *Rolling Thunder: A Personal Exploration into the Secret Healing Powers of an American Indian Medicine Man,* Random House, 1974.

STEVEN F. BRENA: *Yoga and Medicine: The Merging of Yogic Concepts with Modern Medical Knowledge,* Penguin Books, 1972.

DR. HAROLD SAXTON BURR: *The Fields of Life,* Ballantine Books, 1972.

MARY ELLEN CARTER AND WILLIAM A. MCGAREY: *Edgar Cayce on Healing,* Paperback Library, 1972.

ANNE DOOLEY: *Every Wall a Door: Exploring Psychic Surgery and Healing,* Abelard-Schuman, 1973.

MARC DUKE: *Acupuncture: The Extraordinary New Book of the Chinese Art of Healing,* Pyramid House, 1972.

VIVA EMMONS: *The Roots of Peace,* a Quest Book, 1964.

JOHN G. FULLER: *Arigó: Surgeon of the Rusty Knife,* Thomas Y. Crowell Company, 1974.

SALLY HAMMOND: *We Are All Healers,* Ballantine, 1974.

BRIAN INGLIS: *Fringe Medicine*, Faber and Faber, 1964.

J. W. KILNER: *The Aura*, Samuel Weiser, 1973.

HELEN KRUGER: *Other Healers, Other Cures: A Guide to Alternative Medicines*, Bobbs-Merrill, 1974.

GEORGE FREDERICK KUNZ: *The Curious Lore of Precious Stones*, Dover Publications, 1971.

GEORGE LAKHOVSKY: *The Secret of Life: Cosmic Rays and Radiations of Human Beings*, True Health Publishing Company, 1951.

FRANKLIN LORE: *The Power of Prayer on Plants*, a Signet Book, N.A.L., 1959.

GAY GAER LUCE: *Biological Rhythms in Human and Animal Physiology*, Dover Publications, 1971.

W. E. MANN: *Orgone, Reich and Eros; William Reich's Theory of Life Energy*, Simon & Schuster, 1973.

THE MEDICAL GROUP THEOSOPHICAL RESEARCH CENTER, LONDON: *The Mystery of Healing*, a Quest Book, 1958.

MAURICE MESSÉGUÉ: *Of Men and Plants*, Bantam Books, 1974.

FRANK PODMORE: *From Mesmer to Christian Science: A Short History of Mental Healing*, University Books, 1963.

ARTHUR E. POWELL: *The Etheric Double*, The Theosophical Publishing House (London), 1969.

NICHOLAS M. REGUSH: *Exploring the Human Aura: A New Way of Viewing and Investigating Psychic Phenomena*, Prentice-Hall, 1975.

NICHOLAS M. REGUSH, ed.: *The Human Aura*, Berkeley, 1975.

KARL VON REICHENBACH: *The Odic Force: Letters on OD and Magnetism*, University Books, 1968.

EDWARD W. RUSSELL: *Design for Destiny*, Ballantine Books, 1971.

HAROLD M. SCHMECK: *Immunology: The Many-edged Sword*, George Braziller, 1974.

LEWIS THOMAS: *The Lives of a Cell: Notes of a Biology Watcher*, The Viking Press, 1974.

GORDON TURNER: *An Outline of Spiritual Healing*, Warner Paperback Library, 1972.

RITCHIE R. WARD: *The Living Clocks*, a Mentor Book, 1971.

AUBERY T. WESTLAKE: *The Pattern of Health: A Search for a Greater Understanding of the Life-Force in Health and Disease*, Shambalah, 1973.

G. T. WRENCH: *The Wheel of Health*, Schocken Books, 1972.

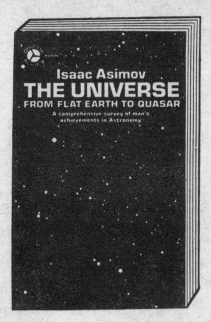

# DISCUS BOOKS
### DISTINGUISHED NON-FICTION

## A SELECTION OF RECENT TITLES

**ERNEST HEMINGWAY: A LIFE STORY**  Carlos Baker  50039  $4.95

**THE EXECUTION OF CHARLES HORMAN**
Thomas Hauser                                      49098  $2.75

**THE BIOGRAPHY OF ALICE B. TOKLAS**
Linda Simon                                        39073  $2.95

**TO DANCE**  Valery Panov with George Feifer  47233  $3.95

**TOO STRONG FOR FANTASY**  Marcia Davenport  45195  $3.50

**BUDDHISM**  Alexandra David-Neel            46185  $2.75

**GAY AMERICAN HISTORY**  Jonathan Katz       40550  $3.95

**GERMANS**  George Bailey                    44917  $2.95

**EINSTEIN: THE LIFE AND TIMES**  Ronald W. Clark  44123  $3.95

**THE PASSIONATE SHEPERDESS:**
**APHRA BEHN 1640-89**  Maureen Duffy          41863  $2.95

**POE, POE, POE, POE, POE . . .**  Daniel Hoffman  41459  $2.95

**DELMORE SCHWARTZ: THE LIFE OF AN**
**AMERICAN POET**  James Atlas                 41038  $2.95

**GEORGE SAND: A BIOGRAPHY**  Curtis Cate     43778  $3.50

**MUNGOBUS**  Raymond Mungo                    42929  $3.95

**QUASAR, QUASAR BURNING BRIGHT**
Isaac Asimov                                       44610  $2.25

**THE CONCISE ENCYCLOPEDIC GUIDE TO**
**SHAKESPEARE**  Edited by Michael Rheta Martin
and Richard C. Harrier                             16832  $2.65

**THE FEMALE IMAGINATION**
Patricia Meyer Spacks                              28142  $2.45

**CORTÉS AND MONTEZUMA**  Maurice Collis       40402  $2.50

**DIVISION STREET: AMERICA**  Studs Terkel     40642  $2.50

**THE RADICAL THEATRE NOTEBOOK**
Arthur Sainer                                      22442  $2.65

**THE AWAKENING OF INTELLIGENCE**
J. Krishnamurti                                    45674  $3.50

DRT 6-80

**DISCUS BOOKS**

### DISTINGUISHED NON-FICTION

(2) DDB 6-80

**DISCUS BOOKS**

DISTINGUISHED NON-FICTION

Wherever better paperbacks are sold, or direct from the publisher. Include 50¢ per copy for postage and handling; allow 4-6 weeks for delivery.

Avon Books, Mail Order Dept.
224 W. 57th St., New York, N.Y. 10019

(3) DDB 6-80